CHRISTIAN JOURNALISM
FOR TODAY

Christian Journalism for Today

A Resource Book for Writers and Editors

Containing Addresses Delivered at
The Christian Writers and Editors' Conferences
Philadelphia, Pa., and Green Lake, Wis., 1948-51
Collected and Edited under the Supervision of

BENJAMIN P. BROWNE
Conference Chairman

THE JUDSON PRESS
PHILADELPHIA

CHICAGO   LOS ANGELES

Contents

PART FOUR: HOW TO DO THE JOB

Foreword

THAT dreams of dreamers do come true is evidenced by the pages of this book on Christian journalism.

Some years ago in a Philadelphia suburban home, the dinner dishes having been cleared from the table and the family dismissed, two men sat over their coffee cups till well past midnight, discussing the problems and potentialities of Christian publications. That lively sharing of minds happily evoked common glowing interests and shining goals. Specifically, the need for a greater impact of Christian ideals upon American life by means of Christian publications was first explored, then excitedly resolved into dreams of destiny. The desire to rescue church school teaching materials from the dull gray into the attractive and entrancing led to the establishment of a conference for the training of writers with a Christian purpose. It was hoped that through this training these writers would become skilled craftsmen. The power in the hands of such men, when fully committed to the kingdom of God, was seen in all its glorious possibilities.

It had been my rare good fortune that night to be the dinner guest of a man of inspired vision and boundless energy, the Executive Secretary of the Board of Education and Publication of the American Baptist Convention, Dr. Luther Wesley Smith. By every measurement a magnificent man, he was eager to lend support to the project, not only with his interest, but with an enabling financial appropriation.

Thanks, therefore, to the stimulus of midnight coffee, the enthusiasm of kindred spirits, and the grace of God, a Christian Writers and Editors' Conference was launched in the summer of 1948.

This conference, now held at the famous American Baptist Assembly, Green Lake, Wis., is at the present time preparing for its fifth and largest summer session; and its leaders have yielded to a persistent demand that as many as possible of the addresses given in former years be put in permanent form. This book, therefore, brings together most of the addresses which have been made at the conferences held from 1948 to 1951 inclusive.

In order that the book might be kept to a reasonable size, all of the addresses have been much condensed. Some material, excellent in itself, has been omitted because it duplicated material presented by speakers in preceding years. A number of the addresses have been transcribed from wire recordings, and this fact explains the frequent and not unwelcome informality of style. It is believed that the addresses included are sufficiently representative to indicate the variety and balance of the instruction and inspiration given each year. We are grateful to all of the speakers for permitting the publication of their addresses.

So far as can be ascertained, this is the first book of this specialized character to be published. Because it is definitely focused on Christian journalism, it is hoped that it will provide valuable resource material for schools of journalism, colleges, and theological seminaries. It also should give much practical help to individual writers.

While the Green Lake Christian Writers and Editors' Conference has been initiated and promoted in the manner explained, we have gladly shared our resources on the broadest interdenominational basis. We have been happy in the co-operation accorded the conference by a number of denominational groups. A score of denominations have been included in both the attendance and the leadership. Two similar conferences have grown out of this conference; they have been organized by persons who caught the purpose and enthusiasm of our conference and have desired to spread its influence.

As chairman of the conference and as compiler of these addresses, it is proper that I should express sincere thanks to all the members of the staff of the Division of Christian Publications, who gave gladly of their time, strength, and skill to make the conference possible; to Rev. and Mrs. John W. Thomas, both accomplished writers, who have served as conference chaplain and hostess respectively; to Miss Ann Tatman, registrar of the conference, who secured from the speakers copies of their addresses; to Dr. Robert G. Torbet, whose discriminating taste gave the manuscripts their present general arrangement and first editing; and in particular to Dr. Miles W. Smith, book editor of the Judson Press, whose long experience, rare talents, and invaluable services as an editor have been most helpful in bringing this book to completion.

BENJAMIN P. BROWNE

Philadelphia, Pa.
May 1, 1952

PART ONE

What Is It All About?

TRAINING WRITERS WITH A CHRISTIAN PURPOSE

Benjamin P. Browne

*Dr. Benjamin P. Browne is the Executive Director of the Division of Christian Publications, Board of Education and Publication of the American Baptist Convention. Under his resourceful and energetic supervision, the Board's periodicals have made marked gains in typographical excellence, reader appeal, and spiritual emphasis. He has led in the development of a new curriculum for Christian education, including improved teaching techniques, increased use of colored illustrations, and provision for home co-operation in the church school task. His recognition of the part which Christian journalism must play in the solution of contemporary world problems has led him to devote himself indefatigably to the promotion and direction of the Green Lake Christian Writers and Editors' Conference, of which he is the capable and genial chairman.—*M.W.S.

A COLD WAR is on between Christian ideas and ideals and the utterly pagan propaganda and secular environment of our times. Convinced and dependable Christians constitute a minority group who are living in a hostile climate and fighting for survival. Modern civilization tends first to ignore, then to obscure, and finally to obliterate the Christian conceptions from all of life. It is almost true to say that the mass mind has become so thoroughly secularized and so drugged with gadgets and sex as to be incapable even of understanding what the lofty concepts of the Christian faith and heritage are all about.

If Christian forces as represented by Protestants intend to be more than a negative and negligible power in shaping the future of American culture, then there is desperate need for creating a school of writers and editors who are impregnated with the Christian faith and dedicated to making the Christian ideals regnant. And what Christian leader can be content with less than the vision and the determination to guide and to mold American life after the magnificent heritage which alone holds hope for the saving of the world?

We are not interested in securing writers of Christian purpose merely for denominational publications, vitally important as this objective is. We must train thousands of writers who can flood into American life until news reporters, fiction and feature writers, magazine publishers, and book authors are craftsmen committed to captivating America for Christ. If Christianity is to be rooted in America as the pattern of our culture, then we must be interested in more than writers who can sit in little denominational cubicles penning articles for limited circulations. Our vision must embrace the horizons—the mountains, the valleys, the cities, the towns, and the plains of America. We must plan a campaign to influence the vast publishing enterprise reaching across the years to a high goal of commanding power and influence. We must bring the Christian faith to bear upon the secular life and culture of our day.

Now, the modern world is quite content to make peace with us if only we will stay in our cubicles. With a morticianlike smile it will accept Christianity as "a nice sideline." If we will consent to keep the Christian religion in its own compartment, it will give to the church the back page in the Saturday night paper, or a column in the way-back section of the popular magazine, while the front pages are strictly reserved for war, murder, strikes, scandal, sex, politics, divorce, finance, science, and sports. But we are not prepared to settle for less than making the Christian message all pervasive, all permeating, and all important.

The English scholar, J. B. Phillips, strikingly translates a biblical passage (2 Cor. 10:5-6) as follows: "Our battle is to bring down every deceptive fantasy and every imposing defense that men erect against the true knowledge of God. We even fight to capture every thought until it acknowledges the authority of Christ." The transmission of the Christian faith and the permeation of all society by the Christian way of life are priority demands for Christian writers, editors, and publishers. Indeed, one may now say with Toynbee, "The salvation of civilization rests here with the propagation of Christianity at its widest and most redemptive strength."

The annual more than three-billion-dollar publishing enterprise in America represents the greatest flood of printed materials in all history. How much, however, of this vast industry has given moral and spiritual strength to our nation? How much represents the work of culture-vultures whose perverted pulps, propaganda slicks, and comic horrifics have poured deadly poison into the blood stream of the republic? How much is the truth being deliberately concealed or distorted despite all of our vociferous self-congratulation and back patting about our wonderful free press?

One trembles with fright to remember that the infinitesimally thin film of ink, just .00025 of an inch thick spread as print on a page, may carry the culture and enlightenment or the evil and deterioration of our civilization to millions both here and abroad, thus shaping the destinies of peoples and nations to unborn generations. Shall this potent film of ink be used by some new Jefferson to create a Declaration of Independence, by some future Lincoln to write a Gettysburg Address, or by some modern to write a *Forever Amber*?

Not only is the character of much of the present flood of literature deplorable, but there is the further disturbing fact that there has been a serious decline of readership of the religious press. It is startling to remember that three quarters of the reading material of Americans was definitely religious in 1840. Today the religious press, Protestant, Catholic, and Jewish, has less than one-tenth the readership of the secular press.

The grave responsibility resting upon Protestants for a more aggressive journalism is pointed up by one of the last statements made by Dr. Alfred Whitehead. He put the problem on our doorstep: "Whether the re-formation we are now passing through will be fortunate or unfortunate will depend upon comparatively few persons, and chiefly upon the members of the Protestant clergy." That pins us down to a strategic stand like that of the Lacedaemonians at the Pass of Thermopylae.

1. *The need of writers saturated with Christian ideals is vitally important in the wide fields of public opinion represented by newspapers and periodicals, by reporters, and correspondents.*

We are plagued with unfair journalism. When Cardinal Spellman calls Bishop Oxnam a "bigot," the charge is printed on the front page of a New York newspaper. When Bishop Oxnam replies, it is hidden on an inside back page. Something about scandal among the clergy gets tremendous coverage. But to get favorable publicity for the Protestant clergy on the front page of a great metropolitan daily is almost as difficult as reaching the peak of Mount Everest.

Once I became so irritated by this state of affairs that I offered, in a paper of which I was then the editor, a reward of twenty-five dollars for anyone who would send me a front-page double-column headline favorable to any Protestant clergyman in any great newspaper in the three cities of Boston, New York, and Philadelphia. The reward attracted a good deal of attention, but I waited a year for any results. Finally one of my New York friends said, "I have a tip that Dr. Harry Emerson Fosdick of the Riverside Church is going to resign. That will be on the front page of the *New York Times,* and I'll be around to claim the reward." As a matter of fact, when Dr. Fosdick's resignation was made public it appeared, as I recall it, on about page 26 of the *New York Times,* and my friend got no reward. At long last, the reward was dragged out of me by a woman in Boston who produced a two-column picture from the *Boston Post* of a minister seventy years of age standing beside his bride of twenty-six. I entertained grave doubts whether or not this news was wholly favorable to the Protestant ministry, but the lady claimed that she was entitled to the reward, and I paid her and that closed the matter.

Our Roman Catholic friends are wise enough to be training right now in their parochial high schools in New York City over one thousand journalists most of whom they expect to put to work as reporters on daily newspapers. If one wonders why so much news is slanted favorably toward Roman Catholic activities and so little toward Protestant, this may be part of the answer. Why should we not encourage youth of journalistic talent and of Christian backgrounds and ideals to become able reporters of news so that the millions of Christians in America may find that the public press promotes truth, righteousness, justice, good will, peace, and sobriety? The field of news abounds in exciting adventures of goodness for reporters who have the Christian insight and the Christian interest at heart.

To the credit of the Bruce Publishing Company, let it be said that this company, in loyalty to its own faith, has dedicated its facilities to the development of "an indigenous American Catholic school of fiction." The company asserts that they propose to give encouragement to the rise of such a school as will "portray the grass roots of Catholic faith in the United States." It is no less worthy for Protestants to dedicate themselves to that expression of the Christian faith which makes for freedom of mind, liberty of soul, and the growth of democratic institutions. This is not to ignore the important fact that there are multiple issues in the moral and spiritual realm where Catholics, Jews, and Protestants may present a united impact through the press. Such issues as brotherhood, the fight against race prejudice and injustice, the demand for clean and honest government, the need to resist communism, the securing of permanent peace, and the separation of church and state should find us standing together.

2. *The solid moral steadfastness of our Republic requires a galaxy of writers of moral purpose and editors of enlightened Christian conscience.*

A well-known magazine, one of a trio, announces itself as "the most potent editorial force in America." Another proclaims its purpose—"to create the first great American century." These magazines claim a readership circulation of twenty-eight million. We must concede that here is a tremendous impact upon American thinking, American standards, and American habits. Therefore, it becomes alarming to realize that these three magazines are reported to have carried in a recent year the enormous total of 898 pages of attractive liquor advertisements, many printed in brilliant four colors and some in fascinating double-page spreads. These 898 pages of paid liquor propaganda went repeatedly month after month and often week after week into twenty-eight million American families!

Consistently these ads associated the drinking of intoxicating liquors with those objects which Americans ardently desire—success, distinction, graciousness, beauty, prestige, charm, gaiety—with nary a scintilla of a hint that liquor carries deleterious and devastating effects. The fact that these ads are reported to have netted a revenue of $12,751,000 in a single year is not to be overlooked. (It is interesting to note in contrast that due to the strong convictions of the late Cyrus Curtis, *The Saturday Evening Post* to this day carries no liquor advertising, and reportedly refused recently an offered liquor advertising contract of fifteen million dollars.) One trembles to think of the kind of American century which the liquor advertisers seem determined to forge upon American youth as the propaganda

B

chains are riveted blow by blow, week by week. Most assuredly we either must call some of our present editors and publishers to repent at the mourners' bench or discover and train editors and publishers of ennobled conscience to whom the Christian ideals of moral strength, alert sobriety, and heroic righteousness are pre-eminent concerns.

3. *The imperative need of Christian pens is pointed out by the fact of the studied omission of religious motivation and fact in much of the current writing.*

. Dean Weigle of Yale expressed recently to a group of educators his distress over printed materials provided for the schools of New Haven to celebrate the tercentenary of that historic city. The materials were read in all the public schools and widely distributed. Dean Weigle indicated that the writing omitted reference to religious motivation as having had a decisive part in the founding and development of New Haven. Whenever the facts called for a clear admission of religious motivations (and they were powerful among those sturdy New England Puritans) it was merely stated that they did not like this, so they did that. Thus the school children growing up would never guess anything about the rich Puritan convictions and profound stirrings which created the new colony, which gave to it its tremendous tradition, and which almost invariably marked its development and pattern during the first 100 years. Dean Weigle emphasized that this way of dealing with history is not only inaccurate, but positively misleading. It is history in distortion. It apparently was written thus to placate a secularized public, as well as certain religious groups. Allusion to the motivation of the Puritan religion was not considered desirable.

We need a generation of writers sensitive to our lofty traditions. Too many popular writers have entered into the prevalent conspiracy of silence with regard to the dominant Christian heritage and convictions.

4. *We need Christian writers to supply the general public with better reading than the current literature which so largely reflects the disintegration of Western society and the vulgarization of American standards.*

The American mind is being drugged with perverted, pornographic pulps, pouring putridity from the presses and corrupting the morals of this great nation. One need not wonder at the low moral tone in national and city governments when one reflects upon a typical American newsstand. It has been said that if J. Fenimore Cooper were writing his famous book today, the publishers would probably change the title to *The Lust of the Mohicans*. Writing has largely abandoned the vertical plane not only for the horizontal but often for the low horizontal. Under the specious plea of picturing life, one detects actually much less the art of portraying life than the art of easy money. Some publishers are under suspicion of producing impure books in order to mark up pure profits. Of our modern drama some wag has said, "Modern plays on Broadway are just the Kinsey Report with gestures." J. Donald Adams remarks that today one must look sharp at book jackets and advertising to see whether one is being urged to buy a book or a brassiere.

Nevertheless, let there never be a doubt that religion remains the most exciting subject in the world. Only its friends are to blame for having overlaid it with a coat of dull gray. The public, if given a chance, will now and again give the religious writer the spotlight at the center of the stage. A recent year is loudly eloquent in demonstration of this fact that religious writing meets a great human hunger. Numbered among the first ten best sellers during 1949 were *The Big Fisherman, The Seven-Story Mountain, The Greatest Story Ever Told,* and *Peace of Soul.* The last named sold just slightly under *The Big Fisherman,* the top-selling fiction book of the year. As runner-up, and close to the first ten, was *Peace of Mind* which had first been rejected, it is said, by twenty publishers before acceptance by Simon and Schuster. Another great seller is *Guide to Confident Living* by Norman Vincent Peale.

Visitors to Topeka, Kansas, still have pointed out to them the parsonage of a Congregational church, the residence of the late Charles M. Sheldon, whose book of another generation, *In His Steps,* had a circulation of ten million copies and was translated into twenty-three languages. The greatest single book order in America was for a religious book, when Sears, Roebuck in 1913 placed with Harper and Brothers an order for one million copies of *Ben Hur* by General Lew Wallace. There is ample proof that religion can get reader-attention once we get the flame of genius holding the pen. "The more's the blame" that we have too often and too easily surrendered the field to the immoral, the irreligious, and the irresponsible. We may rejoice today at the new turn being taken by popular publications. The roots of religion which lie so deep in the American soil are shooting forth again. Religion is getting attention. Even secular editors are discovering that religion can be exciting news, and they are learning that there is a public demand for this theme. It is almost impossible right now for a popular magazine to escape the publication of at least one religious article. This field now offers great challenge to the bold and the daring who have original ideas and adventurous plans. Religion is the most wide-open field in journalism in America today.

5. *Now we must also train writers for our Christian publications.*

There is a serious dearth of writers and editors trained to serve Christian publications and dedicated to writing with a moral and Christian purpose. This lack is appalling in the field of writers of curricular materials and Sunday church school texts. Recently we were informed that a major denomination was caught in the shortage of writers equipped to create new Sunday church school texts. It was reported that as a result, the editor-in-chief had to throw himself into the emergency and through late hours in the night write texts at three different age levels. Any editorial executive who confronts a vacancy in his staff knows at once the turmoil and panic that seize him when he must begin a search for trained and experienced assistance at some special age level.

Now this problem becomes acute if we desire writers who not only have a knowledge of curricular needs, but also possess a creative style of vivid power and vital warmth. There is a vast vacuum made by the lack of lesson writers of captivating style and convincing power. Of course, the demands are enormously severe. Think of what we require of these writers—biblical knowledge and accuracy, theological understanding, familiarity with the techniques of progressive pedagogy, awareness of the psychology, vocabulary, and interests of the different ages of childhood and youth, together with clarity in style, gripping power in composition, and facility in production—not to mention the ability to understand the quirks of pastors, the complaints of parents, the prejudices of churches, and the idiosyncrasies of the editor-in-chief. *It is one big order for mighty small pay!*

Nevertheless we must rescue the church school text or quarterly from its inherited dullness, which has so long served to develop in the child a prejudice against religious literature and which he carries over into adulthood. Let it be said with flaming letters that truthful writing need not and must not be prosy. Theodore Roosevelt was right when in 1912 he told the American Political Science Association, "Unless writing is vivid it will not be truthful, for no amount of dull painstaking detail will sum up the whole truth unless the genius is there to point the truth." The power of vivid colors and racy language can be employed to command attention to the most important texts a child will ever read.

Three hundred years ago John Bunyan wrote a book of perennial fascination in simple picture words of breathless suspense—a book which bridges all ages, as much loved by children as by adults. The persistent influence and endearing charm of *Pilgrim's Progress,* written by an untutored, imprisoned preacher, ought not only to prove beyond a doubt the possibility of writing about religion effectively, but also to challenge us with an immense discontent that we ourselves are not able to achieve a similar objective which is so much desired.

Since public school texts have in recent years been vastly improved, must we continue to produce Sunday church school texts that are unattractive, unimpressive, and unlikable? Is not the magnificent and glorious message of the Christian gospel worthy of attractive and compelling form which is suited to win enthusiastic attention and cherished affection?

Recently the red-letter day for which I had long lived arrived like a bolt out of the blue. A lawyer from a distant city was at our receptionist's desk asking to see the writer of one of our new senior high texts. Since the writer lives 1200 miles away, the receptionist ushered the attorney into my office. This attorney teaches a class of fifteen boys of high school age. The boys had so much enjoyed the current church school text that they had commissioned their teacher to come one hundred miles to our office in order to meet the writer of the text and to gather all possible information about him to relay back to the boys. It seems that the text had been made so interesting that the boys' curiosity had been aroused about the author. Their instincts were correct, for he is an interesting man of unusual personality and consecration. I supplied the teacher with available information about him to carry back to the boys. Then still somewhat doubtful, I said, "You really mean, do you, that your fifteen boys actually *enjoyed* this Sunday school text?" He shot back, " 'Enjoy' is much too mild a word. They not only enjoyed it, they were thrilled by it." When he departed I walked up and down the concourse of our office, beside myself in jubilation.

Too much of our curriculum writing is suspicious of the imagination. We suffer from the deadly detail of trained incapacity. We need emancipation from the jargon of the trade and the wearisome clichés of professional Christian education. We need a fresh breeze to blow through Christian literature. We need some "Jack the Jargon Killer"—a man like Winston Churchill who, when he was Prime Minister, once wrote in protest against the heavy phrases used in government circles, "This is bastard English up with which I will not put."

We need writers who can give punch to great ideas. We recall Nelson's famous words to his fleet at Trafalgar Bay, "England expects every man to do his duty." Someone has said that a modern public official would have said it this way: "England anticipates that in regard to the present emergency, personnel will duly implement their obligations in accordance with the functions allocated to their respective age groups in order No. 605." Surely such deadly language would have been enough to have defeated the English and to have changed human history.

We need writers who appreciate the simple, direct, and colorful language of the Bible. George Orwell somewhere contrasts the power of a simple Bible verse with its expression by a writer of modern political science. The author of Ecclesiastes wrote: "I returned, and saw under the sun, that the race is not to the swift, nor the battle to the strong, neither yet bread to the wise, nor yet riches to men of understanding, nor yet favour to men of skill; but time and chance happeneth to them all." Orwell describes the way some scholar might express it today: "Objective consideration of contemporary phenomena compels the conclusion that success or failure in competitive activities exhibits no tendency to be commensurate with innate capacity, but that a considerable element of the unpredictable must be invariably taken into account."

There is the further need, since our folkways, traditions, and denominational prejudices and preferences are what they are, to require writers to have some understanding of the limitations which may beset the average teacher in the average church. At the same time they must have some exceptional skills in knowing how to write the truth in persuasiveness and in love. There is no difficulty in finding writers who glory in shocking pious people and who take great delight in hurling, in the name of personal integrity, verbal bombshells into the quietude of a church congregation. Yet it is not too much to expect that writers will adopt techniques suited to gaining an entrance for the truth, since we do have a case to present before the jury.

In modern life people prefer to talk about "the mortician" rather than "the undertaker"; a man prefers to purchase "a used car" rather than "a second-hand car." By the same token, there are inoffensive ways to express prophetic Christian truth. If we expect to instruct and lead our people, we must see that our writers shape ideas not to arouse resentment but to win acceptance. We may bristle like porcupines over the prejudices and limitations of many of our church people, but it will be wise for us to curb our inner irritation and to write the language of persuasion and appeal.

To lead our people, we must have writers who are willing to discover and employ the wisest methods of expression. For example, an honest senator, when he was asked, at the end of a big banquet, for a solution to the food shortage after the war, bluntly replied, "Eat less." Members of the opposite party were not slow to set this in the light of brutal advice. On the same problem, that suave public relations expert, Charles Luckman, also told the American people to eat less, but his words were chosen with care. He suggested to the public, "economy in the use of foods through personal restraint." Nobody objected.

6. *We must recruit and train these much-needed writers for the much-needed periodicals and church school texts.*

There are several possible means by which this can be done. *The first is the school of journalism.* Writers for the highly specialized fields of religious curricular materials require richly-stored minds of penetrating insights and experiences of depth and background and of literary wealth. The best techniques and skills of journalism cannot atone for lack of basic biblical and religious knowledge, nor for the absence of training in the arts and sciences, nor for a lack of understanding of human experience in all its pathos and tragedy. Spiritual things must still be discerned spiritually.

However, there are hopeful signs in schools of journalism, and the religious field of journalism is gaining prestige. A number of institutions have established majors in religious journalism. Several seminaries are now offering courses in religious writing.

It is still a major responsibility of editors and publishers to discover and train writers. An editor must be a talent scout. He must go on voyages of exploration and discovery, if he would secure talented writers and editors.

The second means is the writers' conference. The Green Lake Christian Writers and Editors' Conference began in the summer of 1948. Such a conference plan provides a partial answer to the problem. Its purpose is to train writers, to discover new writers, to enable editors to compare notes and keep abreast of new ideas, to provide a fellowship among craftsmen. The Green Lake conference is on the widest interdenominational basis and is building, by means of scholarship aid, a school of promising young writers. This conference has plans for the creation of a National Foundation of Christian Writers and Editors, with year-round headquarters and an executive director capable of conducting clinics in religious journalism in colleges and universities across the country. The plan anticipates creating scholarships for students in this field. Few or no scholarships exist in any American school for students who are preparing specifically for religious journalism. This is appalling in a "Christian nation," where the power of the press is tremendous. Plans propose subsidies to improve the quality and effectiveness of the religious press in the United States.

The third method is the Internship Plan. We invite to our office for the summer period, varying from six to eight weeks, four college students who give evidence of possibilities in the field of journalism. They serve as interns at a subsistence salary. The results leave us enthusiastic and hopeful. Something about this Internship Plan has appeal. It is like teaching one to swim by taking a fellow out in a boat, dumping him overboard and saying, "Now sink or swim." Usually he finds a way to swim. These interns take serious assignments and learn a variety of secrets behind the editor's "Iron Curtain."

A fourth plan is talent discovery through diligent search and en-

ticement of new contributors. The search may take several forms, such as visits, manuscripts, or prizes. The award method, I presume, has been employed by most editors. Several denominations have had outstanding success with this method. The study of unsolicited manuscripts is important. One of our editors recently brought me an unsolicited manuscript and remarked, "This writer has exceptional ability." Today he is on our list of talented writers.

On the other hand it is simply astounding how stupid we are in not recognizing talent when it confronts us. The *Christian Century* recently had great success with a special article which through reprint has had a distribution of over 250,000 copies. Imagine my amazement to discover that this writer had written an article for us many months before, but we had failed in our perception of her gifts and rejected her manuscript. It is fair to say that we are back camping on her trail. The *Christian Century* and *Baptist Leader* are now rivals for the same heart and the same pen of the same fair maiden.

The best writers are often shy and timid and need encouragement to come out of their retirement. The editor must become a prospector for gold. Indeed, he needs to carry a Geiger counter to discover the hidden uranium of writing ability.

The fifth plan is the recognition of the significance of the editor and writer in their influence upon the public. Did not Carlyle say, "Is not an able editor one of the rulers of the world?" I fear, however, that but little public recognition is given to the editor. In fact when one listens to pulpit prayers one never hears petition for blessings upon writers and editors. I have put this test to many religious assemblies. "How many of you pray for ministers, missionaries, teachers, doctors, and nurses?" A sea of hands goes up over the congregation. "How many of you pray for editors and writers?" A great silence follows. Then to save the face of the congregation usually someone far back puts up a faint hand, which I can only hope is honest, although I remain in doubt. Nevertheless, why should we not lift up in our prayers those who so mightily influence our generation by the power of the pen?

I also observe that in youth conferences where we challenge young people to full-time Christian service, we never challenge them to dedicate their talents to the service of Christian journalism. We ask them to sign up to become pastors and Christian educators and missionaries, but we do not exalt the call of the Christian craftsman in the field of journalism. Yet, who can doubt that this field remains of incalculable dynamic influence?

One thinks of the Supreme Teacher. With only a handful of followers in Galilee, he was so confident of the power of his words that he had the sheer audacity to declare, "Heaven and earth shall pass away, but my words shall not pass away." Past the crashing of empires and above the crumbling of thrones, his words stand with inexhaustible vitality as the rallying point of hope for our day and generation. Truly did he say, "The words that I speak unto you, they are spirit, and they are life."

The Word of God is our book of life-giving inspiration, and the pen dipped in its flame has power to move and to endure. No wonder the dying Sir Walter Scott, from his wheel chair, said to his son-in-law, "Lockhart, bring me the book." And Lockhart, glancing over the shelves of the great library at Abbotsford, said, "Sire, what book?" To which Scott replied with a reprimand: "How can you ask? There is but one book."

When from this fountain of life we draw our inspiration, our words live forever. "The grass withereth, and the flower thereof falleth away: but the word of the Lord endureth for ever."

THE FUTURE OF CHRISTIAN PUBLISHING

LUTHER WESLEY SMITH

Dr. Luther Wesley Smith, after highly successful pastorates in Columbia, Mo., and in Syracuse, N. Y., became in 1938 the Executive Secretary of what is now the Board of Education and Publication of the American Baptist Convention. In this responsible post he has given brilliant direction to the publishing activities of the American Baptist Publication Society (The Judson Press). In addition to many other significant denominational services, he conceived the idea of a great American Baptist Assembly for the training and inspiration of all types of Christian workers; and by his courage, vision, and industry he arranged for the purchase of the magnificent grounds and buildings at beautiful Green Lake, Wis., where the Christian Writers and Editors' Conference is held annually.

THE FUTURE of Christian publishing is dependent, as it always has been, upon the merit and effectiveness of the printed word as a medium for expressing the ideas, the ideals, and the feelings of man. The printed word may appear in various patterns and dress, but it is still true that it has a mission in the transmission of thought and culture which it would be hard to exaggerate.

We are often tempted to view with alarm the inroads upon the publishing enterprise of first the movies, then the radio, and now television. But in point of fact, although the children of America gobble up the "funnies" with an avidity which dismays us—particularly if we observe how they prefer these tabloid presentations to that which we write—nevertheless, it is probable that the amount of reading done by the present generation of children, youth, and adults exceeds in quantity severalfold the amount of reading done by all ages a generation ago. As I think of the reading done by children today, in comparison with that done by the children of my day, it is clear that the printed word as such is still an important factor in the experience of folks. And I believe it is destined to be even more so in the unfolding years.

The printed word has unusual power to convey ideas related to reasoned convictions. When the individual begins to think about the deeper truths and the ultimate facts of life, the printed word becomes a medium of peculiar cogency. It will always be so. When one sees before him the words that bring to life ideas which touch the well-spring of his convictions, fears, or faith, he can take the time with this medium to meditate and to interrelate the thoughts brought to life before his eyes. Thoughts partly dim and confused come to birth out of his own meditation. So the printed word comes to have a unique authority for the individual. It is no happenstance that the individual says to himself unwittingly: "It must be true; I saw it in print."

So great is the power of the printed word that often it is our despair. Yet it ought also to be our constant challenge. God has placed in the hands of the writer and editor an instrument of amazing potency. It is a two-edged sword; and neither television nor any other instrument will turn its edge!

Nothing is so powerful, we are told, as an idea whose hour has struck. When William Tyndale risked death that he might put in the hands of every ploughboy the Bible in his own tongue, he was bearing witness to his faith in the power of the printed word, especially the printed Word of God. That God could and would speak directly to men's hearts out of the Scriptures, and that men had direct access to God—that was an idea whose hour had struck. Once it was set marching through the minds of men, it released the mighty tide of the Reformation.

One can think of other ideas whose hour had struck. In every case, whether they were ideas rooted in truth or in the evil nature and ambitions of men, it was the printed word which set those ideas to marching. Many striking illustrations of this fact will immediately come to mind.

There was *Uncle Tom's Cabin,* which kindled the fires of the Abolition Movement. There was Sheldon's *In His Steps,* which gathered up the enthusiastic loyalty of the American Christian Youth Movement, so strong at the turn of the century, and which set the hearts and minds of men on the question: "What would Jesus do in my place?" In recent decades there was Karl Marx's epoch-making writing, and there was *Mein Kampf,* the book that convinced millions that the evil incarnated in Hitler was as good as the truth, and a lot more practical in our kind of world.

What, then, is the idea whose hour has now struck? Has the answer come as a flash in the night? Who will express it in living tones? Who will give it tongues of fire? Whatever the idea is, it must have the printed word to set it on the march through the highways of men's minds.

When my daughter Laura was twelve years old she became ill with the "flu." The devoted boy friend came over with tokens of his remembrance. One thing which he brought, because he knew it was "great stuff," was a big armful of comic books. No, his other arm was not filled with Sunday school papers. It never occurred to him that the latter would be received eagerly. But why should not our Sunday school papers be so thrilling and interesting that children will want to share them with friends in their neighborhood?

They tell me that the newsstands sell books on love and true romance not by the dozen, but by the ton. Why do youths, from good homes and underprivileged homes alike, keep the presses of the land pouring forth such pulp? That is one phase of the publishing enterprise that is not being imperiled at the present time. Why? Because the subject of love is intensely interesting to every growing youth as he begins to sense his own increasing relationship to this inward driving force.

But is not every youth eager to succeed, to achieve? Is he not desirous of learning how to win friends and receive their approbation? Is he not deeply concerned to "be somebody"? And how are all these interests related, and how is he, as an individual, related to "success," which is the big idea of our day? Some years ago *American Magazine* leaped into leadership when it began to publish in each issue a success story of how some American boy made good in a big way. Would not any high school or college youth who is dreaming of the possibility of becoming a doctor thrill to the story of Albert Schweitzer, if it were told in words that did justice to the life of that great missionary?

Religious novels have similar potency. But why are there so few of them that really stir one's imagination and command reader attention? Other novels are devoured by millions. Why should not religious novels, through their fictional characters, tie into the deep and soul-stirring experiences of life in order that he who runs may read what God, Christ, faith, sin, and righteousness mean in life today?

An ancient saying reads like this: "Where there are books there is no past." The past is gathered up into the living present through the printed word. But with equal truth it may be said: "There is a past only where there is reading." Without the printed word the past is lost. The gigantic task of passing on our culture from one age to the next depends upon the printed word. But who will read unless the printed word is indeed a living word?

The future of the Christian publishing enterprise is more significant and promising than any words of mine can suggest. Methods will help—new patterns of thought, new dress for our ideas, new and more efficient co-operative planning. Why should there not be Protestant Bookstores instead of weaker denominational stores which are in competition with one another? Why not a Christian Writers' League to stimulate the writing of books of merit for children, youth, and adults? Why should there not be Christian pamphleteers who will proclaim the new age of "the Parliament of man, the Federation of the world"?

The spoken word is carved in air; the printed word is cut in granite. It is still true that he who wields the pen shapes the future. Because I believe that God's will and his truth will prevail, I believe profoundly in the unfolding influence and power of the Christian publishing enterprise. It is simply the hands and feet which we give to the printed word.

PART TWO

What Do You Have to Say?

WRITING WITH A CHRISTIAN PURPOSE

RICHARD W. GRAVES

Dr. Richard W. Graves is Editor-in-Chief of Publications, the Board of Christian Education of the United Presbyterian Church in North America. It was in 1935 that he was called from the pastorate to serve his denomination as an editor; since 1945 he has been Editor-in-Chief. Included among his responsibilities is that of editing The Christian Union Herald. *He is a valuable member of the Uniform Lesson Committee of the National Council of Churches. Recently an attractive volume of his editorial-essays was published. It bears the intriguing title,* Saints and Silhouettes.

EARLY in the fifteenth century, a boy was doing what all boys have done from time immemorial; he was cutting his initials in the bark of a tree. The only difference was that this boy—whose name incidentally was John Gooseflesh—instead of cutting his initials *into* the tree, was cutting them *out* of the tree in block letters made of wood. He took them into the house, laid them on the table, and arranged them in the order of his name. His mother, who was a dresser of parchment, had a pot of dye bubbling in the corner on red-hot coals. Somehow as John Gooseflesh passed the edge of the table where he had the letters of his name carefully laid out, he knocked one of them off into the pot of dye. Trying to get it out of the pot of dye quickly, he burned his fingers and dropped the letter on a piece of pure white parchment. When he whisked the thing off the piece of parchment, he saw with a sense of awe, for the first time in the Western World, a printed letter. In that moment a new idea was born.

As Samuel McCord Cutters has put it, "When a new idea gets into an unfurnished mind it has the time of its life." That is exactly what happened with John Gooseflesh. Twenty years later, this lad—

C

who by that time had taken his mother's name and was known as John Gutenberg—had worked out the first press using movable type. Surely there is something symbolic and significant in the fact that the first book printed on that press was the Bible.

Think of the huge number of the Christian writings that have been pouring from the presses from that day down to this. They have been of every conceivable form—books, magazines, sermons, hymns, Sabbath school lessons, and many, many other forms which, though varied, equally deserve to be designated Christian writing, for all of them represent writing with a Christian purpose.

Writing with a Christian purpose! What is that kind of writing? Perhaps I am old-fashioned, and perhaps I represent an old-fashioned denomination, but I am going to say that writing with a Christian purpose is "writing that is slanted toward the conversion of sinners and the edification of saints." That is an old, old phrase, but I do not believe it can be much improved.

In all our lives we shall never read anything profounder than those words of the prologue of the Gospel of John: "In the beginning was the Pattern, and the Pattern became flesh and dwelt among us." In all of our writing with a Christian purpose, there has got to be that note of the evangel.

We are indebted to our Quaker brother for giving us that phrase so magnificently descriptive of our civilization, "a cut-flower culture." That is precisely what we have. Cut flowers can look good for a time, but because they have no rootage, they do not last long. There is much that is fair, much that is lovely, much that has magnificent eye-appeal about our civilization, but where is the rootage of it? It must be in the eternal soil of God, in the Pattern which once for all became flesh and lived among us here in our world. We beheld his glory, the glory of the only begotten of the Father, full of grace and truth.

Our writing, if it is to serve a Christian purpose, has got to be writing pointed toward bringing mankind, our readers, under the lordship of Christ, who is the incarnate Pattern and who gives to life both meaning and the beauty of holiness. Some people think, these days, that holiness is a prissy word; it is not. Holiness, according to its good Anglo-Saxon root, simply means whole. The root is exactly the same for the words "whole," "holy," "healthy," "heal," and "hale." All holiness is wholeness. Therefore, everything in our writing, in all of its varied types—whether curriculum, story papers, or what not—if it is to be holy writing, must minister to wholeness— wholeness of body, of mind, of spirit, and of relationships.

We must approach the total person in our writing: the mind, the emotions, and the will. God gave us a magnificent charter for appealing to the reason of men when he said, "Come now, and let us reason together." God, who implanted reason within us, honors every effort we make to meet the reason, the mind, of those for whom we write. We must not be content with that, however; for we should write also to the feelings of people. That is where many of us who represent the larger Protestant churches have fallen down rather badly in recent years. There is in people an enormous amount of latent emotion waiting to be channeled. It is too bad that it has been channeled into everything under the sun except Christian living. Why should not these emotions be harnessed to something big instead of to so many little, trivial things? We should write not to exploit emotions, but to seize upon them and channel them for the kingdom of God.

We also should write for decision. Horace Bushnell made a magnificent contribution to Christian education by teaching Christian nurture. Now the pendulum has begun to swing away from the idea that nurture is all that is needed, that one may develop naturally into Christian discipleship without any crises that call for decision, which was never really Bushnell's idea in the first place. We now know— and Bushnell, of course, must have known it all the time—that one does not enter into Christian discipleship that easily. There are crises for adults as well as for young people; they come to points where they simply have to make decisions, costly decisions. Therefore, we must point our teaching not only to men's minds, with their fine sense of interpretation and their ability to harness the emotional drive latent in men, but point it also to men's experiences of choice, of decision, of crisis, out of which they will emerge a different people than they were before.

A LITERATURE OF HOPE

LAWRENCE E. NELSON

Dr. Lawrence E. Nelson brings to his discussion of "A Literature of Hope" a wealth of factual information and an optimism which is most enheartening. He is the Director of the Division of Languages and Literature, the University of Redlands, Redlands, Calif. In addition to his experience as a teacher of literature and of the art of good writing, he has produced numerous college textbooks of wide circulation. He is the author also of that entertaining and highly informative volume, Our Roving Bible.

FRANK W. BOREHAM, the Australian Baptist preacher who wrote such an incredible number of fascinating essays (now being reprinted by The Judson Press), has one intriguingly entitled "Hatpins and Buttonhooks." He had captured the phrase from an elementary-school boy who announced one day that he had just made an important discovery: some sentences end in buttonhooks [?]; others in hatpins [!]. When this topic was handed me, it ended in a button-hook—"A Literature of Hope—question mark." I immediately threw away the buttonhook and grabbed a hatpin. "A Literature of Hope—exclamation point."

That's the way it looks to me, and I'll tell you why. Then you can judge for yourself.

The most hopeful book in the world is the Bible. It is also the most widely distributed. Such has not always been the case. As late as the year 1800, there were in the world only about four million copies of the Bible. It is now estimated that more than 1,600,000,000 copies of the Bible or parts of it have been distributed, with marked effect.

Within the past ten years, two Gallup polls have found that the Bible is becoming more widely read, both by older people and by young people. *Publishers' Weekly* has reported increased buying of the Bible by lay people for their own use. *Business Week* has noted "a significant preference for 'study' Bibles over 'show' Bibles; purchasers insist on large type, references, and marginal notes." New and more readable translations abound.

But let us turn from the Bible to so-called secular literature, to see what the trend is there. Not long ago a book called *Fifty Years of Best Sellers: 1895-1945* included in its preface this statement: "The 1890's saw the end of one period of great popularity for the religious novel, but during the 1930's and early 1940's this type of fiction regained its hold." It listed in order of sales 169 books which since 1880 had sold a half million copies or more.

Of the fifteen most-sold books, five are highly religious. Leading all others was Sheldon's *In His Steps,* with eight million copies. The other four were *Ben Hur, Song of Our Syrian Guest,* Hurlbut's *Story of the Bible,* and *The Robe.* Lower on the list, but selling more than a million copies each, were *Strength for Service to God and Country* and *The Song of Bernadette.* Then came such titles as *The Birds' Christmas Carol, Magnificent Obsession, Quo Vadis, The Story of the Other Wise Man, Green Light, The Keys of the Kingdom, The Apostle, The Sky Pilot, The Citadel, The Inside of the Cup, In Tune with the Infinite, Quiet Talks on Power,* and *The Christian's Secret of a Happy Life. The Big Fisherman* appeared after the list was compiled.

The conclusion is inescapable: for the past seventy years the American people have been, and still are, intensely interested in fiction and non-fiction dealing with the impact of Christianity upon human lives. They buy such books, read them, and profit tremendously by them.

In 1860 the Boston *Post* tabulated some of the best sellers up to that time. Of twenty titles only three were religious: Abbott's *Young Christian,* Ingraham's *Pillar of Fire,* and Malcolm's *Bible Dictionary.* On this earlier list, no religious book ranked higher than seventh. Today a larger number of religious books are included among the best sellers, and they rank higher on the lists.

A similar trend is occurring with religious plays. In 1917 Myrta McGinnis listed 205 "modern morality plays and plays containing morality elements," written in various countries since 1838. Forty were written in the *sixty years preceding 1898;* 165 in the *twenty years following.* Similar results are reported by two other people who have investigated different types of religious plays, especially in America. No wonder William Lyon Phelps of Yale wrote, "One interesting feature of twentieth century drama has been the notable increase in the use of the Bible as dramatic material." In 1931 the New York Public Library issued a list of 1,948 plays based upon the Bible.

By 1938, newspapers and periodicals were commenting on the surprising increase of religious plays on Broadway; and the Los Angeles *Times* was remarking: "Plays are reflectors of trends. Has the long-talked-of revival of religion set in? Will the movies catch the contagion?" Quite obviously, for at least half a century, drama has been finding an increasingly deeper rootage in religion.

The same trend is true of poetry. The average book of verse published between 1910 and 1920 contained almost twice as much poetry about Christ as was contained in similar books published in the 1890's.

In both Great Britain and America, the use of the Bible is still increasing, and at a more rapid rate than formerly. Moreover, it is the body of ideas in the New Testament, and not merely the picturesque and dramatic portions of the Old Testament, which is causing the principal increase.

The various objective and statistical studies are notable in two respects. They indicate unanimously that writers are leaning more heavily upon the Bible for ideas and illustrations than was formerly the case. They also flatly contradict and disprove the widely held idea that the influence of the Bible is fading from current literature. Thus they form an interesting parallel to the fact that the Bible is being sold and read more widely today than heretofore.

This turn to religious books is continuing unabated. The February 3, 1951, issue of *Publishers' Weekly* was devoted almost exclusively to religious books, and revealed that last fall the sales of Abingdon-Cokesbury were up 20 per cent; of Association Press, 15 per cent; of Revell, 30 per cent; of Sheed and Ward (Roman Catholic), 12 per cent. Harper's religious book department reported "one of the most successful years since the war." Grosset and Dunlap consider their new $1.50-reprint series, called "Novels of Inspiration," the most important religious publishing project which the firm has undertaken in many years.

But these are quantitative measurements. What about qualitative measurements? Are our ablest writers using these religious themes? Most people will agree that on a world-wide basis the most significant literary awards of the twentieth century are the Nobel prizes, which yield to each recipient a cash award ranging from $30,000 to $40,000, and in addition vastly increased royalties and world-wide fame. It is significant that many of the most powerful books by these world leaders in authorship are deep-rooted in religion.

The author of *Quo Vadis* asserted that he wrote it to show that Christianity is the only ultimate truth. Björnson, in his two-part play *Beyond Our Powers,* wrestles desperately with the problem of objectivity and religious mysticism. Rudolph Eucken popularized religious philosophy in his *The Truth of Religion* and *Can We Still Be Christians?*

Selma Lagerlöf's tenderly understanding *Jerusalem* and its ruthlessly probing sequel, *The Holy City,* are classics. Hauptmann's *The Fool in Christ* is an incisive criticism. Anatole France's ironic *Penguin Island* and *The Revolt of the Angels* placed him on the Catholic Index of forbidden books.

Freethinking George Bernard Shaw's *Three Plays for Puritans, Androcles and the Lion* and *Back to Methuselah,* and his non-dramatic *Adventures of a Black Girl in Search of God* lend point to his insistence that the way of Jesus, had it ever been tried, offered the only possible cure for the world's ills.

Grazia Deledda's *The Mother* depicts a spiritual crisis in the lives of a priest and his illiterate but devout mother. Thomas Mann's multivolumed *Joseph and His Brothers* has won an intensity of acclaim in which I cannot entirely join, so long as the covers of his books remain so unjustifiably far apart.

The final volume of Undset's *Kristin Lavransdatter,* and several of her later books, each show their chief character wrestling with, and turning to, religion. Although Sinclair Lewis in *Main Street,* and more fully in *Elmer Gantry,* rejected Christianity as he thought it was lived, he could not stay away from the subject of religion. It recurs frequently in his later writings.

Paul Heyse wrote *Mary of Magdala.* Maeterlinck's *The Blind* proclaims that religion has been the leader of the past, is now in a slump, but will be in some fashion the hope of the future. O'Neill's

Lazarus Laughed portrays the man who had seen eternity as the most incurably joyous man alive.

Pearl Buck, while resentful of religion, has never been able to escape her missionary background. T. S. Eliot turned from *The Waste Land* to poetry which is filled with an echoing cadence of religion.

In the light of these multiplying instances, it does not seem unwarranted to say that writers of the highest repute are among those who lean very heavily upon religion in their writing.

A bit of summing up is now in order. As a result of the unprecedentedly wide distribution of the Bible, religion has for the past fifty years been steadily gaining ground in literature of all sorts, all over the Western World, but especially in America. At present, the pace is being accelerated. Among those who are using the Bible are authors of the very highest rank.

Some may object, and rightly so, that this is not the whole story; that there is much rottenness in present-day literature, and a great deal of shoddiness. Of course. There always has been and there always will be such writing, so long as there remain any shoddy, cheap-minded readers. But we must not fix our attention so exclusively and so angrily upon the blemishes in modern writing that we overlook its healthy portions.

Did you ever read the little boy's essay upon Oliver Cromwell? It is very brief—one sentence long, in fact. "Oliver Cromwell had an iron will and a wart on his nose, but underneath were deep religious feelings."

Beneath the unsightly excrescences on modern literature are deep religious feelings, as I think I have fairly and amply demonstrated. All I ask is that you do not become hypnotized by the warts.

IF I WERE WRITING CURRICULUM TODAY

Gerald E. Knoff

Dr. Gerald E. Knoff is the Associate Director of the Division of Christian Education of the National Council of the Churches of Christ in the U.S.A. There are but few persons, if any, better qualified through study and experience to discuss the many problems connected with the formulating of an adequate curriculum of Christian education. His address deals with the curriculum from the point of view of its basic philosophy and also from the point of view of its practical use in church schools of all types.

1. If I were writing curriculum today, I would want to know some of the important trends characteristic of the Christian education movement of our time.

What new emphases are to be found in the Christian education of today as compared to the movement of ten, fifteen, or twenty-five years ago? I believe we find a number of new emphases which are constant enough in Protestant Christian educational circles to deserve to be called trends.

a. There is a new interest in churches in the classical heritage of the Christian faith and belief.

One need not view this new theological interest with apprehension, afraid that it will lead us into profitless doctrinal disputation. That is the excess rather than the normal manifestation of this interest. It is not enough that we hold in abeyance this kind of thoughtful examination and unite only upon the basis of practical jobs to be done. We must also answer the deeper questions: "Why are we concerned about this task?" "What is our common task as Christians?" "What, after all, is this gospel we are attempting to teach?" These are theological questions. They are also questions for Christian education.

b. There is rapidly developing a set of attitudes making possible a new and unprecedented place of influence for the Christian Bible.

The return of an interest in a type of theological thought

grounded in the Bible is not confined to Europe. It is found today also in American church life. Congregations and individuals everywhere are beginning to realize that American Protestantism has not paid sufficient attention both to careful and competent biblical teaching and to quiet and attentive listening to what the Bible has to say to us.

c. Everywhere in the Christian education movement there is a new desire to effect a better working relationship between evangelism and Christian education.

We must frankly admit that religious educators and evangelists have not always been on speaking terms. But it is possible, of course, to exaggerate the differences which have grown up between these methods of communicating the Christian gospel. It is a matter of great satisfaction that these tensions are lessening and that a new and more wholesome understanding is rapidly coming about.

d. A rather widespread search for new curriculum forms indicates that one of our creative curriculum periods may be ahead.

The local church curriculum of Christian education has been much criticized. Many of the criticisms have been based upon ignorance and misunderstanding. But there is nothing fixed or final about the present curriculum. It is likely that the many searches which are now going on for more effective curricular forms will bear fruit within the next few years. Nursery curriculum planning, re-examination of the curriculum for older youth, and the current investigation of a possible functional curriculum for adults, are cases in point.

e. The increased awareness of the educational role of the Christian family has led us to define the roles of the home and the church school with new clarity.

These five developments are found in all sections of the American Protestant world and may be the lines of significant advance in the next two decades.

2. If I were writing curriculum today, I would want to know, secondly, something about the persons who are going to use the products of my mind and heart.

I would want to know something about the teachers who are going to use the curriculum materials which I prepare.

That is not an easy task. Those who will use the Sunday school materials you write will come from every region. They will represent the widest possible variety of training, experience, and religious educational background.

[The average teacher is a woman, of middle age, brought up in church life. She spends less than an hour in preparation, usually on Saturday night. She is generally late to class, and uses few modern teaching methods. But she took her present class because she wanted to serve and she was needed.]

Here, then, with some modifications, is the teacher who will be using your material. She has weaknesses. She has strengths. As she depends upon you, so also you depend upon her. Only as the teacher understands the curriculum and the curriculum makers understand the teacher will effective and sustained learning take place.

3. If I were writing curriculum today, I would remember, thirdly, that for a very large number the products of our pens will be the chief, perhaps the only, continuous religious influence in their lives.

This is a fearsome statement to make. I wish earnestly that it were not true. But I am afraid it is. I would not hazard a guess about the percentage of children for whom the Sunday school is only one of many religious influences in their lives, and perhaps one of lesser importance. But I am sure that percentage is very, very small. I wish that the number were much greater. For much the greater number, the efforts of the Sunday school stand almost alone.

There was a time, of course, when the Sunday school teacher could rely with considerable confidence upon the Christian home and Christian family to assume the major share of the task. Remember Robert Burns' picture of devout Scottish family life in "The Cotter's Saturday Night"? I suspect it would not have mattered a great deal if the children of that family did not go regularly to Sunday school. But how many families like that belong to the Calvary Baptist Church of Centerville, U.S.A.?

Nor can we who are concerned for effective Christian education assume that the general community influences are working with us. We are grateful for the fine moral, cultural, and spiritual advantages which American communities at their best afford. Yet in too many instances community influences are either religiously neutral or actually negative. Tilford T. Swearingen has a helpful discussion of this problem in his book, *The Community and Christian Education.* This is a book, incidentally, which deserves to be better known.

It is true, furthermore, that in many of these communities the inherited level of ethical idealism is not being maintained. In Elton Trueblood's famous words they are attempting to maintain a "cut-flower culture." If the accumulated experience of the human race has proved anything at all, it is that social idealism and high standards of ethical living, for the most part, come and come only from exalted religious faith.

We cannot count with certainty upon the family influences or the community forces which affect the children of our church school. What a tremendous responsibility is ours!

4. If I were writing curriculum today, fourthly, I would try to write as if I were a participant in the life of two worlds; as an interpreter of one society to another.

I think we need to keep vividly in mind that the Christian writer needs to remember that he is just that; a *Christian* writer. That means something more than living a personal Christian life. It means that he has a professional responsibility to discharge; namely, to help make possible a situation between persons, some of whom we call learners, and some of whom we call teachers, a personal situation in which the Christian faith can be communicated, passed on, and to the common enrichment of all engaged in the process. And to help bring that about, a writer must see himself as a citizen of two worlds.

Wendell Willkie wrote of *One World,* the common economic and political concerns of those who live upon this inhabited globe. The idea is familiar to the Bible, for it speaks of those who have been created by one God, Creator of all mankind, and Lord of all nations. But the Bible does not speak of "one world" from the standpoint of ultimate reality. This physical world, the Bible says, was not self-created. It was brought into being by the deliberate creative act of a God, who is, in the words of the Nicene Creed, the "Maker of heaven and earth, and of all things, visible and invisible."

This created world, to be sure, sustains all forms of human, animal, and vegetable life. But it, itself, is dependent on the will of God for its existence at any given moment. Furthermore, according to the Bible, as it had a creation, it will have an end. For the created world is not eternal, but sometime will come to a terminus, having run its appointed course.

On this created world, there appeared, in course of time, a man and woman to whom was given the breath of life, who were made in the image of God. This new creation, Man, was neither an angel nor an animal nor even a little of both. But he was an entirely new creation made by the unprecedented act of God. This is his glory. This is also his misery and agony. For man is a citizen of both these worlds. He is a citizen of the heavenly kingdom. He is a participant also in all the affairs of this earth.

All through the Old Testament runs the same theme. Man, who was created in the image of God, is always restless until he finds his life identified with the life of God. And yet the life of God is alien to him and its demands run squarely counter to all his natural instincts and impulses. The prophetic literature of the Old Testament can be understood best, I think, in terms of the tension created by this dual citizenship.

Nor is the essential message of the New Testament anything different. The Gospels, the Epistles, and all other New Testament writings only intensify this awareness. Man is unable either to have the earthly complacency of an animal or the heavenly serenity of an angelic being. God calls man to himself, confronts him with his holy will and purpose, and in the fullness of time sends to him his only Son. Here, man finds himself confronted by the incarnate Son of God walking among men on Judean hills and beside the Galilean lake.

And what does man do? He misunderstands Christ. He rejects him. He betrays him. Finally, he crucifies him. Only after resurrection are his disciples finally and permanently won. And the New Testament message was that while men were on this earth, they were inheritors of a more than earthly kingdom. No one understood this tension better than the apostle Paul, who cried: "O wretched man that I am! who shall deliver me from the body of this death?"

I believe a frank acceptance of this dual citizenship is the key to serene and fruitful Christian living. We cannot evade it. We must not deny it. It is for us to accept it. And it is for us curriculum writers to write so others may teach and still others may learn to live as citizens of two worlds.

5. If I were writing curriculum today, fifthly, I would strive to keep a vivid sense of identity with God, who in all ages has sought to win the proud and rebellious spirits of men to himself.

According to the biblical tradition, God is usually the initiator in drawing men to himself. To use a musical figure of speech, the Bible is a symphony of life with a major and a minor theme. The minor theme is man's search for God; his restless spiritual striving after holiness and righteousness; the upward thrust of the soul of man; its search for contact with the Divine.

But that is only the minor theme. The major theme is God's search for man and God's encounter with man. To be sure, often the God-searching man meets the man-searching God. But usually it is the man-searching God who meets man. And that man may not be a God-searching man as Isaiah. He may be a God-ignoring man, as Belshazzar, or even a God-fleeing man as Adam. For the most part, the Bible is the record of God's ceaseless and patient search for the soul of man, at least as much as, and probably more than, it is the record of man's ceaseless and patient search for God.

The whole Old Testament reaches its culmination in the New, which begins with the story of the incarnation. And the incarnation is not a story of man rising to God, but an account of God descending to man. "Who for us men and for our salvation came down from heaven, and was incarnate by the Holy Ghost of the Virgin Mary."

Behind all we do in writing, in shaping a curriculum, in the work of Christian education, and in the entire life and ministry of the Christian church, stands this historical and present fact of God. He is a God who is eternally and restlessly seeking to win back to him the alienated spirits of men. It is not always pleasant to encounter God. Frequently men will go to almost any lengths to avoid him. But it is the task of the Christian educator, the task of the curriculum, yes, the task of the Christian writer, to help men see that God is seeking to win them to himself.

In our work in writing a curriculum of Christian education, furthermore, we should remember that we stand as co-laborers with God in this ageless, cosmic endeavor. This attempt of God to win back his alienated children is one which he has always shared with his most faithful servants. In a very real sense, our efforts should be directed toward preparing and writing such a worthy and adequate curriculum of Christian education as will help make it possible for God, through it, to win and woo men back to himself.

How proud we should be, and yet how humble, at understanding our role in this light. The almighty and ever-loving God has granted us a place right alongside him in the unremitting and patient effort to win all men's hearts unto himself. God does seem to use men as the instruments of his purpose. If we bring the best we can produce and if that is used by consecrated teachers in the best way they know how, God will work through them and use them as instruments of his love and power. For he is accustomed to work through the partial, little accomplishments of fallible men and women like ourselves.

THE CHRISTIAN CURRICULUM IN OUR CONFUSED WORLD

Eric G. Haden

Dr. Eric G. Haden for some years has been Professor of Christian Education at the Central Baptist Theological Seminary, Kansas City, Kans. An astute observer of world events and of current issues in the field of religious education, he has made many valuable contributions to the development of the church school curriculum. He is a helpful member of the Curriculum Committee of the Board of Education and Publication of the American Baptist Convention.

THE CHRISTIAN message, if it is to be a full Christian message, must be directed against those things which hurt and cripple and restrict mankind. In this connection, there are two points that I should like especially to make. They are these: (1) A full Christian message neglects none of the values of the redemptive emphasis, yet unhesitatingly it includes the doctrine of Christian *behavior*— a doctrine as vital as any other doctrine. (2) A full Christian message neglects none of the cutting truth that is distinctively Christian.

The full Christian message is a message of salvation through Jesus Christ. Man, by the very fact of human birth, becomes involved inevitably in sin. Thus, he is subject to the righteous and holy God who must condemn sin and who alone can set him free from the dominion of sin. This message is distinctively Christian in that it is both as pessimistic about human nature *unredeemed* as it is possible to be, and as optimistic about human nature *redeemed* as it is possible to be.

Since this is the message of Christianity, and of no other faith, we dare not allow it to be watered down until it is scarcely to be distinguished from a refined Buddhism, or an enlightened Mohammedanism, or a genteel Judaism. If we do not have the message of salvation from awful sin through the free mercy of God, what message have we? If we do not proclaim salvation for time and eternity, planned and provided by Almighty God, our Heavenly Father, through the intermediacy of Jesus Christ, who is God incarnate, and who, as a free gift from God, is accepted by men through the exercise of faith followed by good works, what message have we that is distinctively Christian?

A distinctively Christian message that is going to produce results in this world, that is going to demonstrate a "cutting edge," must be more than doctrinally correct. It must be part of a total curriculum which stresses also another fact; namely, that people who are growing in the Christian life shall not merely develop habits, but such *intelligent* habits as will fit them for living in an unknown and unknowable future.

In the past, so long as we could know that the coming years would bring practically the same duties, the same conventions and manners, and the same standards as those which then prevailed, it was not difficult to outline a safe education, secular and religious. There were some things that seemed established. Universal agreement, so it appeared, made the world *safe* on these points: (1) law was law, and was to be respected; (2) international law protected the innocent and the unarmed; (3) a democratic country was free to enact the laws by which it would be governed; and (4) certain natural laws, such as the primacy of the home and the duties of the younger generation to their elders, were of universal acceptance. These principles seemed secure; they were regarded as conquests which forever separated man from the beast. The term "gentleman" did not need defining; a "lady" was recognized as such everywhere. Futhermore, it was held that the experience of the race had demonstrated that virtue always had its reward.

In such a world, the objectives of secular education and of religious education were readily established and easily projected. They could be "boiled down" to this statement: *Let us teach our youth the virtues of our forefathers; that done, they shall never want for material wealth or health of body, mind, and soul.*

Then, in so short a time that some are still aghast at the reversal, all former values were questioned, found wanting, and rejected. The old standards were declared to be hypocritical, traditional, and without reasonable foundation; sometimes mere instruments for the favoring of the privileged classes. International agreements suddenly became "scraps of paper." Public service came into disrepute. A politician's promise became a synonym for deceit. The regulations of international law designed to curb modern warfare were found to be as ineffective as painted spots to change a leopard's character.

In a world run mad, is there any promise of what tomorrow shall be like? For what kind of future shall we prepare? What things that we now hold valuable will be valuable then? Through what kinds of institutions will man live his life? Which ones that we know now will remain, and what will the new ones be like that take the place of those now passing away? Can we depend upon the monogamous family? upon trade established in the assumption of the honesty of the common man? upon law founded on the human need for order, for the protection of the rights of others, for homes, for commerce, and for government? And the churches, what will they be like? What will be their standing in society, if any? What will be the future of the sects of the poor and the disinherited—the Pentecostal groups, Jehovah's Witnesses, and the others which now are gaining members by the hundreds and thousands? What will be their place and what will be ours?

A few years ago a magazine of national circulation contained an article entitled "Educate Your Child for Chaos." Maybe that is the right attitude, although I have not adopted it. Then there appeared that terrifying book, *Education for Death,* which described the way in which Nazi youth were trained in hardness and blind loyalty to the State.

For what shall we educate? I would suggest that we educate,

D

not for death, but for personal resourcefulness. When teaching re-sourcefulness by every means available, let us do more than turn our attention to the skills demanded by specific situations; let us also direct our attention and that of our learners to developing skill in adapting ourselves to the unexpected. We must expect the un-expected; we must not be afraid of it, but see it as a challenge, as an opportunity of accomplishing much with little means.

We have, therefore, a twofold objective: (1) To help our people store up resources within themselves, resources of knowledge and of skill and of appreciation. (2) To help our people develop skill in extricating themselves from unusual situations by drawing with originality upon their inner resources.

With this twofold objective, we are not choosing between two alternatives. We are not calling for the classical emphasis upon stor-ing up knowledge; nor are we advocating the opposite—a training in technical skills in which knowledge of the classics is superfluous. Instead, we are saying that he is best fitted for living in an unknow-able future who has many skills of hand, heart, tongue, and thought, and who has so large a store of self-assimilated experiences of the race that he never lacks for suggestions as to means which may be employed in solving novel and frightening problems.

Among the available resources we shall always consider the Bible, the Holy Scriptures of both the Old and the New Testament, as the paramount depository of divine wisdom, guidance, and inspira-tion, as well as the only adequate fount of information concerning the will of our Creator God for the salvation of his sinning creatures.

This does not mean that we shall rule out all extra-biblical materials and topics. Far from it! There is much in human history to incline our hearts to God. There is much in philosophy, in the natural sciences, in the arts, and in the discussion of human social problems to open our minds to the enlightenment of God's Spirit. Indeed, all such resources—biblical or extra-biblical, resources of ex-perience and experiment, acquired directly or indirectly through our own senses and muscles—will be needed increasingly in meeting a future that is so uncertain and perilous.

In addition to helping our people to acquire these resources, we must help them to develop habits of using these resources for meeting new problems. Excellent studies along this line have been made and are constantly being made. What this amounts to is training in self-reliance, an objective which secular educators have long shared with religious educators. The subject is being treated today in one journal after another, and far more adequately than I can do it here. There is one word, however, that I would add to the discussion. I would encourage our people to be willing to try the new, to think and to live courageously, even dangerously, in this new age.

The religious education task of the Protestant churches is never done. In carrying it out, we must not be afraid to adventure along unfamiliar paths. New ways of thinking are urgently needed; new ways of living are demanded; a new reformation of the Christian churches is being earnestly sought. Only so can we hope to meet the new dangers of greed, passion, and intolerance which are coursing through the world.

The task of the churches, the task of religious education, is to venture along the new paths of thought in theology, in biology, in psychology, in physics, in law, and in government. Thinking is hard work, yes, even dangerous work. But everyone who has sought to follow Christ faithfully has had to accept the responsibility of thinking and working. The call is for pioneers in Christian thinking and service. The churches must continue their efforts to win the multiplied millions of adults, young people, and children who as yet are unreached by any form of religious instruction.

MAKING THE GOSPEL LIVE IN OUR WRITING

CLIFTON J. ALLEN

Dr. Clifton J. Allen has the distinction and great responsibility of being the Editorial Secretary of the Sunday School Board of the Southern Baptist Convention. The publications of that Board are numerous, varied, and of large circulation. His able address, "Making the Gospel Live in Our Writing," is given here in much condensed form. It reveals his earnest evangelical spirit as well as his technical competence as an editor.

THE WORK of the Christian journalist becomes increasingly significant. He writes for a growing audience. He deals with the issues that affect the welfare and destiny of humanity. He has something to say that answers the deepest needs of the human heart and points the way forward for our bewildered world. If he has wisdom enough and skill enough, he can spread abroad the creative ideas that will change the currents of human history according to the will of God.

De Quincey made a distinction between the literature of information and the literature of power. The first could teach; the second could move the spirit of man. The Christian journalist does both. He seeks to teach eternal values, and he seeks to stir the reader to the noblest action. He endeavors to do this by showing the meaning of the gospel for the people and the problems of our times.

The subject of this address defines our task. To make the gospel live in our writing must be our first and foremost objective. But, immediately, we need to clarify one point. Let us understand that we are not to try to make alive something which is dead. We have no need to try to bring the gospel to life. Already it is alive. The gospel of Jesus Christ is the most alive body of truth in the world. It is a living gospel indeed. Because we have a living God and a living Savior and a living Spirit, the gospel is alive, and it is the power of God unto salvation to everyone who believes it. Sometimes Christian writers have forgotten this. The gospel does not need defense, but rather interpretation. It does not need protection, but rather proclamation.

Our task as Christian writers is to make the gospel live by making it real, by making it plain, by making it meaningful in experience. We are to put something in our writing that awakens the reader to an awareness of the transcendent greatness and goodness of God, something that arouses within him a sense of unworthiness and need, something that quickens in him a hunger and thirst for righteousness, and something that fires his soul with a conviction as to what he can become and do through faith in the Lord Jesus Christ. That is exactly what the gospel was designed to do and exactly what it did do throughout the Roman world in the first century of the Christian era. Just to the degree that we make the gospel live in our writing, our writing will be redemptive and spiritually regenerative. Only then will it be a reconstructive force in the world.

I do not mean by this that our writing is to become preachy. Not every article is to become a sermon. The gospel is not preachy. It is more than a sermon. But the gospel was not given simply for spiritual entertainment or mere esthetic culture. It was given to reveal God and save men. It was given that men might know righteousness, joy, and peace. Its purpose was new life, abundant life, eternal life, hope and strength and security and good will and victorious living. Therefore, our writing must deal with the great creative ideas contained in the gospel. And our objective, no matter what form or medium we may choose, must be one in keeping with the high objectives of the gospel.

Thus we conceive our task as Christian writers: To make the eternal gospel a living reality now; to tell the story of the good news of God's love in Christ so that the sinful, weary, despairing hearts of men everywhere may shout with joy; to relate the revealed wisdom of the Scriptures to the problems and tensions of our generation to the end that men will say, "Let us try God's way"; to show so clearly the power of love and the blessings of righteousnesss and the reality of the life everlasting that our readers will want to follow truth, practice love, suffer with patience, and lose themselves in the service of the kingdom of Christ. We will write to help little children feel safe in the certain care of the Heavenly Father, to help growing boys and girls learn the ways of happy living, to help our youth make an intelligent and full commitment to Jesus Christ as Savior and Lord, to help our young people have the insights and ideals and convictions of Christian disciples, and to give direction and inspiration to mature men and women that they may accept the stern duties and sublime opportunities of life in a manner worthy of the children of God.

Nothing is more important than for us to realize that the gospel is the word of life and that our real function is to share its life-giving truth with a lost world. Indeed, the gospel has power to make alive. It will arouse the conscience and produce spiritual conviction. It will stimulate saving faith. It will create moral passion and stamina. It will inspire a desire for holiness and a zeal for goodness. The gospel has power. It contains truth which is corrective and healing, comforting and strengthening. It imparts hope and assurance. As we make the gospel live in our writing, we set in operation in the world a redeeming and reconciling force.

In the light of this definition of our task, consider the high demands made upon us as Christian writers. What will be required of us to make the gospel come alive in our writing?

First of all, we need a deep conviction that making the gospel live is indeed our task, our mission. I trust that this does not seem unnecessary repetition. I am emphasizing it because I know how easy it is for the primary to become secondary. Such a conviction will keep us near to the heart of God and near to the needs and interests of humanity. We shall be kept from vainglory and play-acting in our writing. A conviction at this point will keep us from a mercenary spirit and from writing to appeal to the baser interests of our reading audience. It will have a great deal to do with the selection of ideas and subject matter.

In the next place, we must write out of a full knowledge of the gospel. I do not mean to suggest that every writer must have a degree in theology. But I do mean that to make the gospel live one must have a thorough grasp of its truth. This is important not alone for those who prepare curricular materials. No matter what age group one writes for or the form one chooses to use, one needs a mastery of the content of the Four Gospels. The simple facts connected with the life and work of Jesus must be known. The background and atmosphere of New Testament times must be known. There is a veritable mine of ideas in the Bible. A full and intimate knowledge of the facts and teachings of the Bible provides the background from which one can draw to relate Christian truth to the manifold areas of human experience.

Again, it follows naturally that we must major upon the great central truths and ideas of the gospel. Whether in fiction or editorial, poetry or drama, reporting a Sunday school class project, or interpreting international issues, some great truth of the gospel may furnish the theme or become the criterion of measurement. We make the gospel live by writing the message of the gospel.

We must go a step further in considering the high demands made upon us, if we are to make the gospel live in our writing: we must write from experience. This is always a prerequisite for effective writing. The best reporting is done by one at the scene of action. The best stories come from the depths of personal experience. This same principle, on a much higher level, operates in the work of Christian writers. We have to experience the gospel to understand it and to feel it, and we have to experience it in order to help others understand it and feel it, and believe it and practice it. Intellectual powers are important and valuable. We need to realize, however, that things which are spiritual must be spiritually discerned. I think this would impress upon us that the deep things of the gospel must be learned under the leadership of the Holy Spirit. They must be received through faith. They must be understood by the insights of love and obedience. In a very real sense, the Word must become flesh again and dwell in us, so that we behold his glory and feel his power in our lives. Then we shall write out of the reality of experience.

THE CHRISTIAN COUNTERATTACK

Paul Hutchinson

Dr. Paul Hutchinson is the distinguished editor of The Christian Century. *Due to his dynamic and prophetic editorial direction, that weekly has become outstanding in its field. Many universities, recognizing his religious and journalistic leadership, have bestowed upon him honorary degrees. He has written innumerable significant editorials and feature articles. He is the author also of many books. Two of the more recent are* The New Leviathan *and* From Victory to Peace.

Christianity is a citadel besieged. The time has come when we must launch a counterattack, beat off the foe, and regain the exhilaration of victory. However, there are limitations to this view. I doubt whether the men who wrote the New Testament would ever have agreed that Christianity could be put on the defensive. For them, Christianity was a faith and a power which, by its very nature and despite all outward circumstances, put all other conceptions and ways of life on the defensive. Nevertheless, in a world gone as far toward madness as has ours, where the old hedonistic cry, "Eat, drink, and be merry, for tomorrow we die," has taken on a new urgency in the light of man's despair, this figure of a besieged citadel furnishes a legitimate jumping-off point for our discussion.

Secularism and materialism and communism—which is materialism exalted to the status of a religious faith—characterize our age. These are enemies which seem to be carrying all before them. Many Christian leaders view with horror the inroads of communist materialism, especially in the East. But it may be doubted whether the communist philosophy of life, with all its strident atheism and its insistence on the pursuit of immediate material ends, is doing any more to thwart the purposes of Christianity than is the secularistic spirit and outlook which has become so prevalent in the West. Prof. Pitirim A. Sorokin, the transplanted Russian who is today Harvard's most distinguished sociologist, calls our Western civilization a "sensate" civilization. By that term he means what we mean when we say it is a secular civilization; his word for it simply sounds a little more academically impressive. It is a civilization based on the gratification of the senses, with a denial in life, and often in word, of the reality or importance of spiritual forces.

These are enemies which we instantly recognize. And the more we know about them and their strength in contemporary life, the more formidable we see our task to be as we try to prepare to launch a counterattack. But these are not all. We have still other enemies almost equally as powerful. There is, for example, the moral relativism of our time—the contention that the very nature of morality, as revealed by anthropology and other social sciences, makes the idea of moral absolutes preposterous.

Relativity has become a byword, a slogan, of this century. I do not for a minute deny its importance or, rightly understood, its validity. But when you get *moral* relativity, you get human tragedy, and are on the way to political and social tyranny. Hitler's world was a world of moral relativism; so is Stalin's. That is to say, when morality becomes relative to the good of the state, everything we have seen of brutality, bad faith, and despotism follows inevitably. The man (or the clique) controlling the state then becomes the arbiter of morality, and is justified by the morality which he himself proclaims.

But there is another enemy which must at least be mentioned. In some respects it is an even more dangerous one. It is more dangerous because it is within the citadel. The ignorance, provincialism, and noisy prejudice of our own Christians make it virtually impossible for us to mount an effective counterattack against these other enemies which I have mentioned. Mind you, these are "good" people, devoted in their loyalty to what they regard as the Christian faith. But they betray us, nevertheless, when we try to come to grips with the unfaith of this age. Never forget that the essence of the attack which is made on Christianity these days, from whatever quarter the attack comes, is that Christianity is superstition. And when Christians of whatever stripe exhibit what their fellows will regard as superstition, they thereby help to pile up our counterattack before it ever gets started.

One more enemy I must name, and it is in many respects the

most dangerous of all those which confront us. I am talking about the loss of a sense of personal accountability so widespread in contemporary society. This is, as you will at once recognize, closely connected with the moral relativism already mentioned. But it is not the same thing. It is the idea that most men have no real freedom of moral choice; the idea that in business, in a profession, or in toiling for their daily bread they are subject to controls which are beyond their reach, and that to revolt against those controls is virtually equivalent to suicide.

For an illustration of what I am talking about, study the dilemma which the scientists are in as a result of their production of atom and hydrogen bombs and of bacteriological weapons. Many of the best of them have been tormented in soul, as you well know. But most of them have finally taken refuge in the assertion: "Well, we are not responsible for the use of our work. If society takes the results of our experimentation and proceeds to wipe out mankind or desolate the earth, that is society's responsibility, not ours."

Yet, our armory is every bit as well stocked as the apostle Paul said it was, and the weapons there look even more effective today than they did when this century was opening. To begin with, the Christian world-view makes more sense than any other. To the ultimate questions—What is the nature and destiny of man? What is the nature of the world and of the universe? Has life meaning? Does man stand alone?—the Christian religion can give better answers than any other form of world outlook. Recently Dr. Charles Clayton Morrison has tried to summarize under five heads the Christian view of the cosmos and of history. It is made up, he says, of these fundamentals:

1. God as the Creator of heaven and earth and all things therein.

2. The whole creation as subject to God's sovereign will and shot through with divine purpose.

3. Man as the creature of God's creative work, but unique among all creatures in bearing the Creator's own image, and therefore free and responsible, and therefore prone to sin.

4. Human history as the general scene of the Creator's self-disclosure, and the Hebrew-Christian strand of history as the particular scene in which the Creator's self-revelation as Judge and Redeemer of man was most clearly apprehended.

5. The life, teaching, death, and resurrection of Jesus Christ, together with the interpretation of this total event by his early disciples, as the ultimate and definite consummation of the Creator's self-revelation in history.

One of the remarkable developments of the past five or ten years has been the appearance of writers who have demonstrated the keenness of the weapons in this armory. I assume that you are all familiar with the work of men like Lecomte du Noüy in the physical sciences, of Leslie Paul and Gerald Heard in the social sciences, and of Arnold Toynbee and Herbert Butterfield in history. Such recent books as Du Noüy's *Human Destiny,* Paul's *The Meaning of Human Existence,* Butterfield's *Christianity and History,* Heard's *Is God Evident?* and his new book, *Is God in History?*—books written by laymen who know all that modern science and the materialistic world-view have to say—make it possible for us who hold a theistic outlook to take the offensive with a confidence which was scarcely possible a few years ago.

Our arsenal also contains powerful weapons in the record of Christian experience and example. Church history can be a fascinating and an inspiring subject. Too often it has been presented in such a way as to make even theological students shun it as a dreary bore. Kenneth Scott Latourette deserves more honor than he so far has received for making come alive the picture of the church as a going concern, an enormously active and important social force, growing in influence through the centuries and never more to be reckoned with than today.

Another good weapon for our counterattack is the presentation of the individual Christian as a triumphant person. The response of our tired, cynical West to a life like that of Albert Schweitzer will illustrate what I have in mind. Perhaps, in this neurotic age in which the psychiatrist has become king and in which mental hospitals cannot be built fast enough to care for the psychotic products of our high-tension civilization, there is need for all these "peace of mind" and "how to be happy though miserable" books. Certainly their sales indicate the presence of a vast market for them. But it is my personal belief that far more good would be accomplished, and a far greater impression made on our bedeviled contemporaries, if we were to spend more effort giving actual examples of the way in which Christian men and women have achieved a triumphant sublimation of self in lives of service and devotion.

There are too many who still think of Christian experience only in terms of an inner mystical soothing of the emotions which sets the extraordinary person apart from his fellows and apart from life itself in most of its aspects. I do not deny the reality of that kind of experience; it surely belongs in William James's categories of "varieties." But we need to do more to show Christian experience in terms of service for others, especially in helping them to overcome the torments of self. Let me, as a Methodist, illustrate what I mean from the story of John Wesley.

If you ask any Methodist what was the secret of Wesley's greatness, he will almost certainly refer you to that classic passage in Wesley's *Journal* in which he tells of his experience at the meeting in Aldersgate Street, London, when he felt his heart "strangely warmed" and, in his own words, "felt I did trust in Christ, Christ alone, for salvation; and an assurance was given me that he had taken away *my* sins, even *mine,* and saved *me* from the law of sin and death." All well and good. But if you read on in that *Journal* you will find Wesley, as late as January of the following year, writing things like this: "My friends affirm I am mad, because I said I was not a Christian a year ago. I affirm, I am not a Christian now." Then suddenly, all this self-doubt, self-searching, self-condemnation ceases, and there is no more of that inner torment to the very end, fifty-two wonderful years later. What happened? To put it very simply, Wesley lost himself in ministering to the desperately needy masses of England, and from the time he began his preaching in the fields near Bristol he was just too busy to indulge in self-torment. That kind of sublimation of self in a life of service and devotion, experienced by hundreds of Christians, can, if we tell the story graphically, be one of the most effective weapons in our arsenal as we seek to counterattack the dark forces which are driving so many of our tormented fellows to destruction.

The first thing we need to do, if the methods of our journalistic warfare are to prove effective, is to raise our standards of technical competence. Beyond that, we need to study our readers more carefully than we have, and discover how best to write for them. Of course, there are different constituencies and needs, and for that reason we must launch different kinds of journalistic counterattacks. But a lot of our effort, I fear, is wasted on writing for types of readers which are almost nonexistent. The religious educators, for example, have been so anxious to prove to the professional educationalists that they know the lingo of the teacher's colleges and the curriculum consultants that they have failed to gain and hold the attention of the rest of us. The same thing, it might be noted, is true of the professional secular educationalists, and the results have been the same. This is one of the reasons why their proposals for improving the public schools often get such a cold reception from the public.

In the next place, we must work harder to know our world and our times. More reading and more travel will be of help, but we should also increase our contacts in many other ways. One thing badly needed by many church journalists, if their counterattack is ever to carry to where the field of battle lies, is to see beyond the church, and especially beyond denominational confines.

Finally, we must counterattack. I put the emphasis designedly on the "attack." That is the hardest requirement which confronts us. In these days it is easy enough to lament the evils in our world; everybody is doing it. But hand-wringing is not enough.

We need, these days, to give our people—and particularly our young people—something to be *for,* and that is not so easy as pointing out things to be against. We need to arouse men to attempt the best that is within the range of possible achievement, tested by the requirements of the moral laws and the New Testament.

PART THREE

For Whom Do You Write?

WRITING FOR RURAL READERS

WHEELER McMILLEN

Mr. Wheeler McMillen possesses unusual qualifications for the discussion of such a topic as "Writing for Rural Readers." He is the capable editor of the highly successful Farm Journal, *and is the author of* New Riches from the Soil, The Farming Fever, *and numerous other timely and helpful works.*

THE ONE REAL essential in writing for rural readers—perhaps it is not necessary for me to mention this—is to have something to say. That applies to writing for almost any kind of readers. I would almost go so far as to say that it is an unchristian act to fill a column or a paragraph with words which do not say anything. If you do, you are wasting the time of your readers.

Rural Americans, by and large, are conscious of their civic responsibility. They believe that good products and materials are produced by work, and by no other method. They believe that if a person is to eat, sleep, work, and enjoy life, he should—unless misfortune has prevented him from being able to do so—make some sort of contribution to society. It should be such a contribution as will entitle him to his food, clothing, and shelter. In other words, the rural American is a sensible sort of person.

It is a little hard to kid these people. They will take only a little kidding, and that of only a certain kind. They like to think that they are idealists. They respond to the appeal of the idealist. I am not sure that they are any more altruistic, any more bighearted, or any more generous than other people, but they do their share. They believe, by and large, in the things that all of us know to be right. So, in writing for them, it is hard to get by with a dishonest approach.

I think it was Henry L. Mencken who once said that one should

E

never underestimate the intelligence nor overestimate the information of the reader. That is a pretty sound statement. Not all of us who came from the land have had opportunity to fill in all the capacity for information that we have, but there is in us a genuine desire always for correct information that is pertinent to the particular subjects in which we are interested. So give the information to the rural reader simply. Note that many passages in the fundamental book of Christianity—in Genesis, Proverbs, and the Gospels—are written in the simplest possible language. You cannot insult the intelligence of any person by using simple words in preference to involved words.

In writing an article, one of the first rules is to throw away the first page and a half, then take the last half of the last page and put that in front. Begin there and rewrite to about one-third or one-half the length, and you will then have a pretty fair article. No matter how learned your readers, no matter how intelligent, they do not want to wander through involved phrases; they do not want to be bothered by even a needless prefix or suffix.

People read for recreation—now I'm not talking about fiction. Why anybody reads fiction, or why anybody writes it except for the checks, I do not know. But people read articles also for recreation. You have to be fair to them and give them some recreation, not hold them to one dreary subject through column after column. If you try to do so, they just won't stay with you.

When you have finished saying a thing, stop. The most important item in the entire stock of the printer is the period. Sometimes I think the next most important item is the paragraph mark, for if we keep the paragraphs reasonably short, we get more readership.

RELIGIOUS BOOKS FOR CHILDREN

MARY ALICE JONES

~~~~~~

Dr. Mary Alice Jones's enthusiastic and inspiring comments on "Religious Books for Children" are the outgrowth of her rich and varied experience. She has served as Director of Children's Work for the International Council of Religious Education, as Children's Book Editor for Rand McNally & Company, and is now Director of Children's Work for the Methodist Church. She knows children's books from the point of view of the educator, the author, the editor, and the publisher. Among her numerous books are Tell Me About God, Tell Me About Jesus, *and* Tell Me About Prayer.

~~~~~~

THE PURPOSE of religious books for children—at least of the "trade books" which are issued by the reputable houses—is to present religion to the children of our country so that it becomes real, vital, interesting, and challenging to their attention. Though the writer of such a "trade book" has more freedom in the writing and selecting of material than generally is afforded him when he is writing a part of a specific curriculum of Christian education, he also has a certain limit. The material selected and the methods of presentation must be free from argumentative or dogmatic statements. It must be written so that the child himself will be able to read it, or at least be able to follow the thought through the pictures as the parent reads the book. It must be in good taste, at all times avoiding excesses and careless references to the unique beliefs or practices of certain sects or communities.

Books of this sort fall into several natural categories. There come to mind first the books dealing with Bible material. In spite of the fact that there are on the market a great many books of Bible stories, it continues to be true that it is difficult to find a collection of such stories about which parents and teachers can be really enthusiastic. The fact that there are so many Bible storybooks on the market, and the further fact that these books have a large sale even though they are not wholly satisfactory, are evidence of the felt need for this type of material.

Rand McNally has an illustrated *Bible Story Book* which now has been in the line for about twenty-seven years. It is old fashioned in its format and illustrations, yet it still sells around 10,000 copies a year. *The Golden Bible,* published by Simon & Schuster, which is to some of us amazingly inadequate, to say the least, has had a tremendous sale. Pelagie Doane's *Small Child's Bible,* in spite of its not too happy selection of stories and its $3.00 price, has had a large sale. We do need more books of Bible stories which observe all the rules of good story writing on the one hand, and which are true to both the spirit and the facts of the Bible record on the other.

Most parents or grandparents or adult friends who buy a Bible storybook for children wish it to be quite inclusive. This means that the book has to be a large one, with a good deal of text and many pictures to illustrate the many stories. The selection of stories presents problems to the writer. Some stories, especially certain stories from the Old Testament, generally are not considered suitable for children, because they are likely to suggest an idea of God which will be confusing to children who have no historical perspective. Yet there is a demand for books which offer boys and girls the opportunity to become acquainted with all the Bible stories. The writer has to be aware of both points of view in selecting and arranging material for a book of Bible stories to be offered in the general market, where there is a freer crossing of age levels.

Bible material for appreciation is also needed in our line of religious books for children. An outstanding example of material of this sort is *Small Rain,* by Elizabeth and Jessie Jones. It is beautifully illustrated with child-life drawings that reflect the spirit of the carefully chosen Bible poems. This book, since it came out, has brought joy to many children, and it still is very useful. Similar in purpose, though smaller in its scope, is the book for younger children, *In the Morning,* published by Abingdon-Cokesbury Press. In a similar mood, I have attempted for older children *The Bible Story of the Creation.* It belongs to this type of appreciative writing.

We very much need good biographies of Bible characters. They are really dramatic characters who have made a tremendous contribution to human thinking. Yet there are good biographies available only of David, Moses, and Joseph. In *Boy of Nazareth* and the earlier book, *The Beggar Boy of Galilee,* we have good story material, biography in fictionized form which reflects accurately the conditions and experiences of Bible times. However, we do need more straight biographical material on the great characters in the Bible. In the new Westminster curriculum, the junior book, *The King Nobody Wanted,* is a biographical approach to the life of Jesus. My new book, *His Name Was Jesus,* is an attempt to give a dramatic retelling of the incidents in the life of Jesus. It was written for older juniors and junior high school boys and girls.

There is another field in which we need religious books for children. It is in the area of straight interpretation of religion. Such interpretation, of course, is given all the time through the curriculum of our church schools. However, there is a need for bringing some of this interpretative material together in the form of a reading book for boys and girls which will help them to summarize their religious thinking and crystallize it. If these books are produced in an attractive form and written in a style which boys and girls will enjoy reading, they can have a wide usefulness, not as a substitute for, but as an important supplement to the religious education curriculum. Florence Fitch's book, *One God,* has had a tremendous influence in interpreting the basic point of view of the three great religious faiths in the United States. *The Ten Commandments in Today's World* is an attempt to give a straightforward interpretation of the meaning of the Ten Commandments to present-day boys and girls. *Tell Me About God* and *Tell Me About Jesus* are attempts to interpret for children a basic philosophy of religion.

Also in the field of specifically religious books are those which are definitely directed toward creating brotherhood and interracial good will. Many books in the general trade line of all the better publishers make significant contributions. The Missionary Education Movement has rendered a great service by producing a number of good reading books for boys and girls. *Li Lun, Lad of Courage,* is an outstanding example of literature which serves this purpose. So also is Marguerite De Angeli's *Bright April.*

It is extremely difficult to get good material in this field. When a writer sets out deliberately to produce a story which develops appreciation of children of other races or nations, there seems to come

a self-consciousness, a sort of deadening fear. Books in this field
which are written as stories must first of all be good stories. It is
not fair to tell a child he is going to have a story, and then give him
diluted information. There is a place for straightforward books of
information about boys and girls of other countries. Children receive
them with appreciation. But if a writer starts out to tell a story,
it must be a good story, a story that will stand on its own feet, no
matter what the underlying purpose may be. Often, when writers
first enter this field, they try to make the child of another race or
nationality appear as "too good" for human nature's daily needs, and
so they repel rather than attract readers. The author of *Li Lun*
has succeeded in avoiding this pitfall, as has also Jean Bothwell in
her books on India, such as *The Empty Tower*.

In writing books designed to develop a sense of brotherhood
and interracial good will, the author has a special problem. He is
dealing with material which is sacred to the American people, which
cannot be handled through "tricky" devices such as building up
suspense, which are legitimate enough in other types of writing.
It is not easy to make the material interesting, stimulating, challenging, and at the same time to preserve the atmosphere of reverence
which is essential.

The material always needs to be tried out carefully with boys
and girls, and then revised and re-revised before submitting it for
publication. Many writers seem to feel that because their children—
meaning those in their own home or in their own immediate group
in the church school—respond to the material, it is ready to be published. Nothing could be farther from the truth. The children will
respond to almost anything presented to them by persons in whom
they have confidence and for whom they have affection. Before
being ready for publication, material of this sort should be tried out
with children who have no personal relationship with the author.

Again, this type of material needs to avoid the tendency toward
obviousness. It is very easy in this field to say the obvious, and
so to appear dull to boys and girls. From the standpoint of the
publisher, there must be found some fresh plan, some new phrasing,
some different approach to old truths to make materials in this field
worthy of publishing.

If the material has a biblical background, a vast amount of

research must be done to make sure that what one says in filling in the chinks in the biblical narrative is true to the whole historical situation. Research in this field is not easy. The geography is not clearly defined. The location of roads is not definitely known. In working on *His Name Was Jesus,* for example, I had a great deal of difficulty determining how to have the characters walk from one place to another. Should they go by riverside, or through a desert? Should they walk through fields of ripening grain, or through rocky country? Should the trees be full-blown and green, or should they be grubby and brown? Should the roads be paved or should they be dusty? It is difficult to get realism into the background for our characters because of our lack of accurate information on many of these points. The Bible record does not give us the detailed itinerary of many of the biblical characters. And when it does mention place names, the towns have changed so that we cannot be sure of their location. These are real difficulties, but we must do the best we can. Careful research in this field is rewarded, for as a result of it the material becomes more alive, vital, and real.

The writing, of course, must stand up with the very best in the children's field. We can ask for no quarter, no concessions, because the subject with which we deal is "the most important" of all. The people who buy books for children in the bookstores do not give us that advantage. If we want religious books for children to reach the ultimate consumer, they will have to compare favorably in the eyes of the buyer with other books which are offered in the bookstores for his attention.

Format, paper, binding, pictures, all of these mechanical matters are especially important in religious books. To present such a book in a cheap format with inadequate binding, with crude pictures, and bad paper, does not magnify the subject matter.

The cost of good books is no minor matter. Publishers must foresee a fairly large demand for the books before they will be willing to assume the risk of publishing them. Yet when the books do meet the need of the public, they have a wide distribution. From this point of view, some of the religious books for children have been among the most successful of all the books for children published in recent years. If writers have a deep conviction that they have something to say through this medium which needs to be said to children, and if the tryout of the material with groups of children shows that the children are ready to receive it, then it is worth while to send it to a publisher. Furthermore, if the writer is willing to co-operate with the publisher in accepting a modest royalty or payment to permit investment in good material and workmanship in the manufacture of the book, and if the publisher is one who has his fingers on the pulse of the people, the chances are that such a book will be useful to the constituency for whom it is prepared. It then will be worth while, from the standpoint both of the author and of the publisher, to devote time and money to it.

Of course, the market for such books is one in which there is a great deal of competition; so all good manuscripts submitted, in the very nature of things, cannot be published. Unfortunately it sometimes happens that a manuscript selected for publication is not so good as some which are rejected. This is not due to any purpose on the part of the publisher, but to the many circumstances of personal and professional relations and interrelations which operate in all of human life.

There is a large buying public which visits the bookstores, but which is not related to any church. To attract this public so that children otherwise without religious education will come to appreciate and respond to these books presents an opportunity for reaching the unchurched children of our country. The field of religious books for children to be offered through the regular trade channels is, therefore, a field worthy of the best endeavor of writers committed to using their skills in the religious field.

READER INTEREST IN CHILDREN'S PAPERS

NANCY K. HOSKING

Nancy K. Hosking is an associate editor of that very popular juvenile magazine, Jack and Jill. *The high literary standards of that magazine make it outstanding in the secular juvenile field. Her knowledge of children, and especially of their interests and reading habits is based on the voluminous correspondence she has carried on with the children who read* Jack and Jill.

IN MANY WAYS the editors of adult publications and the authors who write for adults have an easier job than those of us who work on children's magazines. This is because most adult publications are slanted to special interest groups. Groups, that is, who have special interests because of their age, sex, or activities—homemakers, farmers, people who want to know about travel, current events, politics, fashions, and so on.

Children's publications, even those limited to a narrow age range, have a difficult problem, because it is necessary to assume that all children in that age range are interested in the same things. This is only partly true, for although the world of children is pretty much limited to themselves and the things they know about, children nowadays know about a great many things.

Reader interest is a kind of thermometer that a magazine editor watches just as carefully as a trained nurse watches the little glass gadget she keeps putting under her patient's tongue. In our office our thermometer is the comment book. This is a big black notebook where a careful record is kept of the comments that come in on every story, article, poem, or play that we publish. These comments are those that the children themselves make in the letters they write to us. Last year we received 18,000 such letters, and since children today are not backward about saying what they do or do not like, we feel that we have a fairly accurate record to go by.

Probably none of you will be surprised when I tell you that

over a period of ten years we have found that the most overwhelmingly popular stories were stories about animals. It does not seem to make any difference whether it is the "Bill Bunny's Busy Day" kind of story or a story about real animals. The children love them.

Fairy stories are a very close second in appeal. *Jack and Jill* is a magazine, let me remind you, that has as many boy-readers as girl-readers. Real-life stories; that is, stories about the activities of everyday girls and boys, come in a poor third. All other story classifications follow after these three.

In their letters the children often say: "I like stories about horses." "I like fairy stories." "I like continued stories." But we have never had a letter that said, "I like stories that teach a good moral lesson." That, of course, does not mean that stories cannot or should not teach a moral lesson, or that children will not like them if they do. But it does mean that it is a good idea not to let your young readers catch you at it.

YOUTH WRITERS MUST KNOW YOUTH

Isaac Beckes

Dr. Isaac Beckes is now President of Vincennes College, Vincennes, Ind. He formerly was Director of Young People's Work for the International Council of Religious Education. In these two responsible positions he has had intimate association with thousands of young people as their friend and counselor. He is unusually well qualified, therefore, to advise those who would write helpfully for the young people of today.

Young people are neither children nor adults. They occupy a kind of no man's land of human existence. In some ways, adolescence is a wonderful period. Youth anticipates plenty of years ahead, the flowering of personality, the dawn of achievement, a job, marriage, and self-sufficiency. Yet in other ways, adolescence is a difficult period, a period to which the reasonably mature adult would not want to return.

We need to recognize that we live in a period of youth movements. Youth movements, as we know them today, are only a century old. In 1850, the Y.M.C.A. was just getting under way. Christian Endeavor did not appear until the eighties. By 1900, everyone, seemingly, wanted to do something for youth. Today, youth organizations are numbered in the hundreds, with expenditures running into millions of dollars annually. It is significant that the leaders of totalitarian states have understood clearly the importance of controlling these youth movements.

A number of very helpful studies have appeared during the last decade. They may help us catch a glimpse of youth in profile in our society. It is reported that among American youth today, between the ages of 12 and 25, there are approximately 35,000,000 believers. Of all American youth, 75 to 80 per cent express belief in God. However, less than 50 per cent belong to the church. Only about 15 per cent have any clear understanding of religion or of the God in whom they believe. Their religious beliefs usually are identified with traditional church activities, not with the larger issues of religious faith and action. The chief interest of young people is to move up the vocational ladder. Social and economic security are major concerns. They have little comprehension of the community or of their place in it. They do not display much awareness of occupying an important place in the scheme of things.

Young people, as a whole, are not delinquent. Although there is, of course, a maladjusted fringe, the percentage who are involved in the toils of the law is not large. Ninety-nine per cent are decent, law-abiding youngsters. Despite the exploitation of sex for profit in our time, they are not sex maniacs. Despite the public pressure in behalf of the use of liquor, they are not drunken louts. All in all, they are better educated and more socially adjusted than the preceding generation; they are probably the best prepared generation of youth in American history.

Young people are a cross section, a reflection, of the adult community out of which they come and into which they disappear. One of the major problems of adolescent education is that young people, in their desire to become an accepted and respectable part of the adult community, stop growing too soon. Even their slang expressions reflect quite accurately the general outlook of adults.

Among the basic interests of youth is a major concern and search for status in society. Emancipation from adults is decisively important to them. Only the weak or crushed fail to break away and to seek a means of self-expression. Young people are, of course, interested in each other, and eventually in the opposite sex. Sex is a powerful factor in the lives of youth, and we should be realistic in our consideration of it.

We hear much talk about careless or improper boy-girl relationships being due to a breakdown of religion as a controlling factor. Such talk probably is wishful thinking. Ever since the days of John Winthrop and his *History of New England,* there have been frequent fluctuations in the so-called liberty of relations between the sexes. These fluctuations have been due chiefly to sociological changes affecting the stability of the population. What young people need to know is that sex can be either a beautiful or a tragic experience; and that it is always powerful—too powerful for them to handle without guidance. It has proved too powerful even for adults. Particularly is sex a dangerous problem in these times when it is being exploited for every dollar that can be got out of it.

Selection of an occupation holds a major interest for young people. "What shall I do for a living?" needs desperately to be changed to "What shall I do with my life?" Nevertheless, preparation for a job continues to be one of the pressing concerns of young people. At present the job is interpreted in terms of prestige, money, home, social advantage, and security. Despite all we may say to the contrary, young people are altruistic. They want to be of service. Perhaps they do not want that service to cost too much, but they will respond to concrete opportunities to do worth-while things for their churches and communities.

One of the most decisive influences in the lives of young people is that of the group with which they associate, whether it be in the high school, the church, the sorority or fraternity, or is made up of adults who for various reasons command their respect. Indeed, one of the major problems of adolescent education is to give them opportunity to become acquainted with adults who are living significant lives.

In view of their many interests, what, therefore, do young people need from writers? (1) The mass of young people need clear, understandable religious materials that they will read, for they are not now reading religious materials to any extent. Such reading material does not have to be "written down" to them, nor need it be "jazzed up" in youth slang, but it does need to be clear. Too many youth books are written for ministers, rather than for the young people themselves. (2) Young people need simple, interesting interpretations of the nature of the church, of the great Christian themes, of the Bible, and of Christian history and biography. (3) They need an interpretation of the place of Christian leadership in society, and some careful instruction as to how a Christian young person should act in society and how he may bear witness to his Christian faith. (4) Certainly, the youth-adult relationships in the church, the community, and the home need clarifying. It is unfortunate that idealistic young people should experience so much frustration in getting emancipated from the well-meaning adults who are concerned for youth's welfare. (5) Social relationships produce issues which demand urgent help; some of these are in the areas of boy-girl relationships, sex, recreation, and social drinking. (6) Above all, young people in our time need an intelligent, yet a devout, interpretation of religious experience. So much of religious experience is, for them, secondhand. They need first-person experience that has meaning for our time. (7) We need Christian writers of such devotion and competency that they can infiltrate, effectively and persuasively, the secular page. We need Christian writers who can make religion so significant that it will have wider meaning and interest.

POINTERS IN WRITING FOR YOUTH

CLYDE ALLISON

*Rev. Clyde Allison, until a short time ago, was Associate Editor of
Young People's Publications for the Board of Christian Education of
the Presbyterian Church in the U.S.A. It was under his leadership
that the popular Presbyterian Youth Fellowship Kit was developed.
Mr. Allison now is engaged in free-lance writing. He is preparing
lesson materials, contributing to religious magazines, and doing
special assignments for the United Nations.*

YOUNG PEOPLE, living in this age of confusion, have an obsession to
be realists, if only to strengthen their sense of security. They want
it to be said of them that they know the score and understand what
makes things tick.

If this means anything, it means, first, that we must be particularly frank, open, and aboveboard in our dealings with young people.
Unfortunately, the church has often substituted shallow, sentimental
piety in place of the directness which young people require. Yet
the church, by proclaiming the gospel of truth, can show that it is
not bound by superficial platitudes; for the greatest realism is faith
in God, who alone is ultimate. Apart from him, the obsession for
realism becomes frustration.

Second, young people long to be significant. They experience
a feeling of lostness amid the confusion of Western civilization. This
is particularly disastrous to their sense of importance. Therefore,
they desire to be found in the place where they count. They want
to join a movement which promises to give them a mission in this
tawdry world. The presence of such a longing in their hearts provides a great opportunity for the church to win disciples of Christ.
If we treat this opportunity superficially, we shall be selling youth
short and leaving our young people to disillusionment and frustration.

We owe it to Christian youth to be honest with them concerning
the implications of Christianity. To build a youth appeal at the

expense of the Christian faith is to belittle the gospel in the eyes
of the young people. It is a deception. Genuine Christianity is more
than an echo of our personalities or a matter of personality development; it is a challenge to discipleship. We must face all the problems
of our human life in the light of the Christian faith in God. There
is no way out of our dilemma apart from the Incarnation, the coming
of the divine Son into our human situation, the sovereignty of God
over all our life, and the fellowship of the Holy Spirit. We must,
therefore, guide young people into a clearer knowledge of Christian
truth, and we must present in no uncertain terms the challenge of
the Christian life and the call to Christian service.

In guiding youth's study of the Bible, the writer's first concern
must be that youth shall hear God speaking to them. To accomplish
this, the writer will use the best knowledge, equipment, and judgment
which God has given him. He must make clear his own understanding
of God's revelation. If we give merely lip service to the Bible, or if
we make an idol of it, but are negligent in using the tools at our
disposal for a thorough study of it, we are unworthy stewards. On
the other hand, we dare not substitute our own ideas for the divine
revelation. To let the word of God be hidden through obsolete language, untenable conceptions, unwillingness to face historical realities,
or sheer neglect, will make us as guilty as those who withhold the
Scriptures from today's youth.

We must lead our young people to see that a true Christian faith
forces a man to take a stand on the issues of life. The man who is
bound by faith to God recognizes that he must do God's will. He
would show himself an obedient son of the Heavenly Father. Let the
church witness to the creative ethical imperatives which are inherent
in this divine, yet human, family relationship.

We need to help our young people realize that our faith does
not lead to individual self-glorification, but instead draws us into
the fellowship of the church. Individualistic religion may be widely
prevalent and quite comfortably at home in many of our middle-
class churches, but at its base it is irresponsible. It leads to spiritual
bankruptcy. Too often there is more fellowship and sharing of life in
the local service club, lodge, or even in the corner tavern than in
our churches. Let us challenge the young people to surrender self-
interest and to find their true selves, not in narrow and selfish cliques,

but in the company of the disciples of Christ in the church, which links together Christians the world over.

Our worship materials should guide the young people to present a corporate response of praise and thanksgiving to God as an expression of their Christian fellowship. Worship points beyond the group to God as the only source of life. It loses its vital power when it is merely an expression of individual self-realization or a matter of esthetics. Worship services should be built for participation on the part of the group. These services, without being stilted, should have those qualities of faith and reverence found in the historic worship of the New Testament saints and in the true worship of evangelical Christians ever since.

If young people are to see the practical relevance of a living faith, we must penetrate, so far as we can, the barriers of theological language and idealized theory. In *Great Is the Company,* Violet Wood tells of the many days which Martin Luther spent with the local butcher, in order that he might penetrate the barrier of the schoolroom and translate the Bible into the language of the people. It is not a matter of language only; it is a matter also of understanding the vital points in youth's experience today. On the other hand, young people rebel against those who, in writing for them, patronizingly adopt a pseudo-juvenile style. They demand directness and honesty.

REACHING THE FAMILY READER

E. LEE NEAL

E. Lee Neal, minister of the Disciples of Christ, served churches in Montrose, Colo., and in Casper, Wyo., before becoming Editor of Adult Publications for the Christian Board of Publication. In addition to his other duties, he has taken on the editorship of the recently launched monthly magazine, Hearthstone. This magazine is dedicated to the fostering and the strengthening of Christian home life in America. To that magazine he is giving brilliant editorial direction.

ARE WE MAKING a rather naïve assumption? Are there any such beings as "family readers"? A quick look at all the activities a family may engage in these days almost convinces one that we are indeed barking up an empty tree. With two radios and a television set in every home, two cars in every garage, two movie houses in every neighborhood, two taverns on every corner, and so on *ad infinitum,* when can family readers find time to read?

There is, however, another side of the picture. More books are being published and sold than ever before, more magazines are being circulated, and, in spite of decreasing numbers of newspapers in local cities, total circulations are up. Yes, the family still is reading.

For a long time the family has been recognized as an important readers' market. Advertising in all of its various forms has always played up the family angle. It has realized that it is the family which will use the vast majority of the products which it proclaims. The great and popular slick magazines are essentially family magazines, and aim their appeals at family readers. What newspaper would dare come to its constituency these days without a regular family page that is greatly expanded and enlarged on Fridays?

In the light of this emphasis upon the importance of the family-reader market, it is time for the church to make the same emphasis. Of course, it cannot be said that the church has been completely blind to the significance of the family reader, but it has not wholeheartedly

F

undertaken to capture family readers for its cause. That it is becoming alert is shown by two rapidly developing movements: (1) The increase in the number of church family magazines. Not long ago there were very few in this field. Now, at least eight cross my desk regularly, and others likely will be launched. (2) In recent years there has grown up a recognition of the importance of the family as a teaching agency, and the family-centered or family-slanted curriculum is becoming the vogue. We may well ask, therefore, "What kind of reading will the family reader read?"

He will read what is pertinent to his needs and pointed at his problems. The material—article or story—must be in the field of his interests. While there are some who will read anything, they are not the ones we need to worry about. It is no trouble to reach them. But to reach the majority, the mass, who have to be clubbed into reading, we must use as our club some particular problem or need that will stop them in their busy whirl and compel them to read. As Jesus well knew, some people will come to a banquet upon invitation, but others will have to be dragged in from the highways and byways.

At the risk of oversimplification, let us use the eleven areas of experience which the International Council of Religious Education, in its *Curriculum Guide*, blocked out as basic to family life:

1. *Health.* This is always an important item of concern to families, but at times the family's concern is intensified into desperate anxiety. Note how often the secular magazines put this record on their turntables. Christianity has a stake in the health of the family: witness the most frequent excuse for nonattendance at meetings— "Didn't feel well."

2. *Vocation.* The varied angles of family interest in this field are legion. They range all the way from motherhood as a vocation to what Junior shall be when he grows up. The mother or father who is not interested in that question is not a true parent. The very roots of the word have a religious connotation.

3. *Friendship.* In a day when the "good neighbor" policy has international significance, though the words perhaps are more honored in the breach than in the observance, the family has a concern here too. The keeping of friendship fences in repair is a need experienced by all families and a serious problem for some.

4. *Economic life.* Perhaps this is too dignified a term for what the family does with its money, but there are few family readers who are not concerned at this point. When one tries to stretch a forty-nine cent dollar to cover a 228 per cent increase in price index, he recognizes it as a real problem in economics. Helping the family to do this is an act of Christian grace.

5. *Sex life.* Although much of the reading matter of our day might make one think that life is 99 44/100 per cent sex, the *Curriculum Guide* comes closer to the actual facts. It presents a truer, saner, more wholesome view of sex. The Christian approach to this problem in family living is a vital issue in which family reader interest can be depended upon.

6. *Athletics.* A walk down any St. Louis street any summer night will convince nearly any skeptic that here is a major interest to many, if not to most, families. Walk long enough and you can hear an entire broadcast of a Browns or Cardinals game. Even the apostle Paul went to the area of athletics for some of his most telling illustrations of Christian living.

7. *Group life.* Here is a catchall area. Into it are thrown all the miscellaneous group relationships of the family which are not touched upon specifically under other categories. How many groups can a family belong to anyway, and still remain a family? Angles and tangles here come by the dozen, each with particular appeal to some persons.

8. *Recreation.* This means different things to different people, but it certainly represents a common area of interest to family readers. It is also an area which gives tremendous concern to the forces of faith in their effort to see that recreation is truly re-creation.

9. *Citizenship.* The relation of church and state is a vital issue in our day, and the family faces it in a specific way in many areas. The payment of taxes, obeying of laws, religion in schools—all are vitally related to family living and pose many problems which family readers must face.

10. *Education.* With our complex civilization making greater demands upon us for an educated approach to life, there are few families who cannot be brought up sharply to face an issue in this area. A good article, aptly titled, will reach out, hold the attention of family readers, and not let them go until it has blessed them.

11. *Religion.* Yes, religion has a place in all this. It is a permeating power that runs through all the areas of life, as well as that specifically delimited area of concern which we know as formal, ceremonial religious activity.

By and large it is likely that most people will read something sometime that hits them sharply within one or more of these eleven areas of family interest and concern.

Perhaps here I should follow the lead of Sinclair Lewis who, when asked to lecture to a group of budding writers on the art of writing, stood up and uttered one sentence, "Go home and start writing." That may be all right for Sinclair Lewis, but not for most of us. In a recent book, *How to Write for Homemakers,* by Richardson and Callahan (Iowa State College Press) I find the following formula: Visualize, Analyze, Organize, Dramatize.

To these four important steps, I would add a fifth; namely, Christianize. This does not mean that every article must be about Bible reading or churchgoing, though there is room for much of that. It does mean that the article must be suffused with the Christian spirit. The best description of that spirit that I know is Paul's "fruit of the Spirit": love, joy, peace, patience, kindness, goodness, faithfulness, gentleness, self-control. The Christian spirit of the article is not necessarily measured by the number of times that the word "Lord" is used, or by the frequency of use of any of the familiar, pious phrases. It is shown by a genuine concern to raise all the thinking and living of the family to the spiritual tone of Christ.

Reaching the family reader has become Big Business. Great corporations are investing millions in it. The church is investing millions in it. What we do to Christianize the family will determine to a great degree what the future of the world will be. This twentieth century dares us to reach the family reader; writers with a Christian purpose must accept the dare.

PART FOUR

How to Do the Job

MANUSCRIPT MECHANICS

JOHN CALVIN SLEMP

Dr. John Calvin Slemp until recently was Editor of Uniform Lessons for the American Baptist Publication Society, and had an active part in the early sessions of the Christian Writers and Editors' Conference. Previously he had been a professor of English literature at Carson-Newman College, an editor of the Sunday School Board of the Southern Baptist Convention, and Editor of the Biblical Recorder, *weekly news journal for North Carolina Baptists. He is now Associate Editor of* Missions, *the monthly missionary magazine of the American Baptist Convention. In addition to having written many articles, poems, and lesson expositions, he is the author of two books:* Christian Teachings for Personal Living *and* Twelve Laws of Life.

AFTER TWENTY years of experience in an editorial office, I am convinced that most writers and editors need every now and then to be reminded of the principles of good manuscript mechanics. Perhaps they have deposited this basic knowledge in the same intellectual attic or basement where they have stored some of the fine points of English composition and literary excellence, feeling no doubt that they would never need it again, but wishing to keep it handy—just in case. So, if someone here thinks that I am bringing coals to Newcastle, let me insist that I am doing so only because in some sections of the city, at least, the fires are running low.

1. Manuscripts should be typewritten, double spaced, on only one side of the page, preferably a sheet of 8½ x 11 inches. Only the original should be submitted, not a carbon or a mimeographed copy. The author should keep a duplicate copy for reference and as protection against possible loss of the original.

2. All pages should be numbered consecutively. In a series of Sunday school lessons, each lesson should have its own series of

numbers. Each lesson should begin at the top of a sheet, and the pages should be clipped together. If, after numbering, additional pages are inserted, the number of insert pages should be clearly marked on the last numbered page before the insert starts. For example, at the bottom of page 6 write: Insert 6a-6c. All inserts should be on full-sized sheets of paper, even though they are only a few lines in length. Brief inserts of a few words or a sentence may be written on the margin, if properly indicated. Fliers (parts of pages), easily torn off in handling, should not be attached.

3. The upper left-hand corner of each page should contain whatever information is required to identify it. A manuscript submitted for publication should include the author's name and address on the first page, and his name and the title of the manuscript on succeeding pages. A manuscript submitted for printing should be clearly marked with the name of the periodical (and section, if more than one) in which it is to appear.

4. Pages should not be tied, sewed, or stapled together, but fastened only with paper clips. Manuscripts should not be rolled. They should be placed flat in an envelope or box. If sent by mail or express, the package, tough enough not to wear through, should be carefully marked with the author's name and address and properly registered or insured.

5. Manuscripts should be typed as nearly as possible according to the editor's specifications. The simplest and most accurate unit of measurement is the number of strokes (characters, punctuation marks, and spaces) to a type or typewritten line. For example, the manuscript count for *Baptist Leader* is 76 strokes to a line. Such a typewritten line will make two lines of type. Now, if an editor desires an article to fill 280 *Baptist Leader* lines (4 columns of 70 lines each), he should ask the author for a manuscript of approximately 140 lines typed 76 strokes to the line. Make sure that there will be enough copy, for it is always easier to cut than to fill. If a one-line subhead occupies on the printed page the space of two lines of text, then it counts as two type lines or one typewritten line. The stroke count in typing is the same for both pica and elite type. The number of strokes is the important consideration, not the size of the type.

6. Quotations that are not to be run into the text (poems or

prose of ten lines or more) may be single spaced, without quotes, as an indication that they are to be set in smaller type. The editor will indicate clearly the size of this type before the copy is sent to the printer. One size under the body type is recommended. The length of the type line may be the same as that of the body type, or if the measurement is wide, the quotation may be indented left and right, as in books.

7. Quotations should be accurate, including spelling, capitalization, and punctuation. Ellipsis marks (three periods following sentence punctuation, if any) should be used to indicate omissions from quoted matter. Brackets should be used to indicate the author's or the editor's interpolations. Letters of permission to quote copyrighted matter should accompany the manuscript. Quotations from the Bible should be from the King James Version unless otherwise directed by the editor. The reference, abbreviated, should be placed in parentheses after each verse or passage quoted. Example: "Whosoever heareth these sayings of mine, and doeth them, I will liken him unto a wise man, which built his house upon a rock: and the rain descended, and the floods came, and the winds blew, and beat upon that house; and it fell not: for it was founded upon a rock" (Matt. 7:24-25).

8. Footnotes, single spaced, should be typed immediately under the point on the page where the reference (indicated by a superior figure) occurs in the text. The footnote should be separated from the body text by two lines (one preceding, one following) running entirely across the page. Here is an example.[1] The advantage in

---

[1] Cf., *A Manual of Style* (Chicago: The University of Chicago Press, 1937), p. 165, sec. 324.

---

placing the footnote here, rather than at the bottom of the sheet, is that it brings it close to the text, thereby making it easier for the printer to transfer the type from the galley to the page form. Footnotes should be numbered consecutively throughout a manuscript (article, chapter, lesson). All footnotes should be written exactly as they are to be printed. Printers should not be expected to expand abbreviated notes and references.

9. If photographs, drawings, tables, or charts accompany an article, these should be numbered consecutively through an entire

article or book. Authors should indicate approximately where they are to appear in the text. Accurate legends should appear under all illustrations.

10. The editor should see to it that all manuscripts have been carefully edited, typed to measure, and cut or filled to fit the space required, *before*—not *after*—they are sent to the printer. Printers should not be expected to edit copy and the overworked proofreader should not be blamed for "mistakes" that are a part of the editor's copy! Inasmuch as typesetting is very expensive, measuring the manuscript to space requirements is good business sense as well as good editorial practice. Here is a slogan for editors to remember: *Cut copy and you cut cost.*

11. Writers should learn early, and long remember, that editors are too busy to do the spadework in manuscript preparation that the writer himself should have done. Most editors lack not only the time, but also the inclination for such work. Writers who are careless in spelling, punctuation, paragraphing, and other details of composition, need not expect to be on an editor's "preferred list." Nor should writers whose sentences and paragraphs are dry, or dull, or dense, or just plain dumb, expect to be there. Writing is more than an art or a gift; it is a science—something to be done according to principles and rules. Therefore good writing is the result of hard, conscientious, painstaking work. Consider, for example, the following—what the writer said, and how the editor rewrote it:

(1) *Writer's paragraph*

For sheer dramatic power the temptation of Jesus is unsurpassed. The narrative is cast into the form which was congenial to the ideas which were current. Vision and parables mingle in this account of the temptations. We must also remember that Jesus exercised a strict discipline during the days of his trials. We are told that he engaged in prayer and fasting as a means of bringing his body and spirit into proper state for meeting his strenuous fight with himself.

(2) *Editor's revision*

For sheer dramatic power, the record of the temptation of Jesus immediately after his baptism is unsurpassed in biblical literature. The narrative is cast in vivid, pictorial form that grips our attention, stirs our imagination, enlists our sympathies. The physical surroundings of the scene of temptation, the period of fasting in which Jesus engaged, his deep searchings of mind and spirit, his steadfast and unalterable commitment to his Father's will—all make this one of the choice passages of the New Testament.

12. Form the habit, beginning now, of reading and rereading a good handbook on style periodically. Use common sense every day, and read your style book at least twice a year.

GATHERING RESOURCE MATERIAL

Violet Wood

Violet Wood is an editor in the service of the University of Illinois Press. She is also a capable writer, and has successfully completed a number of important writing assignments. Her major interest is in biographical material which can be employed to teach a Christian or missionary lesson. She is the author of Great Is the Company, In the Direction of Dreams, *and other widely circulated books.*

SOME WIT HAS SAID that a writer who takes an idea from another author is a thief and a plagiarist, but a writer who takes twenty or more references from twenty other authors is a scholar and a gentleman and is honored for his "brilliant research."

Gathering resource material is just a working name for research, and research is nothing in this world but an over-educated curiosity.

I should like to share with you some of the ways by which I have solved my problems in research and acquired, if not an educated curiosity, at least a semiliterate one.

There are two kinds of research: one for "dead" material and one for "living" material. Dead material concerns subjects on which libraries have reams of stuff; living material concerns subjects on which little or nothing has ever been written.

Two of the books I have written fall neatly into these classifications. *Great Is the Company* was very dead material. It is about Bible translators, twenty-three of them. Only four of the twenty-three were alive at the time I wrote the book, and one of the nineteen, St. Jerome, has been dead a long, long time.

When I first entered the American Bible Society Library in New York City to start my research, I was bowled over by the fact that

86,000 volumes stared me in the face. They ran around the walls of the huge rooms and every one of them—the librarian told me with what I thought was unpardonable pride under the circumstances— was about the Bible, or a translation of the Bible, or a version of the Bible, for the Bible exists in over one thousand tongues. And that was just books!

I started my project in 1946 and referred to the *Readers' Guide to Periodical Literature* for 1945. Under the heading of "Bible," there were several pages devoted to a list of articles, poems, sketches, and stories on or about the Bible. The *New York Times Index* for that year had half a column of tightly packed, eight point type-size references to news stories, items, and features on or about the Bible. The Columbia Broadcasting Company Research Division told me they had devoted about two hundred air hours to broadcasts on or about the Bible, exclusive of time used by "churches of the air" on Sundays. The college at East Lansing, where I was living at the time, offered two undergraduate and four graduate courses on or about the Bible.

Enough is enough. But too much source material is murder. After I had got used to the idea that the Bible obviously was here to stay, in other words after I had stalled around for about a week in utter gloom among the deluge of Bible books, my eternal optimism reasserted itself. People were interested in the Bible—all sorts of people, down through the centuries—whether they read newspapers, magazines, books, or listened to the radio.

My book was to be about translators of the Bible, so I decided to narrow the field to first translators—not necessarily the best, but the first translators. But even that was five times more material than I could possibly study and squeeze into a 60,000 word manuscript.

Since my audience for the book was to be composed of members of all the major denominations in the United States and Canada, I determined to narrow my field still further. I would take a first translator in a major mission land, each of a different denomination. For instance, Judson was a Baptist and the first translator of the Bible into Burmese. No matter how many other Baptist missionaries who were first translators showed up—and one did in Africa— they would be out because I had already chosen my Baptist translator.

By the end of the second week, going daily to the American Bible Society Library from nine to five, with time out only for lunch, I had limited my field to twenty-three missionary translators of the Bible in seventeen mission lands. I made out an index card for each translator and put under his name a list of books by him or about him.

That was fine, but one of my characters was St. Jerome. Most of the books reputed to have been written by him were in Latin or Greek. Nearly all of the commentaries on these books were written by scholars, also in Latin or Greek. My single reference on St. Jerome was the brief article about him in the *Encyclopaedia Britannica.* I could read that, for it was in English.

When I boarded the train for East Lansing I should have been very happy. I was on the threshold of beginning a new book, which is always exciting, but I was not happy. I was wretched. I had spent two weeks of my hard-earned vacation, and all I had to show for it was a bunch of index cards. And one of them, the one on St. Jerome, practically a blank!

I brooded all the way to Buffalo, and went to the crowded dining car to have a melancholy dinner. A Catholic priest came in, and was seated across from me. We began to talk, and I discovered that his home base was Lansing. Remembering that St. Jerome belonged to the Roman Catholics as well as to the Protestants, I asked him if he knew anything about St. Jerome. He was sorry, but he did not. There was a child's primer, *Lives of the Saints,* published, he thought, by Ginn and Company in Boston. I got hold of it through a Lansing parochial school a few days later, but it had nothing to offer.

At that time I was Business and Industrial Girls' Secretary in the Lansing Y.W.C.A. About a week later, at a meeting of social and religious agencies to discuss child delinquency, whom did I meet but the very priest I had last seen on the train. "By the way," he said, "one of the brothers at our parish house wrote his master's thesis on St. Jerome." The meeting was over and I was on the phone calling the Lansing parish house. A very, very tired old voice said he was sorry, but it had been so very long ago and he had moved so many times that he had no idea where he could lay his hands on the old thesis. I asked him where he had done his work. "At Notre Dame," he answered.

That very afternoon the librarian at Michigan State College

wrote the librarian at Notre Dame to see if the thesis still existed and if it might be borrowed. Ten days later I held in my hands the manuscript of a master's thesis on St. Jerome. True, a great deal of it was in Latin and Greek, but the biography, the introduction, and the descriptive commentaries on the Latin writing of St. Jerome were in English.

I then had no more excuses for not getting to work. Six months later the manuscript of *Great Is the Company* went to Margaret Hills for checking for historical blunders. Miss Hills is the American Bible Society librarian. She has been with them for nearly twenty years and has a master's degree from Cornell University in history. After a few revisions, the finished manuscript went to the Friendship Press and was published.

Now if, with the exception of St. Jerome, I had in *Great Is the Company* an overabundance of material, the opposite was true of the book which has just come off the press, *So Sure of Life*. It called for the living material type of research, for it is a biography of a home and foreign missionary, a country doctor who once lived in Malaya and who has been on the Tennessee side of the Great Smoky Mountains for the past twenty-four years and is still there. The material published about him amounted to the following: a score of publicity articles in Methodist magazines and Sunday school papers, a write-up in the alumni magazine of the University of Syracuse, a radio broadcast by Frank Kingdon, and several news stories by roving reporters in Tennessee newspapers. I read all these and again was filled with panic. How could I ever get 60,000 words out of that?

But unlike St. Jerome, Dr. Robert F. Thomas was very much alive. I had just accepted a job on the staff of the University of Illinois and had planned to take a vacation before going to Champaign-Urbana. But it was clear that my vacation would have to be spent in solving this problem of living research. Dr. Thomas and I decided that if I would take my place as a temporary staff member, it would save everyone from feeling self-conscious in the presence of a reporter. At the time, Dr. Thomas had no nurse; so it was agreed that I would do what I could in the medical program. I arrived at Pittman Center, loaded down with typewriter, camera, and lots of quite blank paper. I went with the certain knowledge that I was a sissy, that I was not going to like it, and that if anyone dared to get

hurt or shed one drop of blood in front of me, I would solve everything
by fainting first.

I went on calls with the doctor by day and by night. We rode
in the jeep up and down the mountain trails, slick with mud, and at
night black as a bag of black cats. We were eleven miles from the
nearest phone, seventeen miles from the nearest bus station, and
forty-two miles from the nearest railroad station. Electricity was
confined to the buildings and houses on campus.

An office was set up for me in the waiting room of the mountain
clinic, where I could talk to the endless flow of patients and could
listen to them talk as they waited. I saw Dr. Thomas under all kinds
of situations, as postmaster, as veterinarian, as physician, as baby
doctor, as superintendent of the Pittman farm. I attended meetings
with him and heard him preach in Newport, and went with him
on pastoral calls to the cabins in the hills. I made friends with many
mountaineers, studied their Elizabethan dialect, ate knotties, fat
back, turnip tops, and corn bread. I went to harp-sings and family
reunions and a picnic of Pittman High School graduates. By the
time I was ready to leave I had fifty or so pages of single-spaced
typed notes on the locale and the work, and an overwhelming admiration for the dynamic Dr. Thomas and his wonderful family. With
the help of Mrs. Thomas and the two Thomas boys, I persuaded
the doctor to loan me his diaries. He had kept a line-a-day since
1920. He also gave me his long series of annual reports to his Board,
and his correspondence to family members and friends.

I got on the train at Knoxville to go to Urbana absolutely the
most worn out person in twenty counties. I felt I had lived life to
the hilt, shadowing and haunting the doctor who somehow or other
survives the treadmill of being on the job twenty-four hours a day.

I went home to recover and to think it all over. Three months
after the excitement and the overstimulation had died down and when
I was in the swing of my new job at the University of Illinois, I
sat down and began the biography. Six months later I mailed the
first draft to Dr. Thomas and invited him to slash it and mark it
to his heart's content. He did, he did. For there were plenty of points
where I had gone astray. When the marked copy came back, I rewrote the entire manuscript. At the end of February, I took the
second draft with me on the plane out of Chicago and headed for the

hills. For ten hard-working days Dr. and Mrs. Thomas and I labored over that manuscript, checking and rechecking facts. Dr. Thomas attended only to emergency calls during this visit, but there were always plenty of those. We worked at substituting better stories for those that I had picked, but which did not seem to either of us to come off well. Over and over, day after day, when I felt some scene was cloudy, I would hammer at him: "How did you feel? What did you say? What did they say?"

I got back home and once more sat down and rewrote the entire manuscript. This time I was not concerned with changing the stories or the facts; they had been cleared. I was concerned now with polishing, revising, finding the more exact word, the fresher figure of speech. I made my deadline, April 15, by the skin of my teeth, exactly one year and six months after I had first gone to the mountains in 1948.

I believe you can see from these illustrations that whereas dead material can be handled anywhere, it is not possible to do living research without actually being on the scene. Your writing of factual articles, biographical sketches, and other allied material is not limited by the fact that you live in a place the size of What Cheer. I want to show you that you can live in as small a town as What Cheer, Iowa, and still have as many resources available as if you lived in New York City.

In New York City there are over one thousand private libraries available to the public. These libraries are used by people all over the United States. I cannot list all of them for you, but I shall try to give samples of the various types of libraries and tell what they have to offer the feature writer:

1. *The Russell Sage Foundation Library.* This is a sociologist's paradise. If you are writing a mission story or article and need a description of an atap hut, this is the place to which to write. They either will tell you directly or suggest sources where you can find out.

2. *The Metropolitan Life Insurance Company Library.* Most insurance companies have extensive research divisions and excellent reference libraries. They are the statistician's paradise. If you need to know the per capita income of the Tamils in 1945 or 1890, or if you want to know the number of Anglo-Indians living in Agra today, they will do everything in their power to help you find the information.

3. *The American Bible Society Library*. Anything in this world on or about the Bible.

4. *The International Information Services in Radio City*. British, French, Russian, Dutch, Belgian, etc. Not only will they furnish you with facts but also with pictures. I would say that one-quarter of the mission material I have been able to sell in the past ten years has been made more salable by the fact that the British Information Service and the Dutch Information Service gave me many beautiful pictures for free use in the mission magazines. Yet I have never set foot in the offices of either of them. I carried on the entire quest for information and pictures by mail.

5. *New York Times Information Service*. For current material on national and international subjects, this is an unbeatable source of reference.

6. *All the denominational headquarters libraries and publicity departments*. The American Baptist headquarters, at 152 Madison Avenue, is a valuable source of information and illustrations. The same is true of the Methodist Research Library at 150 Fifth Avenue.

7. *The Missionary Research Library*. Unfailingly helpful on all aspects of mission life, the lands, the peoples, the politics, and the geography.

Every one of the copyrighted books and pamphlets in all of these libraries is also in the Library of Congress in Washington. By paying mailing costs, you may borrow from this source; not directly, but through your librarian who can borrow from the Library of Congress and then loan the material to you in the usual way from your own library. You may borrow through your town library, or through your State College or State University libraries.

But, you say, how do I know what I want in the way of books to borrow? Here is a very brief list of old standbys:

1. *Cumulative Book Index*. It includes books past and present, listed by title and author. Not helpful if you know only your subject.

2. *Readers' Guide to Periodical Literature*. It lists by title, author, and subject the current material that has appeared in national magazines and newspapers.

3. *Encyclopaedia Britannica*. At the end of nearly every article is a bibliography telling the source material from which the article was taken.

G

4. *Who's Who?* In English, German, French, etc. Lists the books written by or about the person you are investigating, if he is famous enough.

5. *Webster's Biographical Dictionary.*

6. *The Statesman's Year Book.*

7. All the official government agencies and bureaus in Washington.

8. State historical associations across the country.

HOW I WRITE FEATURES

Kenneth L. Wilson

Kenneth L. Wilson is now Managing Editor of Christian Herald. Despite his administrative responsibilities he still finds time to write many editorials and feature articles. Prior to his connection with Christian Herald, he was editor of junior high materials for the Division of Christian Publications, Board of Education and Publication of the American Baptist Convention. He designed, and for some years edited, 'Teens, popular story paper for junior high youth.

THE PURPOSE of the feature story is not primarily to spread information but to establish a mood—and not merely a passive emotion. It should do more than make the reader sad or glad. It should cause him to be a better person or a better citizen or to remedy an evil or to give a helpful hand.

If you are going to write a feature story, you must have something to say. The process of finding something to say is called research, which may be nothing more than having kept your eyes and ears open for the twenty or fifty years you have lived. More often it requires investigation in a specific area.

An article will be concerned primarily with one or both of two categories: people or things. An article about a person is known in our circles by the name *profile*. It is generally the result of a personal interview. But a straight interview will concern itself with what a man *says*. A profile will concern itself with what a man *is*. The difference is the same as that which exists between a snapshot and an oil painting.

You see, we must keep coming back to the idea that you are not writing to convey information only, but to get the reader to do something. Perhaps to get him to be more like your subject, or to take heart from your subject's experience, or to go out and do what your subject says people ought to be doing.

Now then, how are you to come by the information you will need—particularly in a profile-type feature? You are after more than facts, such as when and where a man was born. You can get facts of that kind by letter, or often from something already written by or about the subject. In an interview, you are after the information you can get only by being with him. You are trying to find out how he thinks and reacts. You go as a sensitized photographic film, and allow your subject to produce an image on that film.

In the interview you may talk about anything under the sun. When I interviewed E. Stanley Jones some years ago, he had just become a grandfather. We talked babies and children for a while. I remember his saying with somewhat of a sigh, "If it had been a boy, they were going to name it 'Stanley.'" You see, you get a whole picture from such a simple statement. Have you ever heard of him as anything but *E.* Stanley Jones? I was curious about that. So I used his full name in the lead of the story. Where did I get it? That was easy! *Who's Who in America* gave more than one useful fact about Eli Stanley Jones.

At *Christian Herald* we often hang the story of a movement on a personal hook. I am thinking of the United Evangelistic Crusade a few years ago. The personal hook for that one was Dr. Jesse Bader. I talked with both Dr. Bader and Mrs. Bader—and by the way, you can learn a surprising lot about a man from his wife! This paragraph was included in the story, describing their early married life:

"Jesse gave a tenth and saved a tenth from all his earnings," Mrs. Bader reminisced. "We lived on a dollar and a half a week, and in those days a dollar and a half would buy a lot of Aunt Jemima pancakes and sauerkraut." The story went on to describe Dr. Bader's success in his pastorates, and ended something like this:

When you think of them together in Des Moines, working out their destiny over pancakes, Dr. Bader's words on his favorite topic have a new heart-warming significance. "Each local church should not be thought of so much as a field but as a force."

The pancake reference was made casually in the course of the conversation, but it helped to humanize the man and the movement he represents. Someone once told me: "We are not interested in causes. We are interested only in people." It is a good point for a writer to remember.

When I was preparing a picture story feature on Billy Graham and his family, Ruth, his wife, brought up the fact that Billy often prepares his own breakfast when he is at home. She volunteered the information that he gets his own breakfast mainly because he likes scrambled eggs barely congealed and she cannot stand even the looks of them. Now, I do not think that there is any cosmic significance in that; but by using such incidents you get the subject down to where the reader can see him, and look over his shoulder into the skillet, and take sides with either Billy or Ruth.

Does the taking of notes inhibit your subject? Not if you have first become friends. I do not barge in like a census taker. I have come not only for facts, remember, but for a mood. I like to get acquainted. Then it is often helpful to both of us to go over whatever the story is in general terms, returning a little later on to specific points and quotes which you then take down.

I fold several pieces of 8½ x 11 paper once each way, so that I have a firm little pad which I can hold in my left hand.

You will want to know as much about your subject as possible before you ever see him. And there are times, especially when the subject is in the higher echelons of his profession, when you must get down to business immediately, get what you want, and get out. But in those cases you are getting away from the profile, from what a person is, and into what he says. And that is newspaper more than magazine material.

How are you to make an article readable? If you can do that you can sell almost anything that you write; for editors, I believe, generally would agree that it is better for a reader to learn a little about a less important subject than to learn nothing about a more important subject.

Readability is determined by the extent to which the reader projects himself into the picture. A writer has only the same avenue of approach to the person that any other external stimulus has—by way of the senses, to *emotions,* to *will.* You are always shooting at the will, remember.

A literalist would say that the senses come into play because writing touches the mind through the eye. But there is more to it than that. A reader can be made to touch, taste, smell, and hear by means of the written word. The reader is not interested in words, but in impressions, pictures, feelings. Let him feel the texture of the smooth-worn leather covers of the family Bible. Let him smell the stench of unwashed bodies in the Bowery Mission Chapel on a summer day. Let him walk into the pungency of the Bowery Mission clothing department. Here is the way I tried to do that:

> It was no Solomon's Temple. Just a small partitioned-off room at the Bowery Mission. Hardly more than a cubbyhole. And redolent. Good, clean odors—mothballs, and wool and rubber—but not exactly incense. Along one side, a row of suits, overcoats, jackets. In compartments on the other three sides, hats, caps, boots, shirts, things like that.

You have got to get at the reader through his senses. They are his contact with the outside world.

And the emotions! In fiction, yes, you say—but in features? Of course! Here is another paragraph of that Bowery Mission piece:

> Every time Ray Allen pulled open the door, reached for the light chain and walked into the clothing stockroom, for him it was like going into church. Standing in that cubbyhole next to those discarded clothes that had come down from better days, Ray sensed that he was close to the ambitions and joys and sorrows of people. And when you're in that kind of company, God is not far off.

The story went on to tell of some of the ambitions and joys and sorrows in which one suit played a part.

How fearful we have been to attempt to do what Jesus did when he walked the Emmaus road! How afraid many writers are, especially those in the religious field, to try to do even what *The Saturday Evening Post* claims to do! We have looked with distaste upon emotional excesses and rightly so. As churches we have shuddered at uninhibited sects, and as writers at uninhibited publications, and we have said, "Let it never happen to us!" And so we strengthen the hand of those we condemn. "To whom else shall we go?" Americans say. "They alone make our hearts burn within us."

Mr. Hubert Mott, director of our *Christian Herald* Children's Home, and active in welfare circles, told me just the other day that most agencies back off from using publicity with a heart-tug. We do not. And last year, when other agencies were retrenching—when the great Fresh Air Fund was sending out word, "No more children! Our money is used up!"—our Children's Home was expanding its work!

People *want* to be stirred! People are hungry emotionally. *Reader's Digest* knows it. But the churches do not know it—neither their pulpits nor their publications.

So much for generalities. You are interested in the down-to-earth tricks of the trade. How do you put the fizz into feature writing? How do you make it fizz instead of fizzle?

Be specific at every opportunity. "A bird was singing in the trees" is not so appealing as "A robin was singing in the apple tree." I believe that the word "some," used in the sense, "Some men came walking up the road," ought to be deleted from a writer's vocabulary. How many men were there? How fast were they walking? Were they lazing their way along or were they in a hurry? What kind of road was it? Paved or dirt? If they were in a hurry, did their purposeful footsteps stir up puffs of dust as they came?

Make sure that everything contributes to the story. Whatever does not move the reader closer to the conclusion you intend for him to reach has no place in your article. When an editor cuts a story, he cannot touch anything essential. Those of you who resent the slashing of your material may wish to keep that in mind. Added detail may not move the reader very far along the way, for not all articles have the same pace; but every sentence and at least every paragraph must pull its share of the load. I like to write the title first of all. It becomes my theme, my destination.

Learn to use words with exactness. But something more must quickly be said. It is one thing to choose the fitting word, and quite another thing to choose a word beyond the reach of your reader. You are writing to be read, remember—and that is the hardest thing in the world for some writers to do. You are writing for the reader. If he does not know what you are saying, you might as well be writing in Chinese. The purpose of words is to convey meaning. When they cease to do that, they are only so many chicken scratches, whether you get them out of Shakespeare or even the Bible.

The reader likely will get your point, even if he misses a word now and then, but why *make* it hard for him? In the vestibule of Grand Central Station there are perhaps eight doors leading to Forty-second Street. On summer mornings, two or three of the doors are propped open. If you want to go through one of the others, you have to push. You should see the people flocking for the open doors—going out of their way, even, to save themselves a little effort! By choosing the wrong words, you not only are making things hard for the reader, but also you are making things hard for yourself.

Even among the words that wear overalls—words that work for us every day of the week—there are a surprising number that we misuse. "Imply" and "infer" are two. A few weeks ago I received an indignant letter from a reader who was inflamed by the Billy Graham piece I mentioned earlier. He said that I had "implied" that Dr. Graham was able to have a nice home and an automatic dishwasher because he was an evangelist. I answered that I had implied no such thing; that he had inferred it. You might come back at me here and say that in this case at least I had failed to get across my objective to that reader. To that I would have to plead guilty. But since it was the only letter of the sort received, I was not too much upset. You will not get the desired reaction in *every* reader.

"Pier" and "dock" are two other words commonly misused. I did not realize the difference myself until I happened in on John Kieran's television program. A pier, he explained, is the structure; the dock is in the water.

The one book on my desk more dog-eared than any other is the dictionary. There is no excuse for a writer misspelling a word in a story. Nor is there any excuse for his using the word "dormant" when he means "latent"—although I doubt that either means much to the average reader, who would understand immediately if you said "sleeping" and "hidden."

Use facts, but use them unobtrusively. We have already touched upon this in our mention of specific words. A writer may say: "Billy is four years old. He is tall for his age. He has a bad temper. He has brown hair." But how much better to say: "Billy brushed the damp brown hair out of his eyes and looked up defiantly. He was too tall for his four years, and everything about him was too grown up, even his temper."

Say the unexpected thing. This may be nothing more than using the same old expression in a new setting or to express a new concept. Anyone who has ever attended a writers' conference has heard a round condemnation of clichés. But a statement is a cliché only when it is the same old expression used in the same old way.

Incongruity—putting unlike objects or facts alongside each other—is always attention compelling. Here is an illustration of that:

> Macbeth and the three witches bowed their heads while Banquo prayed, "Heavenly Father, use this movie to thy glory." A bell clanged, red lights flashed, the director signaled, "Roll sound . . . Roll camera!" And the witches turned busily to their Kodachrome broth. Bob Jones University was polishing up its motto.

I think that lead took at least several days to write, and I could best answer the question, "How do you write features?" by saying, "With weeping and gnashing of teeth," especially the latter.

Do not be afraid of humor. Write as if you are getting a kick out of it. Now, I do not mean that you are going to jeer at anyone or at any belief. You are merely going to write with natural good humor that can see fun where there is fun. Consider this story about a wheel-chair preacher in New York state:

> The preacher finds some things even in his wheel-chair life to chuckle over—and a grin at one's own trouble speaks eloquently of a man! The baptism of infants has been arranged to conform to the preacher's situation. (Mr. McCahan admits with a sparkle of his eye, "It's a good thing I'm not a Baptist!") The child is placed on the preacher's lap as he sits in his wheel chair by the pulpit. It is a simple enough matter, then, for him to perform the rite. . . . After one morning service when a church family tried to hush their observant daughter, Mr. McCahan laughed away their embarrassment. The little girl was saying, "It's better to be baptized when you're young, because then it's easier to sit on Mr. McCahan's lap." The preacher's wife nods her head at the gleefully recounted story. "I draw the line at teen-agers," she says primly. "They kneel alongside the pastor."

There, the humor comes out of the situation, and reacts with the other emotions brought out in the story, which was a tale of victory over suffering. Right here is a good time to point out that one emotion is always heightened by another. It is said of platform

Writing and Revising

1. In writing your original manuscript, you leave no time to worry about details, for you must write in the pure glow and ardor of your urge and interest. You must "unwriting and blurring" as Carlyle says, with your subject. You must write with a kind of reckless fury. Later you can correct with caution and concern. Let the pen strike while the fire burns and then pause when the mind has recovered enough power to take the objective view point of the reader. When you revise your manuscript, keep the reader in mind.

2. Manuscript surgery. Skillful surgery not only can beautify a manuscript, it can save it. If operating personally. Cut your manuscript to the right length and to frightness. Write it only with the pen but with the knife also. The writer must divest the unfeatured ruggedness to cut out even brilliant passages if they do not fit into his article. The working over of your manuscript may become even more if than the original writing, and frequently takes more time.

speakers, "He had me weeping one minute and laughing the next"; that is not accidental.

Use words of action. Compare, "These children had never before seen the clouds above the trees" with "These children had never before had the chance to measure the speed of a white cloud hurrying past the spearing tip of a giant spruce."

When you have finished writing an article, go through it again and see how many dull words you can replace with words that gleam and jump and run and laugh and cry. Remember that your reader must follow you in terms of his senses. Let him throw himself on the green hillside lawn under that giant spruce and look up at the clouds sliding by. He will love you for it!

Establish a mood. It is hardly necessary to say this again, except that this time we can add that the mood may often be established in the lead of the article. Get your reader into the proper frame of mind from the start. This means that you will have to be in the proper frame of mind yourself. You will have to know what you plan to say, what you hope to accomplish by your story. Never get away from the demands of *mood.*

The mood may be *heart-lifting.* Going back to the wheel-chair preacher story, here is the opening:

> The broad limbs of a 200-year-old oak reach toward the steep-pitched roof of the little white church at Upper Red Hook, N. Y. Across the highway a wind-scarred milestone older than the American Revolution conjures up the rattle of stagecoaches careening down from the Catskills to New York. It is legendary country, rich in brave dreams and stouthearted deeds.
>
> Today, as a thoughtful-looking pastor preaches gently from the pulpit of the little white church, a new tale of courageous faith is being anviled out. For the pastor cannot walk. Chester McCahan is a prisoner of his wheel chair. If one of his feet slips from the chrome-plated rest, he is powerless to move it back. When the telephone rings in the parsonage study, Mrs. McCahan must pick up the instrument and hand it to her husband.

Here is to be a heart-lift, a victory, a smile through tears, in a slower paced article using longer sentences, with an even movement and nothing to bring the reader up short. The story apparently did this with some small success, for Mr. McCahan received nearly a hundred letters and an honorary degree as a result (at least, I like to think that the publicity of the story helped to make him a doctor!).

Or the mood may be *heart-touching,* as in this piece I wrote:

> They looked out of place, those little brown socks. Still pinned together at the top, the brand-new pair lay on the polished desk top. Right beside them was the leather-cornered blotter and just in front of them was a calendar pad filled with penciled notations of people to be seen and important things to be done. On the street below, Manhattan's traffic streamed by tirelessly. To the west, big ships glided leisurely up the Hudson River to their piers fifty blocks away.
>
> While the world's commerce blew its deep-throated whistles and honked its horns, the little brown socks lay on the desk top. No, they weren't out of place. Without them, New York would have been a stricken city and the world a planetary penitentiary. They stood for all the brotherly concern that ties together the fortunes and misfortunes of human kind.
>
> They were God's little brown socks.
>
> God got them from Larry, a 4½-year-old Sheboygan, Wisconsin, boy. The lad's mother wrote, "When we gave our little Larry fifty cents to buy himself an Easter toy, Larry said that he wanted to share his money. He bought this pair of socks, exactly like his own newest ones, for some child who did not have any socks at all."

That article, "God's Little Brown Socks," was about the Save the Children Federation, and the actual socks had arrived a day or so before I visited the office. They lay there on the desk top, worth perhaps twenty-five cents. But the reader is not interested until you make him *feel* something. So the mood you establish may be heart-touching.

Or it may be *heart-stabbing.* I think this might characterize the opening of our last year's booklet soliciting funds for *Christian Herald's* Children's Home, "Mont Lawn." The title of that booklet was, "Blessed Is He Who Gives a Child a Dream." The opening went like this:

> There are no shining dreams along the ill-lighted and dirt-crusted hallways of New York's rickety slum tenements. Once they were proud homes. The best of them have marble stairways—marble that is now gray-black with chewing gum pellets and filth welded to the stone by hundreds of feet. Small crowded rooms open off locked hallway doors. In each tiny three-room flat may be living as many as ten or twelve adults and children. Yes, they live—they breathe—they exist. But in these stifling human warehouses of New York they do not dream.
>
> And out in front is the hot, unfriendly traffic-crowded street, where even sudden death halts the roar and the rush for only a quick, cursing moment. It is a foul street. Some of the neighbors throw their garbage and refuse into the gutters; more often they toss it out

the back windows into the tenement court where it chinks the spaces between rusting tin cans.

No, dreams are not made here. This is only the spawning place of flies and rats—and of despair and crime. Not even a child can yearn for a better way of living if he has never had so much as one small glimpse of the good life. And this is America—Christian America— where the soul of every little boy and every little girl deserves at least one chance to stand wistfully on tiptoe and tingle with the excitement of what a youngster can do and be!

You've got to feel it! You can't fool your reader. In a dozen ways you give yourself away if you're faking an emotion. Yes, it may be heart-stabbing.

Or it may be what for want of better description we can call *heart-stopping*. Last November we used an article on drunken driving. This is the way the article opened:

Twenty-three-year-old Bill was slowing for the curve when a car hurtled out of the turn, weaving crazily. Bill edged his dad's new Studebaker far to the right. "Drunk!" his bride of five months observed indignantly.

Bill's eyes suddenly narrowed. He spun the wheel and sent the Studebaker crunching onto the shoulder of the road. Edna screamed as the oncoming car rocketed directly toward them and then the scream was cut short, her face cleavered in two. She was dead when they pried the instrument panel from her crushed body.

Bill's mother, in the back seat, heard the scream; then ripping metal and exploding glass outraced her sensory nerves. Her first awareness was of bone ends grating in her two legs. Her head was a torrent of pain. She tried to reach upward but her dangling right arm would not obey the impulse. Minutes later an ambulance whined to a halt; a doctor sprinted over, looked, and clenched his teeth. The woman's scalp had been torn away; it hung down inside her coat, a bloody pendant.

The mood being established is one of horror, shock, and then indignation, as the story develops.

A writer is not so much a craftsman in words as a craftsman in moods.

Most important of all to you, the writer, is the reaction of your reader. All your research, all your applied skill of writing, all your acquired knowledge of a lifetime, come together with one purpose— to get reaction, a decision. You can't do it unless you aim for the heart and hit where you have aimed.

FEATURE WRITING FOR RELIGIOUS MAGAZINES

Clarence W. Hall

~~~~~~

Dr. Clarence W. Hall, after a variety of editorial positions, has for some time now been connected with Christian Herald, *first as its Managing Editor and more recently as its Executive Editor. He has achieved distinction not only for his editorial skill, but also for his feature writing. His articles frequently are of a crusading nature and are a ringing challenge to the reader to acknowledge and discharge his Christian responsibility.*

~~~~~~

In these days which have witnessed so mammoth a development of the propaganda media, it is tremendously important that we should have propagandists of the greatest news of all time: the Good News, the gospel. The man who writes for religious magazines differs from the man who writes only for the editor's checks at least in this: his motivation is higher. The Christian writer has a high calling.

As a Christian writer, you should know well the magazine at which you are aiming, and you should know something also about its readers—the kind of people they are, the kind of interests they have, their general age level, their enthusiasms, their prejudices, their yearnings. You can learn much about a magazine's readers, and much about the idiosyncrasies of its editor, by studying carefully some recent copies.

When choosing your subject, make sure that it is of universal interest. Direct your words to the largest number of people in that audience. Too many articles fail of acceptance simply because they are too limited in appeal. They make an editor feel like the boy who, when asked what he thought of his minister, said: "Oh, he's all right, I guess. But he spends too much time answering a lot of questions I ain't never heard nobody ask!"

1. *The News Feature.* This is an article whose main interest stems from an event which has recently taken place or which is about to take place. The important element here is timeliness. You have

got to get it to an editor quickly, or, in the case of a forthcoming
event, in time to make a concurrent issue; otherwise, its value will
be nil. The deciding factor as to its acceptance will be the breadth
of interest which the event holds for the readers.

In searching for a timely topic, ask yourself what is going on
in the world that is of absorbing importance to most people. Even a
secular subject—such as a forthcoming election, an important change
in the United Nations, or a current battle in Congress—can be given
a definitely religious hook.

Read the newspapers, read the news magazines, read your denominational journals. Events are happening all the time which are
subjects for skilled and dynamic treatment. Just stand still and keep
your eyes and ears open; timely topics will come running to you,
begging for attention!

2. *The Achievement or Success Article.* This is a story detail-
ing how a church or an individual achieved success in some field.
This type of article is always popular, for everybody is interested
in success and how it is realized. There are projects galore in the
church field and in the Sunday school; for example, the use of new
and striking methods for building attendance and improving programs in the Women's Societies or in the Youth Department, experiences in connection with building a church, with raising funds, with
putting on a play or pageant.

Here you must be sure that the success is outstanding or unique,
or was achieved by new and perhaps unorthodox methods. Readers,
faced with difficulties in making their projects a success, are hungry
for lively stories telling how somebody else did it.

I cannot emphasize too strongly the importance of keeping your
article away from the abstract and close to the personal experience
emphasis. Projects, whether religious or otherwise, are in themselves dull to everybody except those involved in them. The *Reader's
Digest* formula is this: "When we want to draw attention to a
problem, we wait until somebody has done something about it. Then
we print the story of how he did it."

3. *The Crusade or Exposé Article.* Let us say your magazine
is dead set against the liquor industry and all its ways. Articles on
the evils of liquor advertising, on the flagrant drinking among youth,
on the drinking scenes on the movie screen or television set—all

are good topics if done right. And by "right" I mean done in a manner which is constructive. The article should tell how a bad condition in some locality was cleaned up; it should detail for the readers the steps by which the cleanup was accomplished.

Or maybe your magazine is interested in clean literature and is currently waging war on smut in books. Such a magazine would certainly be a good market for a story on how your town, your school, or your ministerial association went about making an effective cleanup of a bad local situation.

Or perhaps you can uncover an author who has always done clean fiction. If so, tell the story of his lifelong battle—perhaps against the insistence of money-minded publishers—to keep filth out of his books.

4. *The "How-to-Do-It" Feature.* In some respects this will resemble the achievement article, particularly if you enliven it by choosing a person or a group that has done something worth while, and then show how they did it.

The trick here is to make the project seem so important and so easy of accomplishment that it speaks for itself. Since the main strength of such an article is its instructiveness, rather than its human interest appeal, it must be made lively by good writing and perhaps by some elements of personal experience.

5. *The Personality Sketch or Profile.* In my opinion this is the most interesting and popular of all the various kinds of articles. The reason is that, next to himself, the reader is most interested in other persons. He is far more interested in other persons than in mere happenings or abstract ideas. That is why biographies have such an abiding interest.

We like ideas, we like happenings, we like news; but we like to have them incorporated in *people.* We want to know how other people work, and live, and talk, and play. If they have achieved something important, we want to know how they managed it.

But do not make the mistake of thinking that the only great people are the famous people. The latter, of course, are always good subjects for articles, particularly if they can be brought down to the level of the ordinary reader. But there is greatness to be found in many of the so-called "little people" who live their lives and do their work in a quiet but noble manner. Offhand I would say that for every article *Christian Herald* uses dealing with a so-called "name" personality, we use ten dealing with comparative unknowns. Like almost every other magazine, religious as well as secular, we are looking for interesting people who live on the same level as most folks, but whose lives represent something special in the art of successful living.

A phrase much used in every editorial office is "reader identification." When a reader finds a lively account of some individual like himself, and finds that that individual has achieved success in the art of living, he puts himself in that person's shoes and imagines himself achieving what that person achieved. In short, he is stimulated to believe that he too might go and do likewise. That is the best kind of inspirational material.

So much for the business of finding a suitable subject. The next question is: "How shall I write it?" Get your story down on paper, in the rough, just as soon as possible. Memory plays queer tricks. Even though you are exhausted with the gathering of your material, do not put off writing down anything and everything that comes to your mind. If you do, you may forget a striking quotation, a revealing sidelight, or some detail that will make all the difference between a live story and a dead one.

Do not try at this point to write a finished article. Indeed, your writing may wander all over the place, jumping from a bit that might fit into the ending to a sentence or a phrase that might be in the middle somewhere, and from there to an item that might bolster the body of your story.

Now, with all the essentials nailed down on paper, take a breather. Not a long one in which you might cool off on the whole idea, but a breather in which you can sit back and look at your story as a whole. Let it jell, so to speak.

I know many professional writers who maintain that this period of just "sitting and thinking" between research and writing is the most important part of the writing process. Many take a day for it, some as much as two or three days. They do not dismiss the story from their minds—that is fatal—they just give their minds a chance to do some sorting and arranging for them.

Then, when you have the whole thing in mind, and you have some idea of the treatment and emphasis you are going to give your article, make an outline of it. You will need this outline not only for a query in advance to the editor, but also to hold you on the road. There are only a few gifted souls who can keep their ideas in mind and record them without loss of details. Most of us find our story running away with us, or from us, and taking us down all kinds of unimportant byways. You may need to change your outline and rearrange its elements many times, but make one anyway.

Now you are ready to query your editor. Unless you have an assignment in advance, do not risk a lot of useless labor before you have an indication of interest from him. He may want to make suggestions for handling, for length, or for special emphasis.

When you have the go-ahead, you will be ready to go to work on your composition. You are then face to face with the most important part of your story: the *beginning*. The first two or three paragraphs should be something more than a lot of shadow-boxing with words to get yourself warmed up. A speaker can get away with that, but not a writer.

The beginning should indicate at once what the story is all about. This may be done by direct statement, a question aimed at challenging the reader, or a bit of significant anecdote or narrative. Whatever the form, it should be designed to keep the reader on the hook until you can get him into the body of the story.

The editor of *Printers' Ink* once said to Albert E. Wiggam: "I think there ought to be a law passed that all articles should begin with the word, 'When.' If a piece starts with 'When,' you just have to read that sentence at least, to see what happens." There is some validity to this observation, but one should not be too slavish about any one type. Try out beginnings on yourself; see which grab at your interest.

Some like the startling statement which can be a warning, such as: "Within ten years, at the rate we are losing ministers, our churches will be without preachers, and laymen will have to take over." Others like a witty, paradoxical, or even outrageous opening. But in my opinion the kind that is surest-fire as an attention-getter is the narrative opening, providing the anecdote is crisply written and is significant as an illustration of your theme.

Then when you are sure that you have an attention-compelling start for your article, follow through to be sure that the article does not sag, but carries the readers on to an absorbing finish. Keep your writing as bright and as simple as it is possible to make it. Beware of getting bogged down in long sentences and involved phraseology.

Do not be so bemused by the rules of grammar that your style becomes stiff and unnatural. Beginning writers, in particular, sometimes give so much thought to being correct that they fail to be clear.

There are two temptations which should be strenuously resisted. The first is the temptation to write literature. Somehow or other, many charming people who speak intelligently, easily, clearly, and with great good humor and interest, seem to envelop themselves in a sort of academic cap and gown when they sit down to put their words on paper.

The other is quite the opposite. It is the temptation to "write down" to the audience. There is nothing that makes the reader so mad as to realize that the writer is making a conscious effort to "get down to his level."

Then there is the matter of clichés. Avoid them as you would poison. I do not need to tell you that much religious speaking and writing is full of clichés. It is a common fault of many writers to throw in such murderous stuff all through the manuscript. Believe me, there is no surer way of killing a good article and of receiving from an editor that saddest of all forms of communication, the rejection slip.

Your first aim should be for clarity and simplicity of style. Your second aim should be to make your article move along with liveliness and breeziness.

Finally, when you have put down on paper your full story, do not hesitate to write and rewrite it in whole or in part. One of the beauties of article writing is that the story does not have to be told chronologically, nor does it demand the plot sequence which is so necessary to fiction. You will find, in doing your revising, that you will want to rearrange the order of whole sections of the article; you will want to expand undeveloped passages, to cut down or delete passages that are not worth the space they occupy, and to improve and correct details.

Then when you have the arrangement you want, start cutting. You will be amazed at the amount of excess wordage you can delete without hurting your story in any way. Every section, word, sentence, phrase that does not earn its precious space must be eliminated. A

H

good rule to follow when looking at your manuscript in its several parts is: "When in doubt, cut it out."

In your first draft, you should forget wordage and use as many words as you feel you need. But when you come to this revision of your work, think only of tightness and crispness—and be ruthless with yourself. Knock out as much repetitious and unnecessary stuff as you can. And do not be surprised if the editor knocks off more. Just be sure that your piece has unity and strength, as well as a feeling of compactness.

Then when you have revised and perhaps revised again, put your neatly typed manuscript in an envelope, say a prayer, and send it off to the editor.

If he rejects it, even after having given you some reason to believe that he might accept it, do not become discouraged. Above all, do not fly into a rage and throw the manuscript away. There are other markets and other editors. Even if your story should not sell right away, it probably is well worth saving. It represents a great deal of work on your part and can be rewritten at some future date and doubtless sold.

TECHNIQUES FOR THE RELIGIOUS COLUMNIST

HENRY G. WESTON SMITH

Dr. Henry G. Weston Smith, well-known Baptist minister, has served a number of important churches. He now is pastor of the First Baptist Church, Bedford, Ohio. The success he has achieved has been due in considerable measure to his skill in getting newspaper publicity for his church and its activities. He regularly conducts a newspaper column and is the author of The Pastor at Work in Christian Education.

WE SHOULD USE the metropolitan daily as much as possible, but we should not count upon it too heavily in advancing the average local church program. It gives publicity constantly to interchurch work and it publishes accounts of unusual events in local churches, if such events are attractively presented to the religious editor. But for the local church task, the smaller paper that ministers to the community from which the church most immediately draws will produce more help per hour-of-work and per dollar-of-expenditure than the big daily. Use them both, but do not be heartbroken if David's little sling, in the name of the Lord of Hosts, proves mightier than Goliath's spearhead that weighed six hundred shekels. So, whether you have or have not visited the editor of the big paper, you will of course go to see the editor of the paper that serves your own community.

The cost of printing a news item or a "feature" a half-column in length will vary depending on the part of the country in which the paper is printed and the size of its circulation. If the paper has a circulation of 5,000, such an item is likely to cost between $5.00 and $7.00 just to be put into print. That is one reason why small papers do not print three column sermons—a $30.00 to $42.00 reason.

Anyway, the small items serve a better purpose in the local paper. "Names are always good copy" is an established fact of journalism. Even dignified YOU may sometimes very casually have looked for the three-line note about something you did or the guest you entertained on such-and-such an occasion. Oh, you did not care whether it was there or not, of course! But you did LOOK, just the same.

If we are good at reporting and have a frank understanding with the editor that the material which we send him is absolutely subject to his rejection, and "no harm done if he does reject it," we may even get in a little from our sermons now and then. Here is where we shall do well to *study carefully* the mind of the community; for it is only by a proper understanding of that mind, *as it is,* that we shall be able to change that mind to something a little more like what we desire it to be. There are prejudices, old points of irritation, established antagonisms, and feuds. It is difficult to teach someone whom you irritate in the attempt.

If a church expects to have the assistance of a newspaper through its news columns, it would seem only fair that it should pay for some advertising in the paper. Most editors would not deliberately short-change a church just because that church has short-changed them; but if one thinks it over for just a moment, he will feel immediately that the church surely should be as fair as the newspaper in a relationship of this kind. When there is a congenial friendship between the minister and the editor, many good things can be brought to pass.

No one should undertake a project such as the religious column represents, without realizing he is undertaking a thoroughly big job. The gathering and writing of the material will cost him time and effort every week. The copy will have to be ready without fail by the deadline each week. But with practice the writer becomes able to turn it out quite rapidly. When the minister compares the number of people he influences through his column with the number he would influence without it, he may be quite surprised to see how largely the score is in favor of this journalistic venture.

The column which I am now conducting in the little suburban town of Bedford, Ohio, carries the heading, "Ask the Man," with the added words "in the house by the side of the road." I felt that in this rather staid town which had only a couple of thousand population until ten years ago, but which now has multiplied that number by five, it might be well for my name not to appear at the top of the column. Obviously, there is a play upon Sam Walter Foss's poem. People in a community like mine are too inquisitive not to find out who "The Man" is. So, at the end of the first six months, when the people really were talking about who "The Man" might be, we quietly organized a very decent "whispering campaign," which is the very best publicity on earth. By now the *nom de plume* has no more mystery about it than the bell in the steeple. But it is considerably more fun.

I would not want anyone to gain from this discussion the impression that I am suggesting that the minister try to be simply an editorial writer on secular themes. The function of the sort of column I have been talking about is basically religious. The minister has too much to do ever to forget that. But the boundary line between sacred and secular is really not a line, but a sort of no man's land, which is constantly being invaded more and more by the secular, and from which the sacred tends more and more to be pushed back. The religious columnist has the chance to do a little more invading of contested territory than is encouraged in the purely conventional

pulpit presentation. Here is the opportunity to build public understanding and general good will. It is a chance, also, to "come back"
on many points of misunderstanding that can be picked up in the
course of regular parish work. But the definitely religious character
of the column must always be remembered. Since there is a religious
aspect to nearly every question on which light needs to be turned,
the minister who conducts a newspaper column has a great opportunity.

ILLUSTRATIVE RESOURCES FROM THE BIBLE

MARGARET T. APPLEGARTH

*Margaret T. Applegarth is equally well known as an inspiring
speaker and as an author of inspiring books. She is a gifted story-
teller and a resourceful leader of worship. A number of her books
contain worship materials suitable either for private reading or for
use in group meetings. They abound in word pictures which deepen
devotion and enrich one's understanding of the Scriptures. Among
her many books are* At the Foot of the Rainbow, Missionary Stories
for Boys and Girls, Bound in the Bundle of Life, *and* Right Here,
Right Now.

OF ALL THE EXCITING choices in phraseology, the Bible offers by far
the spiciest selection for an author's use. Already over five thousand
book titles have been taken from it by writers; yet it is still possible
to find a biblical phrase so fresh and astonishing that people can be
startled by it!

If you have ever sat in church dismayed over the stolid, lack-
luster state of other church members, you may echo Jehovah's
question: "Can these bones live?"; and make Ezekiel's answer: "O
Lord God, thou knowest." In developing a chapter on this theme,*
I took from Exodus, chapters 8, 9, and 10, the three compromises

* This and the many illustrations which follow have all been drawn from the author's
recent book, *Right Here, Right Now.* Copyright, 1950, by Harper & Brothers. This volume
consists of thirty semidramatic chapters which may be used as worship services. They
set forth, by means of brief biographies, what it means to center one's life on Jesus Christ.

which Pharaoh tried to make with Moses when Moses said, "Let my
people go!" They were: (1) Worship God "down in Egypt." (2)
Leave your little ones "down in Egypt." (3) Leave your cattle and
your herds "down in Egypt." This is a completely modern picture
of church members not eager to worship in spirit and in truth.

Equal astonishment and awareness seem to have come to lacka-
daisical pew-sitters by another chapter called: "Some Said It Thun-
dered, and Some That an Angel Spoke," taken from John 12. Here
half the audience represents the thunder of the dictators of this
earth, reading in loud voices actual pronouncements of Hitler, Musso-
lini, and Stalin. Across the aisle, the other group, in low, quiet mur-
murs, reads (simultaneously with the thunder section) the subdued
but determined deeds of the "underground" forces of Christianity,
where eventually the angels win God's battles!

Still another use of this device of dividing an audience to stimulate thoughtfulness of what the Bible really means is to have all
the men on one side consider themselves Lazarus, just returned to
Bethany; the women, across the aisle, represent Dorcas, back in
Joppa. How would such a rebirth into everyday life affect them
after their touch of glory and wonder? Lazarus repeats Christ's
command: "Unbind him, and let him go!" on beholding the bound
way in which man lives in home, city, and synagogue. Dorcas explains
that after the overwhelming insights of a Last Judgment, with its
endless line of the unclothed and unfed, each with the face of Christ,
she realizes that the few garments she had sewed were "too little,
too late."

This natural dramatic power wrapped up in Bible passages needs
demonstration in our day. For example, in a chapter called "What
Did You Think of the Sermon Today?" eight brief, picturesque parables of our Lord are given by a "preacher" as one-minute sermons
to a small "congregation" up on the platform. Eight different times
they come up and seat themselves, hear a text, a brisk comment, then
leave saying: "What did you think of the sermon today?" Their
instantaneous responses about the fall of the tower of Siloam are:
"Too melodramatic!" "Too overdrawn!" "Too disturbing!" About
the barren fig tree: "Too rustic!" "Too rural!" "Too botanical!"
About the leaven hid in the lump: "Too feminine!" "Too domestic!"

An antiphonal use of haunting texts is always apt to linger in the memory. In developing the thought of the universality of Christianity as "All in the Same Boat," it is possible to have two reading choirs standing against opposite walls on either side of the congregation. One choir reads, at intervals, during the story of the spread of the Christian message by boat around the earth: "He saw them, toiling in the rowing." The other choir responds: "And he came unto them, walking upon the water." For this has literally come true; and in this time of stormy weather, the reading gives reassurance and calm.

There is untapped treasure in naming who and what a modern church member might put into "The Sheet Let Down from Heaven," which Peter saw. What possibilities there are in the sound of the immediate knocking at the door, and in the subtle prompting of the Spirit: "I have sent them!" lest Peter go on being reluctant to carry the gospel to the Gentiles!

What possibilities there are in selecting significant verses from the great prophets and in dressing a group of young men as Sargent portrays those prophets in his great *Frieze of the Prophets,* letting the audience say, as prophet after prophet utters his inspired verse: "Not . . . yet!" "Not . . . yet!" It would show us what "A Metronome Is Playing in Church Nowadays." The discovery of such frank prophecies is a stabbing experience.

If reassurance for youth is sought, then see what recent tiltings and jostlings can be found in Jeremiah 48: "Moab hath been at ease from his youth, and he hath settled on his lees, and hath not been emptied from vessel to vessel, neither hath he gone into captivity: therefore his taste remained in him, and his scent is not changed." All the color, heroism, and ingenuity of youth groups, work camps, and adventuresome Christianity have come from Moab's modern acceptance of being emptied from vessel to vessel, with valor, victoriously.

THIS IS HOW I DO IT

ANNE EMERY

Anne Emery is the author of a number of very successful and highly regarded books for teen-age readers. Senior Year *and* Going Steady *are outstanding. Her reputation as a writer is based not only upon a thoroughly trained literary craftsmanship, but also upon an intimate acquaintance with teen-agers. Her knowledge of their problems and her understanding of their attitudes enable her to write the kind of stories which capture and hold their interest.*

I BEGIN with the idea. Do not ask me where that comes from. It just comes. The longer one works, the faster the ideas come. My first idea was to make real and dramatic for readers the writing of the Constitution of the United States. I was just finishing that book, typing the last chapter, when the next idea popped into my head. I had a Japanese maid working for me at that time, and I thought one day, "I would like to do a story about prejudice, as it affected our Japanese Americans in the last war." Then, when I was finishing that book, we took a trip to the Great Smoky Mountains, where I saw people from the outside mingling with the mountaineers. That trip made me want to write a story laid in those mountains. You see how vague the initial idea was in each case.

When the idea has jelled a little, I begin to outline the plot. For me, thought comes faster when I am at the typewriter, when I can think through my fingers and put it all down as it comes. For many people this is not true; so do not worry if your thought processes operate differently. I write a synopsis of the whole story in a couple of pages. Then I outline each chapter, sometimes as much as a full single-spaced page to a chapter. This may take a couple of weeks. But the ideas are building up all the while. By the time I have finished the last chapter, I can see things I had forgotten to put in the first chapter, so I go back to insert them. I like to put in as much detail as comes quickly to mind, because sometimes I think of things in the preparation of this first outline which would not occur to me again.

Some writers dislike this kind of planning. They prefer to let the story grow as they go along. This is a personal choice. I like to know from the very start where I am going.

I have a great deal of faith in the power of the subconscious to produce successive developments of the plot. I may say here that faith in the power of prayer will contribute enormously to the strength of one's subconscious inspirations. Time after time, when I am stopped by a snag in a plot, I let it go for a day, two days, or three days. Sooner or later the solution comes to mind.

While I am waiting, I do not face a mental vacuum, nor do I fold my hands in idleness. There is always something I can do at the typewriter: developing characters, by-passing the snag and going forward with other lines of the story, or planning background. Sometimes I read books similar to the one I am trying to write. Or I look up background detail, if it is a research story. Or I talk to my high school friends, who are an invaluable source of material.

When I start the actual writing, the synopsis provides a working outline; thus, I always have something to begin with when I sit down. This is the time to write, whether one feels like it or not. I like to compose as rapidly as the story comes to mind, with the mental reservation that I am going to do the whole thing over anyway, so the sooner I have the first draft ready for revising, the better.

The people in my story must live, if I can make them do so. I find it easier to create characters when I visualize concretely young people I know: their manners, their speech, their morals, their opinions, their habits. Do not forget that what goes on in their minds is as important a part of their personalities as the color of their hair and their eyes. Sometimes I write out the characterizations on separate sheets of paper, inventing as many details about each one as I can. Furthermore, the background for them must be real and convincing. The plot must move forward with dramatic suspense. The style must be clear, straightforward, and literary.

The best way to find out how to make characters live, how to make things happen vividly, how to keep your readers in suspense, is to read books similar to the one you are trying to write. Try to discover how that author did it.

You need not be afraid of imitating. If you can imitate a good writer for more than a paragraph, you are fortunate. I worked on my first book, a historical story, with Esther Forbes' *Johnny Tremain* in one hand for a year. I must have read it through a dozen times and studied it, bit by bit, another dozen times. I was trying my best to write a story that would come to life like *Johnny Tremain*. Yet try as I would, I could not do it. There are some natural limitations that neither your subconscious nor your conscious will, can overcome quickly. But what I learned from that author helped enormously.

When I finish the first draft, I let it rest a couple of weeks. Sometimes I am drafting another book in the meantime. Sometimes I take time out to read all the books I can find, keeping a sharp eye for character, plot, background, and mood. In the teen-age field there are not too many books that are really helpful. But even from the poor books one can learn what to avoid.

Now I may return to that first draft, which is going to look different from the perspective of a week's distance. I read it through and add more details to emphasize the personalities. I take out things that do not seem to fit as well as I thought. I make notes of additional action, characterization, background, and motivation for each chapter. Sometimes I add as much as fifty pages to the original story, usually typing this new material on pieces of paper and inserting them where they belong.

Sometimes I retype the whole story on second sheets (I prefer to work on yellow paper, up to the final copy), and revise it again. There was a time, after I sold my first book, when I thought that soon I should be qualified to have a private secretary to do my typing for me. I never reached that stage. But in the meantime I have lost interest in the whole idea. It is helpful to me to type my own work, right through the final copy. Every time I do it over, I change a line, a paragraph, a whole page. There are usually a dozen changes, of words or phrases, on every page—for the better, I think. If anyone else typed the manuscript, some of that final polishing would not be done. And all of it is needed.

Be sensitive about the words you use too often and the adjectives that cheapen your style. Soon you begin to see also what a critic means when he says, "too many adverbs." You begin to purify your taste and to reach for finer forms of expression. All of this effort is deeply rewarding. You grow intellectually, and you grow as a personality. There is no richer satisfaction.

Always you ask yourself, "How is this going to sound to the reader?" The first essential of successful writing is to be aware of other people and their opinions, their feelings, their wishes, and their centers of attention. You must learn to put yourself aside. It isn't "how do I want to express myself?" that matters; but "did I get it across?"

The business of learning to write takes a long time. Kenneth Roberts, who certainly should know, said it was the only profession he knew which became more difficult the longer you practiced it.

If you feel that way, it is a hopeful sign. It means that the reach is exceeding the grasp. It means that with every piece of work you do, you glimpse possibilities as yet unrealized, and you stretch your mind and heart a little farther to try to realize them the next time. When that happens, you are maturing as a writer.

The editor is your first reader. He represents the thousands of readers you are hoping to reach. He knows what they want. If he did not, he would not be editing. He may tell you that you have missed the high point of your story, that if you will rewrite it, he will think about it. This is a critical moment in your professional effort. Prepare yourself from the beginning to trust his judgment, to accept his suggestions—unless some issue is involved so vital to you that you would rather throw the story away than change it.

If you do not want to write what that editor wants, send your story somewhere else. But if you like his work, his magazines, his list of books, if you want to publish with his firm, and he is interested in helping you, then listen to him, co-operate with him, learn to write to his order—and besides selling your work, you will learn a great deal about writing.

In conclusion, then, plan your work before you write. Synopsize your short story or your novel, and try to analyze the plot to discover if there are any dangling threads or unfinished ideas. Begin with characters, and build them into living, interesting people. Write as often as you can, daily if possible, even if you do not feel like it. Read as many books or stories as you can find of the type you are trying to write. Discover the best writers and the best books, and live with them, trying to imitate them and learning from example. And when you finally reach an editor, listen to him! This is how I do it.

TECHNIQUE OF WRITING THE SHORT STORY

Harvey C. Jacobs

Dr. Harvey C. Jacobs is the capable head of the Department of Journalism at Franklin College, Franklin, Ind., and is regarded by his students as a popular and inspiring teacher. He has developed a highly original method of instructing his students in the techniques of short-story writing. The accompanying address (necessarily much condensed) gives an insight into that method.

A short story entered last year in a contest sponsored by a national magazine began as follows:

> Three weeks after Mother died, Daddy went to Boston on a business trip. Two months later, he came back to Georgia bringing with him a pretty young woman, and called us to meet our new mother.

It sounds as though it were getting off to a good start, doesn't it? A story should begin with something interesting—a narrative which reaches out and "hooks" the reader right up into the story action.

This story from which I have just quoted does not have the best beginning in the world, but it does have a "narrative hook." The first scene is set: "Three weeks after Mother died, Daddy went to Boston on a business trip." There is a hint here of the unconventional; and there is even more of a hint in the next sentence: "Two months later, he came back to Georgia bringing with him a pretty young woman." The action and development are begun with the final clause: "called us to meet our new mother."

Any amateur writer can use this beginning and take off, as Stephen Leacock's horse, in all directions. It is the old Cinderella plan, the evil (or good) stepmother, and the subsequent conflict between children and father. There is no end to the types of development which could come from such a first paragraph. The test for a story-beginning is this simple: Does it interest the reader sufficiently to make him eager to read on? This one does. Now let us see what happens.

As the author developed the story, there are the expected two daughters in the home, one pretty and personable; the other less pretty and more reserved. The latter is the heroine, through whose point of view the story is told. The pretty one is given bubble bath soap by the new mother; the other gets nothing. A bit later, the heroine, the not-so-pretty girl, finally gets a date to the high school prom. Her new mother gives her a home-permanent and offers some bubble bath soap to her when she takes a bath. That is the whole story.

According to Mr. Aron M. Mathieu, one of the nation's most experienced editors, that story represents more than half of your competition as a free-lance writer. Can you beat that kind of competition? If you can't, I assume you are trying to beat it or you would not be here.

The beginning of the story led us to believe that a serious conflict was about to develop between the two daughters or between the daughters and the parents. But no important conflict occurred. Furthermore, there was no explanation of the father's sudden decision to remarry. In short, the stage was set, but nothing happened. As many an editor would pencil on the manuscript: "This is a good idea, but it just doesn't come off as a story."

There are as many so-called "systems" for creating a short story as there are writers—and all of them right! They are right because the creative impulse is an individual thing; it cannot be put in a mold and turned out, cold and uniform, like a plastic knob. A mass producer of Western stories once said: "Every story I write is a little bit of me." Perhaps it is only a little bit, but almost every story represents something of the author.

Few authors claim so thorough a knowledge of "formula," whatever that is, that they manufacture their products completely detached from the experiences, the attitudes, the sorrows, and the background of their own lives. One noted author who has made a good living by telling other authors how to write, claims that the study of technique is a waste of time; he says that *the story is the thing,* and that the analysis of plot, characterization, and dialogue may very well tie the beginning author in knots and so clutter up his natural ability, if he has any, that he never will write anything. That may be true.

Most of my students write their first stories with no more dramatic appeal than the one I described a moment ago. Most of them—not all, by any means—*acquire* a better sense of story appeal; they learn that conflict must be resolved to the satisfaction of the reader. What constitutes a satisfactory conclusion depends upon the reader's educational and cultural level, his fleeting whims, and his mood at the moment. Perhaps I should add here that in some literary stories the conflict is not resolved.

What is the purpose of fiction? Even on this matter, the so-called authorities do not agree. Some say it is "escape from the everyday routine." Others say that it is easier for the author to begin his story if he realizes at the outset that he is creating entertainment. But whether the desire is for escape, entertainment, relaxation, information, philosophy, or cultural uplift, the psychologists say that most persons prefer to read that with which they can identify themselves. Consequently, we come to the term with which most authors are familiar, "reader identification."

The basic ingredients of fiction are struggle, strife, and conflict. The story about the two girls was a failure because the conflict was too slight, almost nonexistent. There was a hint of struggle, but the reader was let down. This is the unpardonable sin of short-story writing. You may jolt the reader with shocks, twists, and unexpected turns, but you must come out somewhere near the spot the reader wants to come out. The goal is to have the reader lay aside the story and say, "Well, that's the way I would have done it."

Making conflict convincing is the basic principle of fiction writing. Most writers sweat blood over this. If we knew how to do this, we would all be successful writers. There was a French writer who said there are only four basic conflicts or situations: man as center in relation to himself, in relation to other men, in relation to the other sex, and in relation to God or nature. But how many stories are encompassed in these four dramatic situations!

If conflict is basic and man is central to a story, then our first problem must not be so great as we had thought; for man is generally filled with conflicting attitudes, actions, emotions, and backgrounds. If we put any two men together, we probably have the makings of a story. Thus, the hero and the villain are created; this has been the basic character-pattern of storytellers since the beginning of time.

It is well to state that conflict is the basic element of the short story, and that when the conflict ceases the story interest is probably finished; but you may want a more practical lesson concerning its actual creation. For my college students, I use a simple drawing on the blackboard. I show them that a story is a straight line leading from here to there. At this point I indicate that there is movement in a story. (Please bear in mind that we are discussing the commercial short story. Movement indicates plot, and of course there are plotless stories of the literary or experimental nature. These are much harder to write, and they require great individuality of style and outlook. I do not discuss them because they are not for beginners.) If a story moves, it must have a plot, even though the conflict may be wholly psychological. By this I mean that conflict may be—and most often is—derived from conflicting emotions, and the subsequent movement may be from one basic attitude to another. Thus, when we talk of movement, it is not necessarily geographical or physical movement.

To continue with our diagram, if a story moves over a straight line after we have invented characters and our hero moves from here to there, we probably have about the same type of story that we discussed in the beginning. The homely girl wanted the favor of her new stepmother, the same favor the pretty sister received with no effort at all. There was movement, a little at least; and we moved in a straight line from *wanting something* to *getting it.*

But editors do not buy, and readers do not read, that type of story. What is wrong with it? We want the hero or heroine to have a struggle getting what he or she wants. We want it to seem, *almost to the very end,* that our hero is not going to get what he wants and what we want him to get. Then, when things are blackest, comes what has been called the "sudden reversal" and all turns out to our satisfaction.

So the straight-line "formula" does not work; there must be something added. Let us be very specific and quite elementary. The hero begins at the left side of the line. First, *the problem* must be created and the scene set. He moves along the line to what I call "Number 1 Barrier." This may take 1,000 words in a 5,000-word story, or it may take much less. Depending upon the length and type of story, there may be from one to five major "barriers" thrown up, with logic and conviction, to keep our hero from reaching his goal. I believe it is wise for the beginner to try his hand at stories with exaggerated "barriers" in order to get the "feel" of creating conflict.

The beginner must realize that there are many subtle variations on this theme. I diagram them by showing that the straight line—the movement—must always be there, but the barriers become "dramatic peaks" which lift the reader a little higher each time he hits one. Then in one great dramatic sweep the climax comes and the hero achieves what he started out to get. Each "dramatic peak" in a story plays a little joke on the reader; he thought he had figured out what was going to happen—easy-like and without much pursuit. Then, you take him down another path and again he must hang on for dear life.

Short stories are made up of "scenes." I try to illustrate this part of the construction technique by tying it closely to the "barriers" thrown up against the hero. The average short story of 4,500 to 5,000 words is written in from three to six major scenes. It is easy for the "barriers" to become the "scenes," and, of course, the "pay-off" comes right after the last "barrier"; that is to say, in the last scene. This last scene becomes the climax to the story.

Most beginning authors never get around to a significant climax; they pursue the "straight-line technique." Conflict is not easy to create, but it is especially difficult to carry convincing conflict to the one last dramatic peak.

I am indebted to Mr. Mathieu for a device which I have used effectively. (1) Write the climax of your story in a sentence. (2) Consider whether this climax, when unrelated to your characters and seen by itself, stands up as something of consequence. If not, how can you truthfully say that this climax is important in the future lives of your characters? And if it is not important in their future lives, how can you truthfully say that your story displays high quality writing?

Some writers say that it is useless, if not actually detrimental, to spend time trying to analyze characterization. They contend that characterization is actually a by-product of dialogue, description, and movement; that it should never be isolated. Whatever may be your approach to it, the fact remains that each major character must have certain distinguishing characteristics. They may be human characteristics or they may be social characteristics which grow out of background and environment. For purposes of analysis we may examine these character traits, but in reality they are so closely bound up with all the other elements of the story that it is difficult to isolate them.

Characters must come alive and do the things they are supposed to do. Some authors tag each major character in their story with a list of characteristics which they weave, subtly and artistically, into the description, the dialogue, and the action. Here again, preoccupation with mechanical details may make for mechanical characters. It is better to think of someone you know, and extend his characteristics into the person who is to become your hero.

We could continue at length on characterization, but the beginning author—and the professional too—must be interested in people. He must observe each human personality for all of its quirks and turns. He either will use a notebook or he will store away in his subconscious the encounters he has with unusual people and places. He should be a good listener. Without becoming obnoxious, he must be a walking laboratory looking for material every day. He will become sensitive to faces, figures, mannerisms, gestures—all of these and more. This kind of author will have no difficulty with characterization.

Characters may be revealed in many ways, but one of the most effective methods is to let them talk. This, as all of you know, is dialogue. It is said that many readers make their decision on whether or not to buy a book or magazine on the basis of how much dialogue they see as they scan its pages. In any case, some authors subscribe to the theory that the surest way to revive a tiring reader is to dash him in the face with a cup of dialogue. There is only one better way to keep him awake. You will see it in this passage, for example:

I

> Before the aproned lackey could touch the pistol lying conveniently at his hand, he was staring into the end of a long-barreled Colt. Hack hadn't meant to do it, but he knew the only protection he had in this crooked town was the Colt swinging against his long thigh. "Don't get rattled, fat face." Hack spoke softly. "All I want is what's coming to me. Now get it—and quick."

The first part of the passage is narrative, action! This is the heart of a story, but it would not be much of a passage without the dialogue to make the characters come alive.

Most beginning writers have a tendency to overwrite, particularly in handling dialogue. They know that the goal is natural-sounding speech, yet it comes out stilted and awkward, like this:

> "How do you do."
> "I am most pleased to see you again."
> "You do not recall our earlier acquaintance?"
> "Most certainly, I do. We met at a party given by Montpelier Q. Nerle, son of John P. Nerle, who was a member of the law firm of Finch, Duffy, Nerle, and Jones of Indianapolis."

Think how lost a reader would get if he had to wade through such impossible dialogue! The reader is not interested in trivialities and small talk. He wants movement and action and a character who is getting something done. Let your dialogue and narrative work hand-in-hand to keep your main characters moving. Some stories demand more dialogue than others, but there must always be some.

Beware of putting words into the mouths of your characters merely because you can think of no other way to get those bits of information across to your reader. If your characters cannot talk naturally and crisply and subtly, better not let them talk.

Beware also of trying to make your characters talk the way persons talk in real life. Listen to a conversation, and see how much of it could be reproduced verbatim in a story. Actually, your dialogue must sound the way persons *seem* to talk in real life. Listen to this sample from a *Post* story:

> "And I saw your lovely mother in Paris. Weren't you with your parents?"
> "No, Ma'am; I was away at school."
> "Oh, yes, and your coming down to the island so late—Aren't your parents down this summer?"

"Yes, Ma'am, but I was away at camp."

"At camp, of course. Well——"

It was coming now at last. "Well, I just wanted to tell you, you're a lucky boy to have such a wonderful father. You must be proud of him."

Now, most persons do not talk that way. Take the first speech: "And I saw your lovely mother in Paris. Weren't you with your parents?" Most of us would say something like this: "I saw your mother in Paris, but you weren't over there, were you?" And so on. This is a difficult phase of the mechanics of short-story writing. One has to do it for many thousands of words in order to get the instinctive feeling for smooth, natural dialogue.

We have discussed at some length the three basic elements of the short story: conflict, characterization, and dialogue. We have also thrown in some extras, such as description, the narrative hook, the scene, reader identification, and the climax. Now someone will probably say: "But you haven't told us enough about plot. That's the big problem for me."

My thesis is that plotting takes care of itself, if you have a character who acts, talks, moves, and comes into conflict with another person or with other elements. The plot is merely a vehicle in which your character rides; it is the dramatizing of his unusual qualities as he moves from one point to another. It must be logical. It must hold the interest of the reader, not merely during the opening action and the crucial climax, but during the whole story.

WRITING FICTION WITH A RELIGIOUS THEME

JAMES WESLEY INGLES

James Wesley Ingles, Baptist minister, is now Professor of English Literature at the Eastern Baptist College; previously he was Professor of English Literature at Bates College. He is the author of numerous short stories and several religious novels. Among the latter are The Woman of Samaria *and* The Silver Trumpet. *The last mentioned received an important literary award and has been translated into several foreign languages. Professor Ingles believes that novels and short stories, if properly written, can be made to carry a significant Christian message.*

IN ORDER to write anything of significance, one must feel that what one writes is important, that one has something to communicate. In other words, one must have a sense of mission.

Until we have analyzed our motives, we cannot succeed as writers. For most of us, if we are honest, there is a measure of economic pressure. Frankly, we hope to earn money, either professionally, supporting ourselves entirely by our writing, or semi-professionally, adding something occasionally to our meager income. The prizes offered by many publishers today are highly stimulating. While this mercenary objective is not unworthy as a subsidiary motive and should not be decried, it is wholly inadequate as the prime motive for those of us who are Christians.

If anyone wishes to write well, he must have an inner drive, a desire to communicate something, an urge to share some insight or conviction, or to strike at some evil. This inner drive is essential, if one is to attempt any sustained work in fiction. For, as Browning has Andrea del Sarto admit to his wife after he has caught himself beginning to blame her for his failure to achieve the greatness of Raphael, "Incentives come from the soul's self." The deep drives that sustain us for any extended effort, however, are related to something beyond ourselves.

No man can tell another what to write. Ideas, like incentives, come from the soul's self. The basic principle is to write out of your own experience, your own firsthand observation of life, your own personal and specific knowledge. Relate everything you write to what you have personally known, seen, felt. There is no substitute for authenticity in fiction. There are some areas of life which you know better than anyone else. Draw your subjects from those areas of life.

But a writer must do more than decide on a subject that he knows adequately and that he is moved to communicate. He must also cast it into the form to which it is best suited. Some material should be handled in short fiction and some in the novel form. Furthermore, the writer must know not only what form is best suited to the subject that has gripped him, but also what form is best suited to his own talents. This is an important consideration. Few writers are equally effective as short-story writers and as novelists. If one tends to see his material in the large—expanding, growing, developing, changing—he is essentially a novelist. If, on the other hand, one tends to see life sharply in clearly isolated segments, if he finds that his imagination cannot sustain the longer flight, then probably the short-story form is better adapted to his nature. At any rate, one ought to analyze carefully his abilities in relation to these parallel but very different forms of fiction.

Those who wish to write so-called "Christian" fiction are in particular danger of misunderstanding the nature and function of the art of fiction. This is perhaps one important reason for the general failure of Protestant fiction to maintain high artistic standards. It was G. K. Chesterton, a great Roman Catholic writer, who said that "a good story does not *have* a moral, it *is* a moral." That is a significant distinction. James Russell Lowell, in criticism of his tendency to moralize in his poetry, wrote:

> The top of the hill he will ne'er come nigh reaching
> Till he learns the distinction 'twixt singing and preaching.

As Christians we ought not support the general tendency of our time to disparage preaching. There is no greater, no more solemn, office than that of the preacher, the spokesman for God to his generation. But the functions of the preacher and of the artist are quite different, and the writer of fiction is, or certainly ought to be, primarily an artist. He should have a message, but it must be conveyed indirectly. It is his function to carry truth alive into the heart by way of the imagination.

We are always in danger of riding a thesis rather than embodying a theme. We tend to invent paper characters, two-dimensional characters, in order to illustrate and prove our thesis. That is the curse of many so-called "Christian" novels. The people simply are not real. They are not flesh and blood.

If, then, we are to improve the quality of our Protestant fiction, we must learn how to portray life realistically. Fiction is the art of simulating life. William Dean Howells said that "realism is the truthful treatment of material."

Just here we run into a serious problem. There is, first, our own difficulty as writers to see life as it is and to be honest in our treatment of it. We need to cultivate an almost scientific accuracy of observation. To be a writer of fiction, as Henry James said, is to be a person on whom nothing is lost. The accent and intonation, the dialect and the idiom of the person speaking, the posture, the gesture, the dress, the subtle self-revelations, the peculiar mannerisms—all must be caught by the observant eye and ear of the writer and must be conveyed with a faithful precision that will make the total picture both authentic and convincing to the reader.

And here we come upon a second aspect of the problem. We who are Christian writers often are unfairly inhibited at this point both by editors and by our public. We have been forced by the hangover from Victorian prudery into a sort of parlor-handling of life that is insipid and emasculated. The Bible itself does not suggest any such prudish handling of life. There is no more realistic book in the world's literature than the Bible, but within it all of life is surveyed from the perspective of a moral standard. That is not true of the naturalistic fiction of our time.

The difference between realism and naturalism is the difference between an attempt to see life steadily and as a whole, as Matthew Arnold suggested, and an attempt to reduce all of life to a materialistic level. A realistic treatment of life may be purging, but a naturalistic treatment of it can only be debasing. It denies the essential dignity of man. Ibsen, after his realistic handling of certain social evils, was accused of descending like Zola into the cesspool, but his reply clarifies our distinction. "Zola," he said, "descended into the cesspool to take a bath; I, to cleanse it."

Nothing in life should be outside the range of the novelist's consideration, although the Christian must handle some aspects of life, as any true artist should, with restraint and poetic imagination rather than boldly and crudely. Nothing indecent should be introduced unless it is essential to the material. The youthful writer often longs to shock parental prudery. Something of that attitude seems to characterize many authors today. But the mature writer will know what is essential and what may be omitted.

Although most of the editors of religious journals would probably agree with this point of view, they are forced, unfortunately, by a fear of the prudish among their reading public to impose (in some cases) ridiculous restrictions upon an author's treatment of life. It is these restrictions (perhaps quite as much as the pitifully small remuneration) which discourage our better writers from contributing to our various Christian publications. Some of these writers eventually are lost entirely to the Christian cause.

We have a major task on our hands to educate the tastes of great segments of the Christian reading public so that they will demand fiction of a higher quality, fiction that is an authentic reading of life. How this can be done, I do not venture to suggest. It would seem to me to be primarily the responsibility of Christian editors. I only know that the problem must be faced, if fiction is to be as effective a vehicle of Christian truth as I believe it might be. Perhaps, until improvements are made at the points I have mentioned, the serious Christian writer will have to continue to seek admittance into the larger secular magazines and publishing houses. There are signs of an awakening to moral values already apparent in some quarters. It is the task of our best Christian writers to enlarge the beachhead.

Finally, if we are to save religious fiction from being narrowly propagandistic and at the same time to preserve its function as a vehicle of truth, we ought to note the major characteristics of the kind of fiction that ennobles life. For, while it is not our function to distort life into a pattern such as we might prefer—in which all virtue is rewarded, all vice punished, all church people are good and all good people nice, all problems are solved and all sinners converted—nevertheless, we do have a responsibility to enrich and ennoble life, rather than to degrade and debase it. Perhaps, indeed, that is our chief function as writers of religious fiction.

The primary characteristic of ennobling fiction, it seems to me, is what Arnold Bennett referred to in his *Journal* as an "all-embracing, Christlike compassion." To read the great Russians, Tolstoi and especially Dostoievski, is to understand what this means. Read Tolstoi's classic short story, "Where Love Is, There God Is Also." You are moved profoundly by his compassion for Martin, the lonely shoemaker who has lost his son and his Christian faith, but who is led back to Christ and to a daily meditation on the Gospels by the ministrations of a traveling monk. A reading of that great story cannot fail to illumine unforgettably what Jesus meant when he said, "Inasmuch as ye have done it unto one of the least of these my brethren, ye have done it unto me."

Dostoievski's *The Brothers Karamazov* is easily one of the ten greatest novels in world literature, some think the very greatest. While it is profound psychologically and philosophically, that which most moves the reader is the writer's boundless compassion for all sorts and conditions of men.

This compassion is not the only characteristic of ennobling fiction. The writer who would enrich rather than impoverish life must himself have an abounding faith in the ultimate goodness of life, which of course must be based upon an unyielding faith in the goodness of God supremely revealed in Jesus Christ.

Our great responsibility is to create characters who will exhibit that kind of faith, who will be masters of circumstances, who have "what it takes," as we say, to triumph over the worst that life can throw at them. The secret of the success of Margaret Landon's book, *Anna and the King of Siam,* lay chiefly in the splendid character of Anna Leonowens, that courageous, vital Englishwoman who stood like a rock amid the terrors and corruption of a heathen court. And so it was with that delightful story of a Norwegian-American mother, *I Remember Mama.* And so it was also with that unforgettable picture of a lost way of life in Wales, *How Green Was My Valley.*

We have had more than enough of perverts, malcontents, alco-

holics, suicides, adulterers, dope addicts, nymphomaniacs, klepto-
maniacs, pyromaniacs, monomaniacs, and just plain "heels" as the
"heroes" and "heroines" of recent novels. It is high time we returned
to the basic concept of the hero in fiction. People do not have to
be giants to be heroes. And they do not have to be perfect. But
they do have to be good, and they have to be brave and strong. It is
much harder to create a good character that is convincing than an
evil one. We must remember that goodness without strength is not
admirable, that a static goodness is not admirable, that virtue that
is not tested in the fiery crucible is not admirable. Goodness that is
weak, ignorant, or naïve can only be pathetic. And it is our task
as Christian writers to renew man's faith in his essential dignity and
in God's redemptive purpose for human life. Surely no one who has
read Paton's book can ever forget the dignity and nobility of Stephen
Kumalo, the native Zulu pastor. To have created such a character
is a triumph of fictional art. This is our high calling.

But a Christlike compassion and an abounding faith in God and
in life are not enough to make our writing significant and enriching.
Along with these two great spiritual qualities must go a craftsman's
care.

And just here is where much of our religious fiction falls down.
There are many who set out with a high sense of mission and a noble
purpose, but they have not mastered the art of writing fiction.
They are like children who want to play the piano without mastering
the keyboard.

Fiction is indeed an exacting form of art. Those of us who
wish to serve the cause of truth and the Kingdom through this
medium ought to make a constant effort to improve our technique.
It is possible to write too much and too carelessly. There is no excuse for carelessness in style or awkwardness in construction. Why
should those who serve the King of kings be less meticulous or less
artistic than those who serve the prince of this world? It is to our
shame if we are not making continual efforts to improve.

Most really effective writing is accomplished in an agony of
spirit. Occasionally something will come on the joyous wings of
Inspiration. But she is a most capricious cherub. We are very
grateful for her visitations, but we cannot wait for them. Most of
the time we shall have to "sweat it out" alone. A successful writer

was asked if he liked to write; to which he replied, "No, but I like to have written!" It is the finished product that makes the labor worth while, and though at best it can only approximate the ideal of which we have dreamed, it encourages us to keep trying.

WRITING RELIGIOUS DRAMA

Amy Goodhue Loomis

Amy Goodhue Loomis is Director of the Department of Religious Drama, Division of Education in Home, Church, and Community, Board of Education and Publication of the American Baptist Convention; Director of Drama at the American Baptist Assembly, Green Lake, Wis.; and Director of the Religious Drama Workshop of the National Council of the Churches of Christ in the U.S.A. She has been director of the community theater in Dallas, Texas; New Orleans, La.; and Charleston, S. C.; also director of the University of Michigan Theater. She developed in the Fountain Street Baptist Church, Grand Rapids, Mich., the first department of religious drama to be set up in a Protestant church. She is the author of The Other Woman, Second Choice First, Baker's Dozen, The Beloved Child, Out of Nazareth, *and numerous other plays.*

WHAT, PRECISELY, is a religious drama? Dr. Fred Eastman, for so many years the distinguished head of the Department of Religious Drama of the Theological School of the University of Chicago, implies that a religious play must have a religious effect upon players and participants, as well as upon the audience or congregation. Often the religious play is so moving that it stirs to action—stirs both those who watch and listen, and those who play. Our primary concern, I believe, should be with the players.

If I had written a religious play—one worthy of the time and effort the participants would be asked to devote to it—and wanted to sell it, this is something of the process which I would follow:

First, I would get a production of it. I would be shameless in badgering my friends. I would haunt the telephones and offices of ministers, directors of religious education, teachers, presidents of women's groups, and their like, dangling before their eyes the tempting promise of a production royalty free! Most of these good souls are unbelievably unsophisticated in matters of art and salesmanship and do not see the catch. They will be obligated for no royalty. So, they reason, the production is sure to be a bargain. But you had better not let that hope flourish too vigorously. There will be a production to pay for, even without the royalty. But do arrange for a production, if you possibly can.

Once you have been promised a production, try to attend every rehearsal. Let someone else direct your play. You want to know how it is going to sound and look to that vast group known as "the public." See it through an amateur director's eyes. You will be amazed. Listen and watch with merciless self-criticism. Does it play? Is it really catching the consciences of the participants? Is it having the effect you hoped it would have? No? Then, rewrite the whole thing. If in your honest estimation it is not worth rewriting, throw it in the wastebasket.

But assuming that it can be salvaged, prepare your manuscript properly for marketing. I like the suggestions for such preparation given in *The Writer's Handbook,* published by The Writer, Inc., Boston, Mass. A play is a laborious manuscript to prepare since all the stage business must be underlined to indicate to the printer that it is to be italicized. This requirement is really a wholesome discipline for the playwright, if he is the kind who is inclined to talk *about* his characters, *about* the scenery, and *about* the significance of the motivated stage business, instead of writing a play which renders such directions unnecessary because it reveals them through its own development.

Now, where shall you send this manuscript? You will not like this, but I would send it first to one of the commercial publishers. If the firm is reputable, your play will receive fairly prompt reading; and you will receive either a candid report or a pale, pink rejection slip. If your drama has a chance, you will receive one of those infinitely encouraging chatty notes from the editor. If your play is purchased, you have a fair chance of a good bargain, with the legal details neatly taken care of by the publishing house. Your play will not get very much promotion, but it will be listed appropriately, and you will have the prestige of at least one major league publication behind you.

In the religious publication house, on the contrary, your brain child will undergo at the hands of a committee a routine ordeal that is at once flattening and heartbreaking, an ordeal which should not happen to a comic strip! But if you can survive the endless arguments, the endless mailing back and forth of carbon copies, and still recognize your brain child when the pressure groups are through with the flattening process, you have a chance of specialized promotion that has some value. Of course, I hope you will use this channel, for the denominational groups *need* your product.

A superficial analysis of the market demand for religious dramas as of 1951 reveals that one-act plays are in demand ten to one. Mr. Theodore Johnson of the Walter H. Baker Co. of Boston, Mass., states that nearly half of the religious plays used last year were biblical. Mr. M. A. VanNostrand of Samuel French & Co. says, on the contrary, that biblical plays do not sell as well as plays on contemporary religious themes. This may be, he thinks, because biblical plays are not much as plays. Can we, as writers, change his mind? From the pile of letters on my desk I would say that biblical plays, particularly those based upon New Testament themes, are in demand at least three to one. And, offhand, I can think of only five good biblical dramas. Of the five, three are beyond the means and skill of the average church group. Can we do something about this situation?

Let me warn you, before you plunge, that just because a story has greatness in the New Testament does not assure its greatness as a play. What new approach have you to the well-known story? What new insights have you to offer? None? Then let the story alone! We know it is significant in its present form. Biblical drama, probably, is at once the most needed and the least well-written and well-prepared of any literary form on the market.

Many requests come to all of us for missionary dramas. Missions are urgently, terribly important right now. But many of our missionary dramas are merely propaganda-loaded sermons that never quite come to life. We could use a drama of situation and mood, as, for instance, the trek of the Chinese Christian students westward during and immediately after World War II. We ought to drama-

tize the conflict in ideologies more effectively than it has yet been
done, for India, for China, and for poor, battered Burma. Who is
going to write the drama of character implicit in the life of Brayton
Case, Sam Higginbottom, or even, and perhaps most of all, in the
tragic story of Dr. Gordon Seagrave? We need the plays, but they
must be honest plays, and, if possible, literary plays first of all. Then
and then only will their Christian message come alive.

The market for children's plays is always a tempting one. But
look out! I think it is fair to warn you that the better Christian
educators today are urging that children below junior high school
age make their own plays. Very few churches or church schools
are prepared in physical matters or teaching staff to present formal
dramas for and with children. Anyway, creative drama projects are
much more significant teaching and learning experiences for the
younger members of the congregation. If you doubt that statement,
I refer you with enthusiasm to Miss Winifred Ward's book, *Play-
making with Children.* It will give you some fine ideas for play-
writing, too.

Plays for young people are largely a myth. Young people today
are interested in adult drama, if they are the kind of young people
with enough imagination to be interested in any kind of drama. For
the most part, they resent plays written for youth. But you might
try writing a play *about* today's youth. It ought to be a heart-shaker!

If my remarks seem to have been directed to the discouragement
rather than to the encouragement of writers of religious drama, let me
assure you that the impression is quite correct. In general, I do
believe that we need fewer and better religious dramas. If, each
season, we could be sure of one new one-act play of the dimensions of
An Hour Glass by W. B. Yeats, *The Builders* by Frances Eckardt,
Empty Hands by Helen M. Clark, *John Doe* by Bernard Dryer, or
A Child Is Born by Stephen Vincent Benét, we and the church would
be infinitely richer than if all of us burst into print with a deluge
of the trivial and topical. But we do need that *one* drama annually.

WRITING SCRIPTS FOR RELIGIOUS RADIO PROGRAMS

RUTH DOERR BRIERLEY

Ruth Doerr Brierley, whose address deals so helpfully with the writing of scripts for religious radio programs, speaks out of practical experience gained while a staff member of the KYW Radio Workshop in Philadelphia. She has written and directed the radio presentation of a number of highly effective religious dramas.

THERE ARE certain fundamentals for effective script writing for radio. First, there should be a rough over-all outline which includes the theme of the program, the beginning, and the ending. All available scenes which develop a conflict should be listed. Then a plot-outline can be prepared.

The actual writing involves good characterization and effective dialogue. Each character must possess a distinct personality. Opposites should not think alike on major issues. There should be a balance between weak and strong traits in each character. His identity may be established at once (1) by having the character talk about himself, (2) by having others talk about him, or (3) by having the character converse with others. The central character ought to be involved in nearly every scene, either in person or by implication. He should manifest the growth and change which are the result of circumstances and the passing of time.

Dialogue should measure up to the following requirements: (1) It should fit the characterization and the circumstances. (2) It should describe action. (3) It should set the stage by supplying necessary information. (4) It should convey ideas. (5) It should be concise and simple, avoiding the stilted and academic literary style. Above all, it should be vivid.

The script writer will do well to read his script aloud, for his lines must impress the ear of his audience. Instead of a brief treatment of numerous ideas, a few ideas should be developed thoroughly. The listener cannot absorb a great deal in a single program. Every line must further the plot; there is no time for unnecessary detail. Long, involved speeches should be avoided. The time element must be telescoped greatly.

There are three major purposes for radio scripts: (1) to entertain, which requires the capturing and holding of the listener's interest; (2) to inform, which necessitates getting facts and moral lessons across skillfully; (3) to activate, which calls upon the writer to inspire his listener to act upon what he has heard.

The foregoing hints are as important for religious programs as for those which are general in nature. The sequence of steps to be taken also should be the same.

WRITING SCRIPTS FOR MOTION PICTURES

Alan Shilin

Mr. Alan Shilin is an accomplished script writer, and his professional services are much in demand by the denominations undertaking to produce religious motion pictures. He is the head of Alan Shilin Productions, New York City. Typical of his recent productions is Wings to the Word. *He has been a helpful teacher at the Workshop on Audio-Visual Education conducted each year at the American Baptist Assembly, Green Lake, Wis.*

Script writing for motion pictures is polyphonic writing; that is, it is the writing of words which are destined to be heard, and it is the describing of pictures destined to be seen. Therefore, such writing calls for the creating of an audio-visual chord which has as its basic components picture, sound, and impression.

The script writer must work under certain limitations. One is financial. Usually the low budget for the religious film makes it imperative that the writer make the most of little. A second limitation is literary. He must provide in his picture a complete story. Both cause and effect must be clearly evident. A third limitation is length. There can be no extraneous material.

ing near a lilac bush has greater pictorial value than a subject in a white sari walking along a cement road.

Again, when the photographer desires to personalize his theme or plot and has selected a central character, he should strive to draw attention to that character through the color of his or her clothing. Where there are group scenes, the photographer must consider color in his appraisal of them and strive to arrange the group so as to produce the maximum effect, just as flowers are arranged for the same purpose. (The difference, of course, being that the photographer is dealing with a dynamic situation wherein colors will flow before the eye, ever forming new combinations.)

The color-conscious photographer will soon learn that he has always at his beck and call no less a prop than the blue sky. Anyone who has seen Kodachromes projected will appreciate the beauty and effectiveness of the sky when used as a background.

5. There is always the element of structure to be considered. It is embodied in the following principle: *The sequence is the structural unit of the motion picture.*

Films are not made of shots; they are made of sequences. Given a quantity of excellent unrelated shots, the producer is powerless to convert them into an intelligent sound film. He would much prefer a quantity of mediocre shots in related sequences. Then, at least, he would have the materials with which to create a sound film, strengthened in its deficiencies by a good narration, by optical effects, and by a good musical background.

What is a sequence? It is a series of shots, related in their subject matter, but varying in their settings and angles. By the progress of the action, these shots combine to represent thoroughly a scene. The components of the sequence include the following: (1) establishing the locale, action, or mood; (2) matched action; (3) the cutaway; (4) the close-up.

Even as a paragraph opens with a topic sentence, so does a sequence open with a "topic shot." That is to say, the first shot of a sequence which bursts upon the eyes of the audience should establish instantly the locale, action, or mood (perhaps all three simultaneously) of that which is to follow.

Most sequences open with the traditional long shot which attempts to convey a broad introduction. This is quite natural. One usually steps back to view a painting before one moves closer to it for an examination of its fine details. The same procedure applies to films, wherein we usually open with a long shot and then move in for a closer scrutiny.

It is important, however, that the photographer realize that a long shot selected at random is not always the best establishing mechanism. There are occasions when a close-up can achieve the same purpose in a much more effective way.

The photographer should know, however, that most of his sequences will be opened by long shots. Thus he should strive to vary the norm wherever possible by looking for striking, dynamic, and symbolic close-ups which will do the same job. After the audience has seen sequence after sequence established by long shots, it will have a tendency to sit back and expect the same device thereafter. It is at this intangible point that a close-up establishment will arrest the eye and rivet the attention to a new and higher degree.

A word must be said concerning the advantages of signs and symbols as establishing shots. Where they exist, these are perhaps the best means available to the photographer. What better way to establish a town than to make a close-up of a sign which reads: "Welcome to Green Rock, Maine. Population, 2000." What better way to establish Washington, D. C., than by a shot of the Washington Monument, or London by a shot of Big Ben in a fog, or New York City by a shot of skyscrapers or of the Statue of Liberty? Wherever the representation of an object enables us to drive home instantly locale, action, or mood, we should seize upon the opportunity.

One of the fundamental principles concerning sequence construction is this: *Action threads the sequence together; in motion pictures, the most effective action is "matched."* By this we mean that the action is broken down into separate, artificially arranged, overlapping shots which, when edited, will give the illusion of fluid and natural action.

Cutaways are essential components of most sequences. They are designed to relieve the action, fill out the sequence, and provide additional fluidity within the sequence framework. By the term "cutaway" we mean a diversion from the line of action; literally, a "cutting away from the subject under observation." For example, in a conference room scene we may be photographing the action of a committee member who has risen to speak. We "cut away" from him to make a shot of a clock on the wall. Then we return to him as he finishes his speech and sits down.

All shots in the sequence deal directly with the action in the conference room except that shot of the clock. Why did we bother to make it? (1) We made it to relieve the action. Rather than confine the eye to an uninterrupted series of shots based on one thing, we inserted another. (2) We made it to punctuate the point of the sequence. The committee member was urging his fellows to take action quickly because time was of the essence. Perhaps the committee had met in an effort to raise money to feed the starving population of China. The shot of the clock served as a symbol of the urgency of the meeting. (3) We made it to emancipate the sequence from the grip of time. Without the shot of the clock, the audience would assume that the committee member had spoken for exactly as long as they saw him speak before sitting down. But by inserting the cutaway, the grip of a temporal limitation is relaxed. It becomes a moot point as to how long the man spoke. If the narrator declares that he spoke for one minute or one hour, the audience will find his statement credible.

Nothing can be photographed that will prove of more interest and appeal than the human face. Thus, the close-up becomes something of a culmination or fulfillment in the sequence. We know that the camera must remain fluid, that we are constantly moving toward something. What is that something? It is the human being at the center of the action—the person, his face, his character, as revealed through his eyes and mouth.

The sequence which does not contain close-ups almost invariably falls short in the sense that it is incomplete. It has failed to acquire the elements of personality and intimacy; it has traveled without arriving at a destination; it has missed its dramatic opportunities.

Let us now discuss briefly the problem of sequence transition —a highly important matter in the creation of material for sound films, and one which depends almost entirely upon the talents of the photographer.

The best films are the most cohesive ones. And the most cohesive films are those in which sequence follows upon sequence so naturally that it becomes difficult to distinguish between them. What is the perfect sequence transition? It is an arrangement whereby the final shot of sequence number one is the establishing shot of sequence number two.

What, theoretically, is the perfect film? It is the film that contains absolute unity of time, place, and action. In other words, it is a film which requires only a fade-in at the beginning and a fade-out at the end, a film whose sequences are so thoroughly linked that it creates the impression of being but one sequence.

There are some general suggestions which may serve as a check-list for the photographer in the field with reference to the selection of a theme or plot. (1) Every theme or plot must have a beginning, a middle, and an end. (2) A simple theme is almost always the most desirable. (3) It is almost always better to allow a theme or plot to be suggested by characters, locale, and actual situations than to impose an artificial formula on these factors apart from the scene. (4) It is almost always best to personalize a theme or plot by developing it around a particular character or group of characters. (5) It is usually best to confine the story to action in the present. (6) It is entirely desirable to include a place for humor in order to relieve the dramatic progression. (7) Since this is a motion-picture theme or plot it should, wherever possible, incorporate opportunities for action, camera fluidity, synchronization of sight and sound, and exploitation of color. (8) Since we shall be dealing with unprofessional actors, the theme or plot should require the minimum of performance. (9) The theme or plot should contain all the necessary information in its body. In other words, it should establish locale, time, character, conflict, all in the pictures themselves. (10) These are primarily documentary themes or plots, and they should be flexible enough to include opportunities for significant detail. They should present, as a contributing factor to the story itself, something of how the people live and think.

In formulating a theme or plot, the photographer should subject his idea to three stages: (1) The idea in synopsis form. This amounts simply to writing down the idea. Only when it is recorded can it be referred to, changed, broadened, and evaluated. (2) The idea in outline form. Once the idea has been synopsized, it should be expanded and analyzed, resulting in a list of major scenes. In other words, it should be broken down into a list of perhaps eight phases which are milestones in the story. (3) The idea expressed as a shooting script. This is a further breakdown from the idea in outline form. In it the phases are divided into sequences.

THE WRITING OF RELIGIOUS POETRY

EDITH LOVEJOY PIERCE

Edith Lovejoy Pierce has made a valuable contribution to the Christian Writers and Editors' Conference by her gracious spirit, her counsel to writers, and her reading of her original poems. Many of her poems were first published in The Christian Century. *Two volumes of her verse are now in print:* In This Our Day *and* Therefore Choose Life. *Her poems, rich in their imagery, reveal vivid observation, warm sympathy, and a passionate longing for justice, brotherhood, and peace.*

To WRITE a religious poem, one that is truly religious in its effect, it is necessary to have some experience of the presence of God. It is not possible to sit down and write such a poem because it would be a pleasant thing to do, or because Blank Religious Publication needs to schedule a Christmas poem in July. This does not mean that the religious poet is a greater saint than any other Christian, but only that, for temperamental reasons, poetry happens to be the particular form his devotion takes.

It might be argued that the practice of the presence of God gives a better background for the writing of poetry than the study of poetic forms. But of course the two are complementary rather than mutually exclusive. Certainly the forms without the Presence will result only in didacticism, and at best in an idea presented prosaically in poetic meter without the transfiguring image, which is usually a mark of the Presence.

Take this matter of the image: whether simile or metaphor. There is a poetry of sound and a poetry of sight. The perfect poem combines both, when both are subsumed by the idea.

In the poetry of sound, emotional effects can be produced by various and varying rhythms, as well as by the subtle arrangement of vowels and consonants. (It is as important to order the internal sounds of the line as the rhyme at the end.) But the poetry of sound is hard to translate, since no language can be completely reproduced in another tongue. And even in its original language much of the power of the poem is lost on an audience which lacks a sensitive ear. Every line of a poem should be heard mentally, when not read aloud, and should be written to sound well to the inner consciousness. Take, for example, the line: "The upturned cups of the topmost trees. . . ."

A word may be in order about the Gertrude Stein school of thought. It is not possible to use poetic sounds as musical symbols, pure and simple, for it is not possible to divorce word sounds from their content, or from their overtones of sense or (as in the case of Gertrude Stein) of nonsense. Poetry is always more than sound because it involves ideational content. It may at times lack the emotional content of music, but it cannot dispense with intellection. Sound and sense form the warp and woof of poetry, at least of the poetry of sound.

The poetry of sight is much more fluid, relying less on the mechanics of language and being therefore more easily translated. For its proper effect the image must be seen mentally, not just accepted intellectually.

Simile and metaphor are not merely things seen; they are things seen in context, things seen in certain relationships, strange and original relationships. It is this bringing together of disparate thoughts, objects, or images and the finding of the relationship between them, or the finding of the missing link that joins them—it is here that the intuition and sensitivity of the poet come into play. Herein lies one distinction between poetry and prose.

The symbol is not a substitute for reality, but a device for presenting reality that could in no other way be assimilated in its fullness by the limited mind of man. The symbol is the best way of saying the unsayable. The power of the symbol is the power of suggestion. An assertion states, but does not suggest. An assertion is trapped by a fact. A suggestion is open-ended and points toward the infinite.

The practice of religious poetry may throw light upon the truths of theology. I cannot help but believe that the poet is better equipped to grasp some of the most fundamental truths about the nature of God and his revelation than is the man who is unable to think symbolically. Were the great creeds and doctrines of the church formulated in a day when symbolic thinking was more readily indulged in than it is now? And how can we measure the flattening and cheapening of language that has resulted from modern advertising? Take one word as an example, the word "mystery." What does it mean to a twentieth-century Western man to speak of a twenty-five-cent "mystery" that you buy at the corner drugstore in contrast to what the word "mystery" meant to the apostle Paul?

It is a great mistake to contrast poetry with truth. The saying, "there is more truth than poetry" in a certain statement, shows that we do not take poetry very seriously. But perhaps poetry is the very avenue that can lead us to a revitalized apprehension of religious truth.

A mind that cannot think symbolically bogs down in literalism, so that an image of destruction, say the fire that consumes the city refuse (the Gehenna of Jerusalem) or the grass cast into the oven (which today is and tomorrow is not), becomes the sulphur and brimstone which consume human flesh in a literal hell. Forgotten is the underlying truth, which was to have been conveyed poetically: namely, that a dead and useless spirit will be cut down like an unprofitable tree. "Why cumbereth it the ground?"

One of the greatest poets of the image was Jesus Christ. Whether his poetry of sight was also poetry of sound we shall never know, for his original linguistic expression is lost to us. Certain it is that whatever else he was (and he was much else and much more), he was also a great poet. Nor is this surprising. One would expect the Word of God to express himself in immortal poetry rather than in the turgid prose of after-dinner speeches or the *Congressional Record*.

It is an interesting and perhaps unanswerable question to ask how much the viability of Jesus' words is due to their content and how much to their form. When scholars, wishing to detract from the originality of his message, show how the Golden Rule, for instance, has been expounded in many different Scriptures, they only confirm the vitality of his presentation. Why should *his* particular words survive? There are, of course, other reasons besides the aptness of his language, reasons which have to do with the life he lived and with who he is. But all this raises another interesting question. Is form really separable from content? Or is form in itself an aspect of revelation?

It has been said that art grows not out of forms, but out of the unformed; that it is not culture which produces art, but vital experience. Vital art requires life experience. Certainly a poem should be written from the inside out. The content should determine the form. Or perhaps it is more accurate to say that form and content should be mutually determined. Even more accurately, one might say that form and content should both be determined by the revelation they seek to express.

For myself (I can speak only for myself here), I find that some kind of emotional upheaval is usually necessary for the writing of a poem. Love, sorrow, anger, joy, despair. Lines leap to my mind, but only out of a matrix of feeling, past or present, active or quiescent. I seldom seek after a poem, for the simple reason that I never find one by the hunting method. The writing of religious poetry is not particularly difficult: it is either easy or impossible. Most of the time, the latter! In no form of writing can the author take less pride in his own personal achievement. In writing, as in living, he is "saved by grace."

If poetry is a kind of revelation, it is obvious that the first move must be made by God. Perhaps the hardest discipline is that of waiting in patience for the angel to trouble the waters. All one can do is to lie beside the pool, watch and wait, and perhaps pray, and jump in when the water is stirred. But one must be ready to jump in at the proper moment! Nothing is more trying than the feeling of poetic emptiness, when one must go on living only in faith that a renewed sense of God's presence will bring back the power of poetic expression —a power as completely lost between poems as though it had never existed.

Indeed we are at every moment dependent upon God for life, and for the inspiration which is more than life, or perhaps a higher form of life—a mode of being which is as close to eternal life as anything one can find in this dark world.

Before Pentecost

Waiting for the wind.
Waiting for the breath.
Floating between life and death.
Walking as dream men,
Not knowing the what or the when,
Not knowing the ultimate where.
Waiting for the air.
Wandering through street after street
In a thunder heat,
In a thunder gloom,
Where the hot stones
Of buildings
Rise like uncovered bones
In a street like a tomb.
Day and night, day and night
Knock like a drum,
Like a muted, meaningless drum,
Like a heart that cries:
"When will the Spirit come?"
Clutching at a word,
A promise, a breath stirred.
Waiting for the air.
Continuing steadfast in prayer. . . .

OPPORTUNITIES FOR CHURCH PUBLICITY

Thomas W. Moore

Mr. Thomas W. Moore speaks out of a wide, firsthand acquaintance with all phases of publicity and public relations. At the time of making this address, he was Director of the Community Affairs Department of Forest Lawn Memorial-Park, Los Angeles. He now is the western representative of the Columbia Broadcasting System.

CHURCH LEADERSHIP, when it does not develop a strong and effective public relations program, is pursuing a shortsighted policy. Churches need to use the professional techniques; and, above all else, they need professional publicity budgets. Many denominations with a lavish missionary budget are miserly in their publicity expenditures. They forget that publicity is missionary work. They ignore the fact that through the newspaper, magazine, radio, and television, the church can reach that twentieth-century phenomenon, the American pagan, who can be won to Christian faith only through a growing awareness of that faith's relevance to life and immortality.

It is an axiom that to get publicity you must approach the problem from the side of the editor. If the press is to be lured into helping the spread of Christianity, the church will have to do more than send in sermon announcements or letters complaining about the treatment or lack of treatment of Christian subjects.

In order to rectify this situation, which I am convinced is the basis of the lack of publicity, let us examine first the publicity for American Christianity in general, as distinguished from that for a local church. For many years, American churches of all denominations did absolutely nothing that measured up to the press standards for front-page news stories. Perhaps the churches were not idle; but from the middle of the nineteenth century, when the church inspired the abolition movement in this country, until almost the beginning of World War II, there was little top copy that came across the desk of the newspaper editor. Perhaps it was because the churches were more concerned with theology than with the outreach of Christianity to the unchurched community.

It is most heartening that there is today a resurrection, as it were, of the social application of the gospel; and with this resurrection has come a belated interest in religious news on the part of the major editors of America. The church people of America have begun to re-examine spiritual values. They have moved from analysis to resolution, and from resolution to action.

The churches have begun to speak out. Those of you who can influence the policies, resolutions, and actions of your parent groups should do all you can to bring about a positive stand on all issues affecting the social, political, and economic lives of Americans. Do not become discouraged when you feel that you do not get adequate coverage of such statements of policy. It is a slow educational process that should be part of a planned campaign to bring to the consciousness of editors the importance of Christian views. It will come with time. It has already begun.

For years *The Saturday Evening Post* shied away from anything with a religious character. Now, spurred on by the practical success of *Life* in the field of religious stories, its editors are searching for top religious articles. *Reader's Digest, Coronet, Time, Ladies' Home Journal, Collier's, Woman's Home Companion*—name them all—no longer throw up their hands on religious subjects. Your Christian articles will get a perusal; and if the stuff is there, they will be printed.

When we pass from publicity on the national level to publicity on the local level, we come to the most frustrating and perplexing part of the over-all problem. The relation of church news to small congregations has been impressed indelibly on the mind of the editor. This, too, is changing, but it is a slow process and can be expedited only by an approach to the problem which recognizes the years of conditioning in the wrong direction. Here also our axiom of approaching publicity from the side of the editor comes into play. The local pastor and his publicity chairman need to stop thinking of the newspaper publicizing the local activities of the church. They need to start thinking of the press as a means of bringing to the unchurched, in our chaotic age, the importance of Christian faith.

The media for such publicity are magazines, radio networks, electrical transcriptions, television networks, motion-picture film for television, the major wire services, and the national newspaper syndicates. Let us discuss them one at a time.

Some of the major magazines of this country which in recent years have become receptive to religious articles and stories have already been mentioned. If you wish to "make" one of these major magazines, study its contents carefully. An analysis of *Life,* for instance, will reveal that this publishing organization is interested in church architecture, church art, history of religion, church pageantry, evangelism, and text articles on religious theology. All except the last must be photographic.

There is no set pattern for such articles, but you are wasting your time unless you slant your material for a particular magazine. *Reader's Digest,* I believe, would be receptive to an article under its feature "The Most Unforgettable Character I've Met." If I were the publicist for the American Baptist Assembly, for instance, I would search for the story of a particularly colorful Baptist minister who was in some way connected with it.

Of all the media for national publicity, none is more open than the national networks. They are constantly in need of electrical transcriptions, live television, and motion-picture film for television. Here you have an entirely different problem from that of a magazine. You probably are aware of the fact that the Federal Communications Commission grants licenses to stations with the stipulation that they use a certain percentage of their air-time for public service programming. Religious programs are counted a public service. Here is a mandatory acceptance, and you are restrained only by the measure of your creative ability in competition with others in this field.

Of the opportunities offered by the air waves, perhaps the most overlooked is the electrical transcription. If you have anything to do with the publicity of your next conference, first attempt to get a major network to carry one of the principal addresses. Study the address in advance, and suggest to the speaker ways in which he can make his address one of national interest. The network may be more receptive than you think. The advent of the tape recorder has removed one of the obstacles to network broadcasting in that a program can be recorded without the expense connected with a live program. The recording can be played at a later time, at the convenience of the network.

If you fail at the network level, do not be discouraged. Make an electrical transcription of the address or a fifteen-minute condensation of it; mimeograph this address, and send a letter to the stations you are interested in reaching, enclosing a copy of the script with opening and closing announcements. Address your letter to the public service manager of those stations. Tell him that you are sending him a copy of an address; give him a "who's who" of the speaker; and tell him that you will make an electrical transcription of it available to him at no cost. You probably will be amazed at the response.

Incidentally, there is no better way to break into the radio and television field than by developing, planning, and writing a religious show for television or radio, and presenting it to public service managers of stations with the idea that they carry it sustaining. They will co-operate to the extent of bearing the cost of such programs, if the programs are well prepared and have audience appeal. In this connection, in designing any religious program, keep your sermons down to meditations of not more than two to five minutes. Radio stations and networks often have chased listeners away with weighty sermons; consequently the station managers are allergic to them.

In the field of national newspaper syndicates and wire services, we likewise find a growing awareness of the importance of religion. Wire services, ten years ago, would not cover a religious activity if it was anything short of sensational. The social consciousness of the churches, however, has forced them in recent years to carry more religious news. It is exceptionally difficult to "plant" a story and have it carried on the wire services.

The best approach here is to send them detailed memoranda of the religious activity and invite their coverage. An old trick in this line, and one that despite its age never seems to fail, is to address your communication to all the wire services at the same time. By this I mean, address your note somewhat as follows: "Memorandum to Associated Press, United Press, and International News Service." If your note gives promise of any real news, each will cover your event; if for no other reason than that otherwise the competition will get something that they should have. When the reporter covers the event, the chances are that he will do the job of finding what is most newsworthy. Since time and money has been devoted to the cause, the chances are good that it will hit the teletypes.

In the field of syndication, there can be no substitute for studying the individual features. There is one feature, called "Historic Churches of America," which has a very wide distribution. If you have a historic church, you have an excellent chance of "making" this feature. By studying each feature and by knowing what the editor is looking for, you should be able to adjust your sights to hit the bull's-eye.

Moving now to publicity at the local level, your only change in techniques will apply to your local newspaper. Do not pull out entirely from the routine sermon announcements and advertisements, if that is the policy of your local newspaper. Stay there, if for no other reasons than the competition; but set your mind to creative thinking in terms of what the editor seeks for his readers.

Since an institution is the reflection of a single individual, start, in your thinking, with the head of your church, the pastor. Editors always are more interested in people than in things. If your minister is not inherently able to say and do those things which are newsworthy, the chances are that he can become newsworthy after a brief conversation with you prior to any public utterance or event. Make him the official spokesman for your church, and your church will become known.

In the field of local radio, the same rules apply as for national radio. The field is wide open. You need not be relegated to a time spot of 6:30 on Sunday morning or 11:15 on a weekday night. The local stations have more time available than do the networks; and they have a hard time putting out over the air waves something listenable for thousands of hours a year. They will be responsive in direct proportion to your ingenuity.

Television film offers perhaps the greatest opportunity today for publicity. Station managers can show material on a 16 mm. film. If you are going to burn the mortgage on your church, rent, borrow, or buy a 16 mm. camera and expose 100 feet of film showing the minister lighting a match and the flames that ensue. Send it to the stations and forget it—it is on the air. This can be done economically—you can find ways to cut corners. And do not overlook in radio or television the possibility of religious spot announcements relative to church activities. If cleverly written and cleverly transcribed, they will get air-time.

The fact remains that there is greater opportunity today for Christian publicity, for Protestant publicity, than has ever existed before. The opportunity is there; we should make the most of it. The only way you can fail, in view of the opportunity, is to fail in ingenuity. If all of us as church people can work together with editors and station managers, we shall succeed. We shall then be doing, I believe, what Christ bade us do; namely, preaching the gospel to every living creature.

USE THE PUBLIC PRESS

Paul C. Carter

Dr. Paul C. Carter, by reason of his professional experience, is well qualified to discuss all matters relating to publicity for religious causes. He was for several years a pastor (West Hollywood Baptist Church, Hollywood, Calif.); then, for a longer period, the Executive Secretary for the Allied Temperance Forces, Inc., with headquarters in Rochester, N. Y. He now is the Director of Publicity for the Board of Education and Publication of the American Baptist Convention.

When we set out to use the press, we do well to ask ourselves two questions: (1) To whom are we telling our story? (2) What do we want to accomplish? We are apt to pay more attention to the second question than to the first. We know that we want more people in church and church school. We want to interest more people of leadership ability. We want to attract more folk of means who will help us pay the bills. We desire also to deepen and extend the spiritual life of the church. These are worthy objectives which we want to accomplish.

Who will be our public as we use the press toward accomplishing these ends? Here is a general list that will cover most church situations: (1) your church leaders and board members, (2) your membership, (3) prospective members, (4) the community, (5) the denomination—city, state, and national.

Having determined our public, we should make a list of usable channels and forms of publicity. Here are the media in general use among pastors who are taking full advantage of publicity opportunities: (1) the Sunday bulletin, (2) the parish newspaper, (3) daily newspapers—general news, the church page, sermon reviews, (4) advertising, (5) direct mail, (6) special booklets, (7) radio and television.

We are now ready to transfer this list of media onto a year-round publicity chart. Note that we use the media as headings for the several columns. Along the lefthand column each line is dated to represent a week. This makes it possible for us to plan and record our publicity week by week, month by month. This chart has its greatest value when we fill it in ahead of time, rather than merely use it to record what we have done. It forces us to plan, and it serves as a constant reminder of what we could and should be doing. The spaces on it will not all be filled. But those blank spaces will call upon us for an accounting.

In addition to the general or continuous publicity program of the church, there come times when the pastor needs to lay out a publicity campaign to promote an important event. Special events make news. Here are seven steps that may be recommended in building a publicity campaign: (1) Plant an introductory story. (2) Issue story on sponsorship and objectives. (3) Run general story with more detail. (4) Present story on the committee and its work. (5) Release story of final details and the program. (6) Arrange for the press to interview the principals before the event for last-minute coverage. (7) Aid and encourage the press in reporting the event. If your advance campaign has been effective, the press will be eager to run a full report on it.

As a method of planning and keeping track of a special publicity campaign, we recommend what we call a ninety-day calendar. It usually takes from sixty to ninety days to get ready for a major event, provided we make the most of its promotional possibilities.

The success of a publicity campaign is conditioned to a certain extent by the worth-whileness of the event. You must have an article worth selling. But our trouble usually is not with the quality of the product we are offering, but with the ineffective and unimaginative way it is offered. What we need is consecrated showmanship.

L

Our successful use of the press will depend somewhat upon our understanding of news-writing techniques. News writing requires procedures and a style quite different from essay, sermon, or magazine writing. The news story must have a head. If you suggest your own headline, you aid the editor by indicating to him at a glance what you think is the most important thing in the story. Often enough he will not use your headline. The first paragraph of your news story is known as the "lead." You will doubtless recall the well known formula for the lead paragraph which states that it should cover the answers to those interrogatives: who, what, why, how, when, where. We do not usually answer all six of these questions in any one news story, but they do serve as monitors which prompt us to incorporate the most essential facts early in the story.

Unlike the essay, the news story does not build toward a climax. Rather it starts off by imparting to the reader the most striking facts. The obvious reason for this is that the newspaper editor knows from experience that most of his readers are browsers who rarely get beyond the first paragraph. The lead paragraph, therefore, presents the most significant set of facts that will be found in the story. What comes after that will simply fill in the details.

The body of the news story is composed of those paragraphs necessary to supply the detail that grows logically out of the lead paragraph. Those paragraphs serve to satisfy the curiosity that has been whetted by the facts or issues presented in the lead. A news story should be written in such fashion that if, for lack of space, the editor finds it necessary to shorten it, the concluding paragraph can be sacrificed without serious loss. Ideally, we try to write our stories so that they can stand on their own, regardless of where they may be cut.

As for the styling of the news story, it has been our experience that in addition to following the rules of simple and direct English, it is highly profitable to study the style book used by newspaper reporters and editors. Usually when you ask your local newspaper editor for a style book he is happy to oblige you, for he is complimented by the fact that you are interested in making your news writing conform to the style he is following in his paper.

Style books vary in form. Some of them are issued as simple mimeographed instructions to reporters; others are printed as booklets, particularly those used by chain newspapers. My procedure has been to acquire a style book from each community in which I have served, for newspapers vary in different parts of the country. What is recognized as good style in Los Angeles may be unacceptable in Kansas City or New York. It is also helpful to keep a carbon of one's story as submitted, so as to compare it with the way it appears in the paper. In doing this, it is best to make the comparison over a period of time in order to make sure that the changes which appear represent consistent and established policy in dealing with copy.

Adhere to the policy of turning in news stories in typewritten form, double spaced, and with broad margins left and right. All names incorporated in stories should be complete with initials and first names where possible, and accurately and completely identified. Usually names enhance the value of news stories.

It is often to advantage to accompany news stories with good photographs. These should be action photos or portrait prints of good quality. Glossy prints, 8 x 10 inches, are preferred.

Your parish newspaper will be read. Indeed, it will become very popular if it is kept to the newspaper style of reporting the facts. This will not be true if you load the paper with propaganda and sermonets. If you must editorialize, follow the news writer's style of presenting it in interview form. *Green Laker* is an illustration of news style applied to a publication that might easily become a direct propaganda sheet. Notice the use of news type, action photos, cut lines, and headlines, all of which conform to newspaper style.

The news approach will get the best response all along the line —in the public press, in the parish press, and in the denominational press. This is not to imply that there is no place for essay writing. However, the best use of the public press, parish newspaper, and the news sections of the denominational press requires the discipline of adhering to news style. The experienced news writer finds that he can say about everything that is worth while without resorting to didactics or direct propaganda.

Keep a scrapbook. Like the schedule, it helps you keep track of the amount of publicity you are getting. It gives you a basis for comparing the copy you turn in and the way it comes out in print. This can be your best critic and teacher. It provides a valuable record. You will find that old scrapbooks often yield historical and resource information which cannot be gleaned from any other sources.

Use the public press. Like the nostalgic church bell of the frontier community, the press can call your people to worship and to services of Christ on the modern frontier where "new occasions teach new duties."

WRITING TO METHOD AND MEASURE

GLENN McRAE

━━━━━━━━━━━━━━━━━━━━━━━━━━━━━━━━━━━━━

Dr. Glenn McRae is Editor-in-Chief of Church School Publications, The Christian Board of Publication, Disciples of Christ. He has had an active interest in the Christian Writers and Editors' Conference from almost its beginning. He has written much church school literature, has personally edited a great deal more, and for many years now has carried the administrative responsibility for the entire church school publications output of his Board. Among the courses which he has written are Makers of a Nation *and* A Man Who Wrote Scripture.

━━━━━━━━━━━━━━━━━━━━━━━━━━━━━━━━━━━━━

ASK AN EDITOR of church school publications, "What is your Number 1 need?" and he is likely to answer, "Writers who can write to a teaching situation." Short stories—armloads of them—come every week to the editor's desk. Poetry? It fairly rains from heaven. Editorials, feature articles, informational items, and puzzles fill a sizable basket each week. Yet all these manuscripts, good, bad, and indifferent, do not help the editor to meet his Number 1 need.

What is meant by "Writing to Method and Measure"? It is writing to a teaching situation. The materials we are talking about are lesson, topic, or program materials for groups of various ages; in other words, materials for groups that meet for purposes of learning. Such material is written with a teaching-learning process in mind. It should help those who use it to bring about a creative experience in teaching-learning.

The reason this need is so hard to satisfy is because of the difficulty of the task. Much is required of the writer of this kind of material. He must know the field of the teaching unit; that is, biblical, personal problems, social problems, church history, or missions. He must understand the age group for which he writes. He must be able to imagine a teaching-learning situation and write so as to further the teaching-learning process. In addition he must be able to write. That is to say, he must be able to put on paper whatever he wishes to express, and to do this with reasonable exactness, grammatical propriety, and some measure of inspirational quality.

What editor, in spite of his directions to the writer to the contrary, has not received lesson topic material that was merely a series of essays? No vital use can be made of such material. It may be read and commented upon by the teacher or leader, or it may be used as the basis of a lecture. Such material limits the user as to the methods he may try with his group. The editor desires material that will help teacher, counselor, or leader to carry on a vital learning process.

Since most of such material is written on assignment, the editor gives the writer essential information as to the kind of group, such as church school class or Sunday evening fellowship, for which the unit is to be prepared. The writer learns the sex, age, and background of the students, and the ability of the teacher or leader who will probably use the material when written. The editor provides an outline of the proposed course of study, series of topics, or unit of work. The outline indicates the field, objectives, content, and other essentials. Then the writer goes to work.

First, let the writer put a copy of the objectives of the course or unit before him. He should never file it or lose it. The objectives are his guiding star. Without them he will lose his course. Then the writer makes whatever study of the field of the unit is necessary. As he does this, he tentatively blocks out the sessions according to the number specified. *Each session must be planned so as to help achieve the objectives of the unit.*

Next, the materials for the sessions are written. Here is where the writer must visualize the teaching-learning process. He sees a group of a certain age (children, young people, or adults) in a certain situation (Sunday morning class or Sunday evening discussion group). Here are the objectives of the unit and of that session. Then he visualizes "things to be done" to achieve those objectives, and he writes whatever is needed to help the leader and the group achieve the outcomes that are desired.

The following outline will show the writer's task:

Unit: "The Hebrew Prophets"
For senior high pupils
Objectives of the unit

1. . . . . . .
2. . . . . . .
3. . . . . . .

Session 1.

1. Objectives
    a. . . . . . .
    b. . . . . . .
    c. . . . . . .

2. Teaching steps
    a. First step
    b. Intermediate step
    c. Intermediate step
    d. Final step

Session 2.

Etc.

The writer must visualize the activities of the group as it takes the necessary steps or does the necessary things to accomplish the objectives. The work of the writer is to make the objectives clear and to provide materials that will help to carry on a vital teaching-learning process. For each teaching session, the writer should include the following:

1. A statement of the objectives, expressed in terms of achievements in the lives of the members of the group. These are knowledge, insights, attitudes, habits, and activities. The student's material should be written so as to lead the student to accept the objectives. If students and teacher or the group leader work toward the same objectives, more will be accomplished than if the teacher has one set of objectives and the students another.

2. A variety of material—perhaps in several literary forms—suggesting the steps to be taken to achieve the objectives.

First step. This one is important. It must awaken interest and give the session a good start. None of "Now, children, what is our lesson about today?" There are many ways to start a session so as to arouse interest. The teacher or leader may tell a story, ask a question, recall a relevant incident or recent happening, give a self-rating test, or do any one of a dozen other things. Whatever is done should rub the sleep out of the eyes of the students and bring them to the edge of their chairs. This first step is as important as the lead paragraph in a news story or the opening of a work of fiction.

Next step. These are more "things to be done" to achieve the objectives of the session. Each step should bring the group nearer the desired outcome.

Final step. This should be climactic, round out the session, and give a sense of unity. The teacher or leader in most cases may have to devise this final step in the light of what has taken place during the session. Even so, the writer should frequently provide materials that will help him to take this final step.

The preparation of this kind of material involves the hardest and most exacting kind of writing. The demands upon the writer are many. He must know the group for which he is writing, the situation in which his material will be used, the field about which he writes, and the teaching-learning procedures that should be used. Of course he needs skill in writing. Above all, he is not writing essays on a series of topics. He is providing materials for a dynamic, creative teaching-learning process. His rewards are the rewards of all writers whose written words kindle the light of truth, fashion ideals, create noble purposes, stifle prejudices, blot out sin, set men to serve their fellows, and point to the pathway that leads to God.

TABOOS FOR RELIGIOUS WRITERS

Miles W. Smith

Dr. Miles W. Smith, in his long association with the American Baptist Publication Society, has had rich and varied editorial experience in a number of highly responsible posts. He has served as editor of junior high publications, as editor of adult publications, as Editor-in-Chief of the Department of Sunday School Publications, and, since 1949, as Book Editor and Director of the Book Publishing Department of The Judson Press. He has written many quarters' expositions of the Uniform Lessons and four Judson Graded Courses: The Homeland of the Master, The Light of the Nations, The Way of Wisdom, and Workers with God. *He is also the author of* On Whom the Spirit Came, *a scholarly and inspiring study of the Book of Acts.*

THE DICTIONARY defines a taboo as a sacred interdiction laid upon the use of certain things or words or the performance of certain actions. I shall not use the term in that sense. There is nothing pontifical in what I shall say, no assumption whatever of doctrinal infallibility. The right to worship according to the dictates of one's conscience is one of our four basic freedoms. It follows, therefore, that you can hold any view and write anything you wish—anything at all, so long as it is not plagiarized, is not indecent, and does not constitute grounds for libel. No problem arises so long as you do not undertake to get what you have written published.

That is to say, the restrictions, such as they are, rest not so much upon the writers as upon the editors. As matters stand in publishing houses, the editors are held strictly accountable for whatever has appeared in print. The writer oftentimes never learns how much of a furor his slip of the pen occasioned. The letters of complaint always are addressed to the editor and the publisher, and the publisher holds the editor responsible. The editor should not have permitted the mistake to appear in print. Taboos, therefore, are not arbitrary. They are the outgrowth of editorial experience. The editor has found, perhaps through bitter experience, that every disregard of one of these taboos is an invitation to trouble. Editors, accordingly, tend to become cautious.

What may be printed or may not be printed—if the editor wants to hold his job, and most of them do—is determined by the canons of decency, good taste, and appropriateness to the purpose of the periodical in which the writing would appear. The editor has no desire to stifle originality; on the contrary, he will welcome every creative, constructive approach to a subject that a writer can offer. But the editor's never-ceasing job is to find those dependable, methodical writers who can produce, or who are willing to learn how to produce, those articles and materials which his periodical must have if it is to continue publication. The editor will keep in mind that the final judge of the product is the consumer; that is to say, the reader. If the reader repeatedly turns thumbs down, the publishing house before long will be forced out of business.

I think you will see all this in truer perspective if I remind you that taboos (if we must use that term) are not limited to religious publications; they are equally numerous and equally demanding in the case of secular publications. I do not mean that the taboos will be the same. They vary always with the publication, its character, and its purpose. But there will be taboos, and you will encounter them whenever you undertake to sell to an editor an article which wanders very far from the beaten track.

Certain articles which would be acceptable in a magazine read largely by men would be rejected at once by the editor of a magazine intended for women readers; articles which would be welcomed by a magazine of left-wing political persuasion would be rejected at once by a magazine of conservative leanings. There is nothing to be gained by inveighing against these conditions. There are a few journals which encourage free, even unrestrained, expression of opinion. If you have written that kind of article, send it to that kind of magazine; otherwise resign yourself to not seeing it in print.

I may mention here that writing for periodicals—news, informational and inspirational articles, lesson treatments, and topic developments—is something quite different from writing a book. In a book a man can be more himself, he can write what he pleases and in the way he pleases, he can make his manuscript as long or as short as he desires—and that is good fun. It is not hard to write a book. All one needs to do is to sit at the typewriter long enough.

Even so, trouble may arise when the man who has written the book undertakes to get his manuscript printed. On consulting a publisher, he may discover that the book which he has written, and in which he has taken so much delight, is not at all the kind of book in which the publisher is interested. If you have publication in mind, it is wise to find out what the market is before you proceed. It may save you hours of wasted effort.

However it may be with respect to books, when writing for a periodical one must have regard for that periodical's specifications. If the editor says to make the article 2,000 words in length, he means 2,000; not 1,500 and not 2,500. If the article is too short, the editor will have to pad it; if too long, he will have to condense it. There is always the possibility that the editor that day may be rushed for time or be in an unappreciative mood. You should not be too severe in your criticism of him if he returns your manuscript and buys instead a manuscript which, whatever else it may lack, is of the length he needs.

The importance of observing specifications closely—an importance which should be obvious—will serve to make clearer the situation with respect to taboos. Let us suppose that the writer of a submitted article has included in it, wittingly or unwittingly, statements which the editor feels he cannot safely allow to appear in print. Perhaps he feels that they *might* pass muster, but he does not wish to run the risk of provoking controversy. What shall the editor do?

If the objectionable statements are brief, he may simply cross them out and publish the rest of the article as it stands. An inexperienced writer sometimes will take great offense at such a deletion. He may write that no changes are to be made in future articles without his express permission. He wants to be able to say whatever he wants to say, regardless of what effect his statements may have upon the circulation of the periodical. That attitude usually means that he will not sell that editor many more manuscripts. Professional writers, as a rule, welcome all the editorial attention which the editor is willing to give to their manuscripts. They take the attitude that the editor is a friendly collaborator who, with special knowledge of periodical needs, is assisting them to make their manuscripts marketable.

But what if the questioned statements are of considerable length? What shall the editor do then? If he leaves them out, the article will be too short. Shall he write something of his own devising to take the place of the omitted paragraphs? Or shall he return the article to the writer as unacceptable? Usually there is not time to write the author requesting that he submit new copy to take the place of that which must be omitted. The editor, under these circumstances, has a difficult decision to make.

The writer, naturally, will wish to know what topics or forms of expression the editor finds objectionable. What, then, are the taboos? This question already has had a partial answer. That answer had to be given in generalities. Any statement which is more specific will need to be in terms of a particular publication. (1) For whom is the periodical intended? Obviously, some things may be said in a periodical for adults which would be unwise in a periodical for children. (2) By whom is that periodical published? If by a denominational publishing house, the writer must guard against making any statements which contradict the basic doctrines, polity, and program of that denomination. If by a nondenominational firm, that firm in all probability has a publishing policy which gives rise to its own list of taboos. (3) What is the purpose of the periodical? Perhaps the periodical is being published to improve the teaching procedures in the church. It will be futile to send to that periodical an article recommending a teaching procedure which once was acceptable, but which present-day educational authorities have discarded as not being the best. Consequently, the counsel to know your field and to know the periodical at which you are aiming is of first importance. Except by personal correspondence with the editor, there is no other way of determining what that periodical will print and what it will not print.

It may be well to state here that *how* one says what one has to say is frequently as important as *what* one says. For example, many religious articles turn upon the interpretation of one or more Bible verses. These interpretations may be highly controversial. If an editor permits such a statement as, "All scholars are agreed that . . . ," it is quite likely that some reader will take him to task on the score that there is somewhere a scholar who does not agree. If he is so foolish as to allow an author to say: "This is the correct view, and to hold any other view is a mark of stupidity," let him watch out for an explosion!

There are some things which may be safely said, so long as you smile when saying them. Bear in mind that that smile, that little sign of tolerance and human kindness, cannot be reproduced upon the printed page. You cannot interpret your printed words with a chuckle, a shrug of the shoulders, or a wave of the hand—as you do when making an address or preaching a sermon. Current speech is heard, forgiven, and forgotten; the printed word is hard, it endures, it possesses finality. Rightly or wrongly, what is printed is assumed to be your reasoned opinion, not subject to change; and you will be judged by it.

There are taboos, then, and some of them are religious. But they are guiding principles, rather than *ex cathedra* prohibitions. In some cases, each taboo is nothing more than a convenient rule of thumb for determining what is wise procedure. So far as the publishing house I am connected with is concerned, I do not know of any subject connected with the Christian religion which may not be discussed so long as the purpose of the writer is not anti-Christian and so long as the spirit of his discussion is friendly and constructive. As a rule, we get into difficulty only when we permit statements which are dogmatic, dictatorial, and uncharitable.

THE TASK OF THE CURRICULUM WRITER

Paul M. Lederach

Bishop Paul M. Lederach is the Executive Editor of the Mennonite Publishing House. In addition to having responsibility for a group of churches, he either edits or supervises the editing of the numerous publications issued for the churches of his denomination. By his presence and by his addresses, he has made a significant contribution to the success of the Christian Writers and Editors' Conference.

CURRICULUM WRITING requires a rare combination of attitudes, abilities, skills, and interests. To begin with, the curriculum writer must be a *writer,* one who can write not only clearly and interestingly, but also intelligently and with spiritual discernment.

At the same time, the curriculum writer must be a teacher, acquainted with the best in teaching methods and techniques. He must be a theologian and Bible student, for he must make God's will and way relevant to life and experience. He must know people, particularly the needs and experience development of those for whom he writes, whether they be children, young people, or adults. He must be a churchman, acquainted with the needs and program of the church for which he writes, so that he can inspire loyalty and commitment to the life and work of that church. He must be an individual with a well-rounded personality, with wide interests, with a character that is above reproach, and with the ability to co-operate with his directors and associates. He must be a transformed Christian, with a thoroughly Christian philosophy of life, and with a deep-seated commitment to Christian service and discipleship.

When this kind of individual is found, and is challenged by the possibilities of curriculum writing, and responds to the call of the church, what is his task?

Basically, the task of the curriculum writer is to be an interpreter. He must interpret the fundamental message of the Bible to individuals in the light of their needs and development. He also must interpret the elements of Christian experience and Christian living to individuals in the light of their needs and development. Finally, he must make his interpretation of the message and experience both practical and meaningful to individuals caught in the tensions and frustrations of twentieth-century living and growth. This is no small undertaking.

As an interpreter of the Bible and its message, the curriculum writer himself must have a comprehensive grasp of the Bible and its purpose. He dare not approach the Bible as though it were merely a body of interesting information. Nor dare he approach it as a group of dusty historical records out of the dim, dark past. Nor dare he approach it as a system of doctrines to which everyone must adhere. Nor dare he ever approach the Bible as a group of authoritative documents to prove or promote his own pet ideas or emphases.

The curriculum writer must approach the Bible as the inspired record of God's will and God's way for men. He must see that its message is the very word of God to lost, sinful men. He must see that this message is aimed at men in their deep need. He must recognize that it is the message of the Bible that brings men to God. It is the "good news" that reconciliation between God and man is possible through Jesus Christ. He must recognize that the message of the Bible deals with transformed lives and holy living.

In the light of this message, therefore, the curriculum writer does not spend his time writing scholarly dissertations on the shades of meaning of Hebrew and Greek words or upon the discoveries of scholarly critics, although he himself should be versed in these matters. Nor does he spend his time as the Pharisees of old, who examined the Scriptures as a rulebook for laws and regulations which, if kept, would make one right with God. Instead, the curriculum writer who properly understands the message and attempts to fulfill his task as interpreter, writes so that his audience may see and hear God the Father speaking to every need and area of life.

Important as it is to know the message of the Bible, and important as it is to hear God speak, these are not enough. Jesus was never satisfied when men merely had correct ideas about God. His aim was always to bring men into fellowship with God.

This leads to the second phase of the curriculum writer's task, that of interpreting the elements of Christian experience and Christian living so that men may have fellowship with God in the truest and highest sense.

In this area the writer's task is large. First, he must provide those materials which will aid individuals to experience the Father-child relationship. That is, he must bring persons to experience the reality of *"Our* Father which art in heaven. . . ." He can do this, however, only as he points them to the atoning work of Jesus Christ and its acceptance by faith.

Second, he must provide those materials which will aid individuals to experience the forgiveness of sin. At times he will have to label sin as sin, so that some will sense their need for forgiveness. Others carry in their hearts feelings of guilt, feelings of having sinned beyond God's love or help, feelings of remorse. These feelings are destructive. They may cause character disintegration and emotional upsets. The curriculum writer must help these individuals understand that God is love; that God does not despise the truly repentant soul; and that "if we confess our sins, he [God] is faithful and just to forgive us our sins, and to cleanse us from all unrighteousness."

Third, he must provide those materials which will aid individuals to experience victorious Christian living. The curriculum writer must clarify the provisions which God has made for building strong Christian character and for gaining victory over sinful behavior. He must help individuals say with Paul, "I can do all things through Christ which strengtheneth me."

Fourth, he must provide those materials which will aid individuals to experience the power of prayer. He must help individuals to grow in their appreciation of the place and power of prayer and in their ability to pray. He must suggest prayer techniques and objects for which individuals should pray.

Fifth, he must provide those materials which will aid individuals to develop strong beliefs and convictions concerning the church, home life, and community living. In this connection the curriculum writer must present Christian ideals. He must elucidate principles of Christian living. He must set forth the scriptural standards for life and conduct. It is particularly important that the curriculum writer be aware of the tension which exists, and must exist, between the standards of the kingdoms of this world and the kingdom of God.

Not only should he be aware of this tension, but also he must dare to proclaim the way of righteousness without regard to the fear or favor of man. For example, he must advocate the way of Christian love in a world of hate and war and bloodshed; he must advocate the highest standards of purity and morality in a society of moral decay.

In short, he must promote the life of simple discipleship to the Lord Jesus Christ, the life of unreserved obedience to him and to the teachings of the New Testament.

The third aspect of the curriculum writer's task is to make his interpretation of the message of the Bible and of the elements of Christian experience practical and meaningful in present-day living.

The ability to do this must be resident in the writer himself. That is to say, the writer himself must be constantly seeking to understand and hear the word of God. He must receive the word of God in his own experience. For he too is living in the world. He too is rubbing elbows with society as it is. As a curriculum writer he must be making the gospel practical in his own life and in his relations with others. In this way he himself becomes a witness to the power of the gospel.

The curriculum writer, therefore, must never become an ivory tower fixture nor an armchair philosopher. He must be on the front lines. Thus he will become intensely practical. As a practical man, his writings will be replete with illustrations and "how to" suggestions. In a sense, he will be telling what he has seen God do, what God has done for him, and what God has done for others. He will write to help others come to the richest and fullest type of Christian experience.

As the curriculum writer prepares his materials and makes them as down-to-earth and practical as possible, he must not think of them as ends in themselves, nor as crutches for the spiritually indolent. He must remember that curriculum materials are merely means to an end. Therefore, the curriculum writer is not satisfied till his readers, through the help he has given them, come to the Bible themselves, and there meet God, and there come to grips with the way of Christian living. When this occurs, the curriculum writer has helped to build strong, maturing Christians, who by life and testimony can bring others to Christ.

The curriculum writer has before him one of the most influential tasks in the church. He must nurture children, convict sinners, edify saints, strengthen the church, and extend the borders of the Kingdom.

HOW TO WRITE FOR CHILDREN

MARY ALICE JONES

For a brief biographical note concerning Dr. Mary Alice Jones, turn to her address entitled "Religious Books for Children," beginning on page 67.

WRITING FOR CHILDREN, like writing for anybody else, requires first of all that a person have something to say, and that he be stirred up about it. Here we encounter one of the major problems in the field of religious writing for children. We are definitely limited by the religious publications as to what we can talk about and as to what we can say about the subject chosen. There are numerous taboos, numerous prejudices, which we must observe; and there are also numerous perfectly legitimate limitations placed upon us. Moreover, especially in curriculum writing, we have to write on assigned subjects. This is less true with respect to the story papers. Nevertheless, even those who write for the story papers frequently are asked to prepare material on a definite theme and for a specific purpose. These writers then try to stir up within their souls an enthusiasm for the subject assigned to them, and more often than one would expect, they succeed. It is true, however, that all too often writers are asked to write on a subject for which they have no zest, that they are given a time schedule so short that it becomes difficult for them to secure the necessary data to make their writing accurate.

This is, so far as I can see, a limitation which we shall simply have to accept and with respect to which we shall have to do the best we can. I do not see how, in the field of religious education, an

M

editor can avoid assigning specific subjects at specific times to writers. I do not see how he can wait for a writer's enthusiasm for a particular subject to coincide with the curriculum outline prepared by the curriculum committee of his denomination.

But this does pose a problem for the editor who feels the need in the children's field for material which he would like to think of as great literature as well as lesson material with a purpose. When a writer has to suppress a tremendous urge to put on paper a boiling-within-her story of a "Gingham Dog and Calico Cat" and set herself sternly to work developing a story to illustrate the truth that peaceful negotiation is a better way of settling a dispute than fisticuffs, the chances are that the editor will lose a good fanciful story and get instead a mediocre "teaching" story. But, as I said, I do not see how in the present state of the world we can change this situation. The most the editor can do is to be aware of it and, so far as he can, assign to authors subjects on which he knows they have both information and enthusiasm; and he then should give them as much freedom as is permissible, in developing their material along the line of their own inspiration.

In the field of fiction for our story papers, where we have more freedom, it seems to me that the editors ought to develop some plan for securing contributions from more of our topflight children's writers. This might be done, if they were to get together and offer a good price for the serial rights for first-rate books written out of the author's own enthusiasm and basic interest.

A second essential of good writing for children is that one should know the audience for whom one is writing. During the past fifty years there has been a tremendous increase in studies into the nature and interests of children. Carefully arranged charts have been prepared after thoroughgoing research by such students as Dr. Gesell of Yale, showing what reactions, what vocabulary, and what interests are likely to be in the ascendancy at each age as the child progresses from infancy through early childhood and on to early adolescence. On the basis of the enormous body of data which has been collected and presented, we have today a much clearer idea than we ever had before of what capacities we may expect of children at various ages. At the same time, comprehensive studies have been made of how children learn, what it is that attracts attention, and what it is that makes a lasting impression. We can be reasonably sure, therefore, that certain types of stories will be interesting to a large number of boys and girls of a given age, and that certain subjects will be attractive to them when presented in the form of accurate information. These studies have been of great help to the children's book editors and to all other persons who have been concerned with material for children.

Though it is true that we know more about children's interests, limitations, abilities, and ways of learning than we ever knew before, just at the time when we were thinking that we had a good blueprint of what children of various ages may be expected to know and may be expected to be interested in, we find ourselves plunged into such a tremendous world situation that all our careful charts are thrown out of gear. Boys and girls of today are being forced to learn much more rapidly than ever before. They are having to face up to much more far-reaching problems, to know much more about suffering and destruction and hatred than was the case when our generation was growing up. Consequently, their interests are much broader and more inclusive.

Children are raising basic questions and are needing not the superficial, all-is-well type of answers, but really sound answers to all sorts of questions that probe deeply into the meaning of life. In mission study groups they heard, for example, about the thrilling progress that had been made in Korea toward the development of a flourishing native Christian church. It was pointed out to them that Korea had made more progress than any other nation in Asia, had a far higher percentage of Christians than any other country, had more churches, more kindergartens, and larger attendance at Bible conferences. Then all of a sudden they heard that Korea had become a shambles; its churches had been destroyed, its schools disbanded, its fine Christian leaders executed or taken into exile. Why, they want to know, did such things happen to Korea, when Korea, of all the countries of Asia, had made the greatest and most significant response to the gospel?

The point is that with boys and girls of this generation we need to be extremely careful not to undershoot their store of knowledge and the depth and breadth of their interest; whereas in the last generation, when writers were just becoming conscious of child study, the problem was to avoid overshooting the mark. Some of the writing in our curriculum material and in our story papers for boys and girls seems to me to undershoot the basic interest and the sweep of concern which we find in present-day boys and girls.

Problems of suffering and problems of evil which ten years ago we would have thought should be reserved for adolescents, maybe even late adolescents, now must find a place in the curriculum for juniors. Knowledge of geography which ten years ago we would have felt could not be depended upon until grades six or seven, now can be presupposed for grades four and five. While this is true, we are finding also that the public schools are playing down interest in historical background, and that we are going to be able to depend less and less upon general information on early culture. This means that we shall have to give more attention to Mediterranean civilization, Greek civilization, Egyptian civilization, and Babylonian civilization than we needed to do when we could depend more generally upon a knowledge of historical background gained through public school studies in the intermediate grades. Apparently all this is going to be pushed up to junior high school or even high school. So in this area we shall have less, rather than more, upon which to build.

Let us check for a minute some of the outstanding interests of boys and girls in the field of fiction, judged solely by the types of books which have the largest sales. We find that animal stories rank very high, especially dog and horse stories. The most popular are those in which human beings and animals both have part, and in which each plays his natural role rather than a fanciful role. If animals talk, it is better to have them talk to one another, rather than to human beings. Few books in which animals take the roles of human beings have as high a degree of popularity for children past six or seven as do books which deal more realistically with animals.

Cowboys and Indians continue to be very popular, although some of the children's book editors and librarians report a decreasing interest recently in these subjects. I do not know whether this is just a temporary slump or whether it marks a trend.

Realistic stories of present-day boys and girls engaged in normal, present-day activities seem to be received with a good deal more enthusiasm than stories with historical background. There seems to be a definite resistance to historical stories. However, a really good one does go over. This presents us with a sales problem in writing good fiction with a biblical background.

When the hero is a boy rather than a girl, we have a much larger sales potential. Girls will read about boys, but boys will not read about girls to any considerable extent. When boys and girls both appear as characters in a story, as is frequently the case, it is better to let the boy take the leadership.

Generally speaking, boys and girls do not like subtle books. They like them to be straightforward, with black and white definitely delineated. They like the hero really to be the hero, to behave like a hero, and to come out on top; yet they do not want the hero to be too good. If he is, they get very much annoyed and will have none of him.

Right here we run into a serious problem when we are writing material in the field of world friendship or when we are writing material to "teach a lesson." In our material in the field of world friendship, we wish to play up boys and girls of other races and national origins, so that their good qualities show up. There is danger of overdoing this. Children will not admire these boys and girls if they appear to be nothing more than plaster saints.

It has been difficult to get good books about Negro boys and girls. If we tell good stories in which a Negro boy behaves in a normal fashion, with a normal share of failures and limitations, or possibly with downright orneriness, we are accused of being prejudiced; on the other hand, if we make him a model child at every point, the boys and girls who read about him will not like him and our purpose will be defeated.

The same is true when presenting material about persons from other countries. Some of the books prepared by the Missionary Education Movement have been criticized at this point. Some say that they make the boys and girls of the various nations and the conditions under which they live appear entirely too idealized. It is difficult to get good material of this sort, as every editor knows—material in which the hero stands on his own feet as a person, behaves normally, wins respect because of what he is rather than because the author lays it on with a heavy brush to make him appear better than he actually is.

The third point to remember, in connection with writing for

boys and girls, is concerned with the importance of the writer knowing how to write. Inevitably, some reference to this phase of the subject has been made already. When one has something to say, one writes with zest and enthusiasm. If one knows one's audience, one is likely to sense the points at which writing will interest or fail to interest that audience. And after all, what we mean by knowing how to write is knowing how to interest one's audience.

There are no rules which a person may memorize and follow with the guarantee that the results will be a good book, a good story, a good article, a good piece of lesson material, or a good bit of inspirational writing for a given age group. It just does not work that way. A person has to be enthusiastic about a subject and eager to share that subject with a particular age group before he can begin to be a writer, and no amount of technical training can make up for deficiencies in these first two phases of the job. On the other hand, some persons who have never had a course in story writing and scarcely a course in composition have been among the most dynamic writers we have had. Very often, courses in story writing are deadly dull and confuse rather than inspire writers. Nevertheless, there are certain techniques which a person needs to observe if he is going to be shipshape in his writing.

To begin with, after a subject has been selected, it should be definitely limited. Sometimes an author who has started a story finds that he must limit it. It is better, if possible, to limit it in advance. Obviously, this saves labor. Less obviously but equally important, it is likely to make the story a better story. If one is going on a thousand-mile journey, one makes preparations different from those made for a twenty-mile journey. Similarly, if one is going to write a story which encompasses a lot of territory, the preparation is different from the preparation one would make if the story is to be on a smaller scale. A "bobbed off" long story rarely makes a good short story.

Having limited the subject, it is a good idea to plan pretty well how one is going to develop it. I do not mean that a writer can ever know exactly how a story is going to develop when it is begun— it sort of develops itself. However, it is better—so it seems to me— if we can know to some extent the general line of development we are going to follow, so that we can get our material together and get our background all built up before we begin to write. If, for example, we are writing a story laid in some particular part of Palestine, it is well to know, in so far as this is possible, whether during the season of the year at which we are placing our story, it was hot or cold; whether the persons were walking by a riverside or through a wheatfield; whether the flowers were blooming and fragrant or whether they were dry and dusty. If the author can go beyond this and know also the shape of the leaves upon the trees, he will feel reality and therefore give a sense of reality to the reader.

Similarly, in dressing the character. Even though the story is not to be illustrated, if the author is going to write vividly, he must know how the character was dressed. For one thing, this will keep him from running into difficulties in his writing, and for another, it will give him more of a sense of the reality of his character. If the character wears a robe, there are certain conventions which must be observed. There are certain conveniences in having a robe and certain inconveniences. All this will be in the writer's mind whether he mentions it or not, and often a tiny turn of a phrase with reference to a costume will spell the difference between making a character stand up and letting him "flop."

Some of the best of the children's writers find that a collection of folders—one on food, one on dress, one on climate, one on unique ways of talking in the region used as the setting—is very helpful. Often a vast amount of material is collected in order to give vividness and reality to one brief sentence, and if a person is interested in good writing, it is well worth the effort.

But there has to be something more than a background to a story. More important, of course, is the character (or the characters). To keep each person in character from beginning to end requires careful attention even in a short story. Each character must stand in the sort of relationships that he would naturally have with the other characters. All of this is of the essence of good writing.

The children sense any artificial manipulation of the characters. Once a character is established, he must continue in character to the bitter end, no matter what that does to the writer's scheme. I had an interesting experience of this sort with my fifteen-year-old niece recently. She had been assigned the job of writing a short story to illustrate the principles of short-story writing, which she was studying in her literature course. She very sensibly elected to write a story about a summer camp, since she had been to summer camp for five years and knew something about such camps. She got her characters lined up and her plot moving, and then she ran into difficulty. She came to me and asked me what to do. She said that she wanted one of her characters to act in a certain way; then she added, "But I know she wouldn't do it." She had sensed a problem faced by all writers who are sensitive to their job. If a character will not do something naturally, the writer has no business forcing him to do it.

Of course, the incidents must move along, one following the other both logically and from the standpoint of the interest and development of the story. Boys and girls like their stories well knit. They would not be able to tell you this, but I have observed that when an author contrives the incidents so that they come together in the way that *he* wants them to do, rather than in the way they naturally would develop, the result is a story which is not very popular.

Sometimes stories are bogged down with unessential incidents. It often happens that one can reduce a story in length by as much as a third by eliminating unessential incidents and remarks. The chances are that such a reduction will strengthen 99 per cent of all stories in their first draft. Often a writer has collected a lot of material and feels that it must be used; so he crowds in incident after incident. Sometimes these incidents are in themselves interesting as they give intriguing sidelights. But the writer must discipline himself and ask the questions: Does this incident move forward the essential plot of the story? Does it develop essential aspects of the character of the hero or of one of the lesser characters in the story? In other words, is this incident necessary to the story?

Similarly, with bits of description. Sometimes the author becomes enamored of the scene and wanders around telling a lot about it. In children's materials it is well to reduce description to an absolute minimum. Instead of stopping the story to describe a lake, it is much better if the description of the lake can be woven into the incident. Let the characters walk around the lake, and so give an idea of its size; or let them row across it, or fish in it, or swim in it. This is a far better way to convey how a scene looks than to use descriptive words. Children can best imagine what a thing is like if it is presented to them in terms that call up images of action; they get less help from words that merely paint a picture on a flat canvas. If one is describing a hot day, let it be in terms of how a character felt as he played ball, or as she washed dishes, or as he climbed a hill or studied his lessons. Weave the overtone of hotness into the activity, rather than pause in the activity to report the thermometer reading!

Conversation is one of the most difficult phases of writing for a beginner to manage. The characters become confused. They become stiff as pokers; their phrases do not clip lightly. Yet conversation is a far better way of revealing a character than is talking about him. Through what he does and what he says, the reader, especially the child reader, comes to know him.

A good way to begin is to take down the conversation of some persons of the same age as that of the characters about whom you are writing. If one is writing a story about ten-year-olds, for example, listen unobtrusively to ten-year-old conversation on the playground or at church or in the back yard or wherever one can listen unobtrusively. Take notes; put down words and phrases; keep at it until you get a feeling for the way children of that particular age are likely to talk in normal conversation. Then keep working at it until the conversation in the story begins to take on some of the life which the conversation on the playground had. Make the conversation of ten-year-olds differ from that of mature persons or learned persons or primitive persons, or crude persons. In other words, through differences in conversation, lift up each character and make it sharply delineated.

Then there is the actual choice of words to be considered. There have been vocabulary word lists prepared for each age level. These indicate what words can be comprehended by children of each school grade. These lists, I think, are only of general use to persons who are writing for boys and girls. To stick rigidly to a word list when one is writing a story or a bit of poetic description is somewhat deadening, and may result in a wooden, uninspired piece of writing. A writer who knows children will not hesitate to use a word not on the word list for the age for which he is writing, when it is the best word to use in that situation. He will know that an alert child is quick to sense the meaning of a word when it is used in its context, and he will not sacrifice literary quality or accuracy on the altar of adherence to a word list, no matter who drew it up!

Personally, I never pay any attention to word lists when I am writing for children. I go ahead and write the way I think the story should be written. Then I ask my secretary (lest I should become prejudiced) to run over the material, checking it against the word list for the age span for which I am writing. I do not even want to know the individual words that are off base, but only whether I am away off base or just a little off base! If she tells me I am away off base, then I go over the material myself and try to simplify the words, not checking them against the word list, but checking the more difficult or unusual words against my own sense of what would be hard for a child to understand. In this way I reduce the number of "big" words. Then I ask her to check it again, to see if my score has come down to a reasonable figure. If she reports it has, I let it go at that. Persons who are writing for textbooks are required to adhere rigidly to the word list, but persons who are writing for general reading or for inspirational reading must—so it seems to me—have much more freedom than is accorded them by arbitrary word lists.

Let us assume now that the story or bit of informational writing or inspirational writing, as the case may be, has been written. It is now in first draft. Then it must be revised, and re-revised, and re-revised. When I was editor of children's books with Rand McNally & Company, some of my best writers completely rewrote their manuscripts as many as eight times and polished and revised phrases and sentences many more times than that. There were ten complete rewritings of my manuscript, *His Name Was Jesus.* It takes such revising to get a manuscript in proper shape for publication. I have heard of writers who dashed something off and sent it to the publisher, and the editor had it set in type and distributed it that way. I am sure this has sometimes happened, but neither in my own experience as a writer nor in my experience as an editor have I ever come across a manuscript of that sort. The more delicate the writing, the more repeated revision is necessary. If one is doing a bit of devotional writing for boys and girls, each word becomes tremendously important. It is as if one were working on a miniature, rather than a mural. Every thin line takes on increased significance.

After one has written and revised a manuscript, it is very helpful to get a person of the age group for which it is written to read it or to listen to it. I know, of course, that a child who likes an adult friend will like whatever that adult friend writes. Frequently a writer, when sending his manuscript to the editor, will assure him that it is a good manuscript for that age group because he has read it to his own children and they have loved it. This is not a very reliable criterion. Personal relationships are important, and a child who loves an adult will likely love what that adult writes. Nevertheless, in spite of this difficulty, if a writer can try objectively to observe the reader or the hearer of his material and "size up" his reaction quickly, he may get much help. Then there are adult friends who can give counsel, if the writer is really seeking constructive criticism. Honest and friendly criticism is what a writer needs most, for it is impossible to be wholly objective about one's own creation.

In conclusion, if you wholeheartedly believe in what you have written, even though no one else seems to believe in it, do not become discouraged. Keep on working upon your story, and if it really is good and worthy of publication, the chances are that some editor will recognize that fact some day.

MAKING THE BIBLE UNDERSTOOD IN
CHURCH SCHOOL LITERATURE

GUSTAV WIENCKE

Dr. Gustav Wiencke is an editor of the Parish and Church School Board of the United Lutheran Church. Among his editorial responsibilities is The Parish School, *a monthly magazine for church school workers. In addition to having written a great many articles and lesson treatments, he has edited numerous elective courses for young people. He is a competent Bible scholar and is a member of the Uniform Lesson Committee of the National Council of the Churches of Christ in the U.S.A.*

As WRITERS we know that there are no "five easy steps" to the quick solution of the problems of our task, no one-two-three rules for interpreting the Bible in the actual process of developing and writing church school literature. Therefore, we propose to view the task of making the Bible understood from four angles, and to do so out of the actual work of writing church school materials.

The first angle of approach is how to make people interested in understanding the Bible. People agree that they ought to read the Bible, ought to learn how to understand it, ought to know it. But they must be helped to understand it, and they must find pleasure in doing so. While commentaries ignore this question, the church school lesson writer may not do so. Commentaries assume reader intent, interest, and intelligence. Lesson writers dare not make that assumption. Commentaries dwell on dozens of technical matters, often leaving out the forest because of their interest in the odd-shaped leaves on some of the trees or in the curious ferns behind stones.

Among the methods of arousing interest in understanding the Bible are the following: (1) Develop the drama that is inherent in the biblical passages. (2) Raise a problem which will point up the way in which the biblical teaching can be related to life situations. (3) Appeal to an experience of biblical personages with God as a basis for development of the theme. Be specific in describing those details of the situation which will bring it to life.

The interpretation of a Bible passage requires the development and use of certain skills: (1) Read with wide-open eyes, noting the details which reveal the reactions of individuals, their attitudes and responses to situations and conversation. (2) Look for handles for organizing the passages. Keep in mind the need for clarity, and for drive to the lesson. Develop a rough sketch of the lesson; decide on the sideheads, teachable Scripture sections, material for the pupil's book and for the teacher's guide.

Resources for biblical interpretation are numerous: (1) libraries, especially those of theological seminaries; (2) Bibles in modern-speech versions; (3) journals, such as the *Biblical Archaeologist* and the *Expository Times;* (4) standard reference books, such as commentaries, Bible dictionaries, histories of Israel, lives of Christ; (5) special books on individual books of the Bible, such as Luccock, *Acts of the Apostles,* and Lowrie, *Short Story of Jesus.*

Recognize also the limitations under which you work: (1) Mechanical limitations, such as space, and the fact that the Bible exposition is not the whole lesson. It is rather a means to an experience, to an attitude, to an action. (2) Then, there is the limitation placed upon the writer by the layman's range of understanding. Usually, academic explanations leave the reader in a fog. Such explanations will help the writer to gain a broader background and a greater sureness; however, they need not appear in the finished writing. Short paragraphs and easy-to-understand words are best for the average reader.

(3) The writer must remember that many laymen have limited historical background and see in much biblical material little relatedness to their own life. To make matters more difficult, words in the Bible (e.g., holiness, repent, mercy, wisdom, love) do not always mean the same thing to people today that they did to people long ago. (4) Another limitation comes in the degree to which a reader, or even a writer, is able to understand a Bible passage in the larger context of Christian experience, biblical revelation, and historical background.

PART FIVE

*From Behind
the Editor's Desk*

AN EDITOR SPEAKS FRANKLY: AN INTERVIEW

BEN HIBBS

Ben Hibbs is the widely known editor of The Saturday Evening Post. *Upon his graduation from the University of Kansas, he was for some years a newspaper editor in various cities. From 1929 to 1940 he was Associate Editor of* Country Gentleman; *from 1940 to 1942 he was Editor of that magazine. Since 1942 he has been directing* The Saturday Evening Post. *He has received honorary degrees from Northwestern University and Temple University. In 1947 he received the University of Pennsylvania journalism award.*

It should be explained here that Mr. Hibbs did not address the Christian Writers and Editors' Conference, but attended one of its sessions and very graciously consented to being interviewed. The occasion was informal, and the answers which he gave to the questions asked were wholly extemporaneous and without any thought that later they might be published. Such was the interest in the interview, however, that with Mr. Hibbs's generous permission the stenographic record of the interview is included in this volume of addresses.

How do you discover authors and find stories for The Saturday Evening Post?

We have to break our materials down into several different kinds. As far as articles are concerned, we accept them from free-lance writers. However, about 90 per cent of our articles are done on assignment. We have a great pool of article writers. Some work solely for us; others write for us and other publications also.

We get ideas in many different ways. Sometimes they come from those in our office, sometimes from the authors themselves. Over a period of years we have gradually accumulated a group of writers, and know what they can do best; consequently, many of our articles are assigned. We have staff writers who do writing on various subjects—medicine, science, aviation, certain types of business, and so

N

forth. One of our associate editors is a trained medical man. He writes medical articles, and passes upon articles written by others in this field before they are published.

I would say that 90 per cent of our fiction is unsolicited. We work with short story writers, and talk with them frequently.

Other types of material, such as back-of-magazine boxes, are sometimes arranged for in advance; much material comes in unsolicited. The unsolicited manuscripts number in the thousands. Most of the cartoons are received in the form of rough sketches. They are returned for completion, if we can use them.

How much editing is done?

We do a great deal of editing. Frequently we buy an article which has a lot wrong with it. The subject is good, so we buy it and turn it over to our rewrite man who rewrites it; then it goes back to the author for final approval. Or the article may be almost right, with only a few things to fix. Cutting is our biggest problem. Not more than 10 per cent of the articles we buy are printed exactly as they were written. There is a great deal of cutting.

In fiction, we always do cutting in the serials. We are trying to get the writers to write their short stories short. Perhaps the ending is not right. In that case, the manuscript is sent back, and the author is asked to change the ending, clear up indefinite points, and cut his manuscript. Not so much work is done in our office on fiction as on nonfiction.

Do you buy materials through agents?

Seventy-five per cent of our fiction comes through New York agents. Probably not more than 20 per cent of our articles come through agents. There are some fiction writers who do not bother with agents.

Where do you get your poetry?

From free-lance writers. We have no poetry writers on our staff. Very little poetry is purchased through agents.

Would you detail some of the counsel which you give your writers?

When a writer starts out on an article we usually sit down with him or else we write him very carefully about what we want in the article. That does not mean that we try to write it for him before he gets his material. We expect him to have latitude. But as a help to him we very often suggest sources where he can get material that otherwise he might not know about. After he has finished the "leg work," he may write a long report or come into the office to discuss the article with us and to get advice on what we would like omitted or included. During his research he usually finds ten times as much material as he can use.

With fiction, the advice we give to young writers is concerned primarily with what to do and what not to do to make a salable story. If a story is good, yet not good enough to buy, we have men on our staff who will help the writer to make a salable story out of it. Agents sometimes do this type of work. The really good agent should be able to help the writer at this point.

How do you train writers of promise, even though you are not able to take their material?

We have a staff of editorial assistants. Every morning when the mail comes in, the manuscripts are divided into two piles — first class and second class. The first class goes to the staff of associate editors. The second class goes to the reading room staffed by editorial assistants. They go through these manuscripts very carefully. If they find anything hopeful, they send it to the associate editors. The people in the reading room are bright, alert. We spend hours and hours each day writing long letters to hopeful young writers who seem promising. The development of these young writers is our bread and butter. I think all major magazines do this. If these young writers show some real promise, we frequently have them come in and talk with us.

How personal is your contact with writers?

Writers never get a form letter. Instead, we work very closely and very carefully with them. Most rejections, however, do have to go back with a rejection slip.

What are the principles on which you make a decision regarding a manuscript?

Intuition. People who work on magazines have to have a seventh sense which tells them what great masses of people like to read.

The first principle is in the form of a question: "Is it interesting?" But if we chose only the manuscripts that will get the largest readership, we would have a one-sided magazine. I often say to our staff that I look upon the *Post*, not as a magazine that every reader should read from cover to cover, particularly since it comes out every seven days, but one which serves a large and varied bill of fare each week. It is hoped that thereby each reader will find in the magazine five or six things which interest him. We cannot expect everything to please everybody.

How much do you depend upon readership polls for your decisions? How do you discover reader interest?

I do not depend very much on the daily mail. It is interesting, and all letters are carefully answered. But I do not think one gets from the mail a true indication as to how one is doing. An editor very rarely hears from a person who agrees with him. That which crosses people's views is what stirs up mail.

Some years ago we started a Gallup-type poll which is conducted by a subsidiary of the Curtis Publishing Co. This is done twice each month. A copy of the *Post* comes to my desk with everything in the magazine stamped with percentage figures. The figures show how many people read the whole of the article and how many people started the article and stopped; they show what articles the readers considered excellent, good, or only fair. This report also is broken down by groups, by age, and by sex. Of course, these polls have to be adjusted scientifically—geographically according to towns and cities, and according to newsstand purchasers and according to subscription readers. We have come to the conclusion that the poll is pretty accurate—within 2 or 3 per cent. It shows us how well we are doing our job.

We depend upon readership polls to a great extent, but not entirely. For example, when we found people were not reading foreign articles as avidly as they did during the war, we did not discontinue that type of material. Instead, we got our men in the foreign field to build more human interest into their articles. By dealing with individual people rather than with broad abstractions, we were able to get the foreign news across in a more interesting way, and readership went up again.

Can you relate any sudden change in reader interest? Does reader interest change during certain periods of the year?

Anything about the Russian threat is read avidly today. People are much concerned about this—as much as during the war years. During the war, if we had listened to what people said to us about the interest of the reading public in the war, we would have cut down the amount of war material we carried. Everyone said, "Won't it be wonderful when the war is over and we won't have to read about this horrible thing any more!" People indicated that they were fed up with war material, yet throughout the entire period of the war there was not a single one of our surveys but what showed that the war articles were rated higher in readership than anything else in the magazine. Readership of war articles was a good 20 per cent above everything else in the magazine, including fiction. During the war period we gave about 60 per cent of the article space to the war and to war topics. People wanted to read about it, despite what they said—obviously because the war was close to everyone. It touched every home in a personal way, and had a vital bearing on every business enterprise.

If we were to follow readership polls exactly, you would see a quite different type of *Post*. You would find that in the summer it would be filled with very light stuff. We do tend that way a bit in the summer, but we do not let the magazine become unbalanced. We feel that we should run articles on world affairs, even though we believe we could sell more copies for a time if we changed the character of the magazine. But in the end, it would mean losing the very best type of readers we have. We feel that a magazine such as the *Post* has a duty to perform. We would not care to turn it into a fluffy publication.

What are some of your taboos?

Just certain principles of decency. There are some topics, such as raw sex, which we do not handle. Also, there are some fields which we make no attempt to cover, simply because we do not feel they belong in the *Post*—such as gardening, cooking, and home-making. We have been pleased with the reception of religious articles and stories. One story about a minister won the largest fiction readership we have had in the last six years.

What is your proportion of fiction and nonfiction?

Half and half.

How do you get all the manuscripts read quickly?

Our plan was established many years ago. We think the humane thing to do, for the sake of the author, is either to buy or to return the manuscript quickly. We get to look at a lot of material which ordinarily might go to other magazines simply because we handle it faster. We keep material moving from one desk to another. We have a large enough reading staff to do that. We do not think that a manuscript has to be read by more than two or three people. In most cases our decisions are made within twenty-four hours. I take manuscripts home each night and pass them on the next morning. This is the first-class material. The second-class manuscripts sometimes take ten days to two weeks to be processed, but most of them are handled in a week.

How controversial do you permit an article to be?

We do not shy away from controversy. I believe that editors should publish what they think is true on a topic. We also believe we have the right to take sides. Sometimes we publish the other side. We publish many articles with which we do not agree. Even though we do not agree, the article may still be interesting.

What place do cartoons have in religious publications?

I think they are good in any publication.

Do you feel that your magazine gains by refusing liquor advertising?

Yes, the character of a magazine is what sells it to subscribers.

Payments for materials?

For short stories we pay $850 to $3,500. A beginner starts at $850 and works up to $1,750 or $2,000. If he is really good, his price may eventually rise to $2,500 or $3,000, and occasionally even higher.

Articles bring from $750 to $3,500, usually plus expenses. Short articles from $400 to $600. The highest price we ever paid for article material was $175,000 for a series of ten, or $17,500 per installment.

How often do you hold staff meetings?

Every Friday. The meeting usually lasts for only twenty minutes. A staff conference is just a clearinghouse for information, since decisions have to be made day by day.

THE EDITOR'S UNEASY CHAIR

GLENN McRAE

For a brief biographical note concerning Dr. Glenn McRae, turn to his address entitled, "Writing to Method and Measure," beginning on page 164.

EVERY EDITOR sits in an uneasy chair. If he sat in a rocking chair that squeaked, the squeaking in most offices would be in unbroken rhythm, varied only by its intensity. Why is the editor an uneasy creature and his chair an uneasy one? There are many reasons.

The editor's work is filled with imponderables. In every situation he faces there are unknown factors. Every task he performs involves a tussle with unseen powers. His world appears to be in a state of perpetual crisis. Even routine matters may become calamitous.

Take the filing of a letter. In my office filing a letter occasionally means that that letter has gone to that land from which no letter ever returns. If that letter contains a contract or someone's poem, the loss is little short of tragic. (Or is it?)

Then there is the morning mail. That neat pile of letters on the corner of the editor's desk is to him a haunted thing. He knows not what evil lurks therein. How many readers have written this morning to point out a typographical error in last week's editorial and to hint at carelessness and inefficiency in the editorial sanctum? How many have sought to communicate their rage because of disagreement with some view expressed in a recent periodical? How many of those letters were written to apply choice epithets to the editor's distant person? Is that delicate missive on top of the pile from that poetic member, in good standing, of the pen woman's club? Is she writing to thank the editor from the bottom of her heart for accepting one of her poems, even though the editor, ever since buying it, has been asking himself, "Why do I have such weak moments?"

Take the processing of a manuscript. There is no task on earth that has the possibility of more errors than the preparation of a manuscript for the printer. To describe adequately the editorial operation requires military phraseology. A well prepared manuscript involves only a brief, sharp skirmish. A carelessly written manuscript, especially in the curricular field, calls for a major campaign, a long-drawn-out siege. Only the spirit of I-propose-to-fight-it-out-along-this-line-if-it-takes-all-summer will bring victory. For such a siege, the editor needs an unlimited supply of materials—pens, pencils, scissors, paper knives, paste pots, a calendar good to A.D. 2500, paper clips, pins, stapler, scratch pad, ham sandwiches, ice packs, coffee, and a shot of penicillin. Then with a bit of luck and the help of a kindly copy editor, he may deliver an acceptable manuscript to the printer.

I have a notion that the editor's uneasiness is due, not solely to his work, but to the constant fear of what he may become. Will he, before the sunset of life, become a finicky, comma-grubbing, semi-colon-uprooting, cantankerous creature? Will he come to delight only in taking sentences apart? Will he reach a point where he cannot read a book without pencil in hand to make editorial corrections? Will he chide his wife at the dinner table for the long sentences in her conversation and her excessive use of exclamation points and dashes?

But if there were no fears in his life and no uncertainties in his work, the editor would still be an uneasy soul. Day and night there hangs over him a dank, ominous, menacing cloud that threatens him every moment and robs him of peace of mind. What is it? The deadline. Every job that the editor undertakes must be finished on time. There is no postponing of the hour when the editor's periodicals shall be put to bed. He cannot put off until tomorrow the tasks of today.

I should like to define a deadline. A deadline is the point in time at which the writer should deliver the manuscript to the editor; and if the writer fails, the editor, not the writer, dies.

So you see the editor is an uneasy creature and he sits in an uncertain chair. Yet I would not dwell upon this uneasiness. Rather I would speak of the relationship between writer and editor, a relationship essential to the most creative work.

When an editor invites a writer to write an article for a magazine, a study course for a Sunday morning group, or a series of topics for Sunday evening fellowship meetings, he really asks the writer to join with him in the creation of something that neither of them can create alone.

How can the relationship between writer and editor be made cooperative and creative, and how can they work so that each makes his best contribution?

First of all, writer and editor must recognize the part each has to play in the writing enterprise. The editor at the outset contributes an idea for an article or conveys and interprets the description and purpose of a study course as developed by a curriculum committee. Uninspired as an editor or a curriculum committee may seem at times to be, nevertheless the interpretation of the purpose and point of view of those who planned the article or course is the editor's task. An article is planned as one of many articles, and a course of study is part of a total curriculum for the church. The writer who is to create a part of the whole must work with the total plan in mind. The editor interprets the specific writing assignment in terms of the total undertaking. The writer, for his part, contributes his specialized knowledge of the subject, his experience in that field, and his skill in writing.

If writer and editor are to join in a creative enterprise, they should have a personal conference at the very beginning. At that conference they must look at the enterprise in its larger aspects. Purpose, point of view, content, and scope should be reviewed. Such preliminary conferences go far toward making the relationship of editor and writer mutually helpful. They develop an *esprit de corps,* a feeling that "we're doing this together"; both writers and editors come to see that they are engaged in a great enterprise. We are seeking through our work to change the very character and life of the children, youth, and adults of our churches. We are not timeservers. We are the creators of a new generation.

These conferences are important for another reason. They give the writer opportunity to contribute to the planning. Writers are not merely to be handed a blueprint and told to go to work. They know something of what should go into the blueprint. It is well for the editor to make possible this contribution by the writer.

Before work begins, there should be a clear understanding about many details.

1. *The fee.* The fee may be large or small, but whatever it is, let it be made known at the beginning. The editor should not pass it off with the remark, "We'll see that you are paid for this." I like to tell the writer early in the negotiations that for this kind of writing my Board pays so much. If the fee mentioned is not satisfactory, then neither writer nor editor needs to lose any time. The fee should be stated in a letter or memorandum to the writer.

2. *Schedule.* A schedule of work should be planned. The dates when different stages of the work are to be completed should be set. Sometimes a preliminary outline is required. If outline and manuscript are to be reviewed by a committee, the schedule must be lengthened accordingly. The date when the finished manuscript is due in the hands of the editor—that is, the deadline—should be set. Put this schedule in writing.

The writer should be certain that he can work as rapidly as the schedule requires. Some writers work faster than others. Some jobs, because of the research and background reading required, take more time. Both editor and writer should take these factors into account when making out the schedule of work.

3. *Length of manuscript.* The editor must tell the writer how long a manuscript is desired. It is wasteful to submit 50,000 words when only 40,000 can be used. It is equally wasteful to send only 30,000. The editor knows the size the printed page is to be and the kind of type to be used. Careful calculation will enable him to tell the approximate length the manuscript should be.

4. *Quotations from the Bible.* If quotations from the Bible are to be made, what version should be used? There is usually an editorial policy that must be followed. There is generally a policy concerning quotations from modern versions. The writer will need to be informed at this point.

5. *Copyrighted material.* Should copyrighted material be used? As a rule, copyrighted material should be used sparingly. The editor will have a judgment and no doubt a policy concerning the matter.

One thing about copyrights should be kept clearly in mind. A copyright is title to property. The permission of the owner must be secured before using his property. Penalties for the violation of the copyright laws are severe. Writers and editors will find little inspiration looking through prison bars at white clouds floating by.

If copyrighted material is to be used, there should be an understanding as to who will write for permission to use it. Some editors prefer to do the writing, others ask the writer to do so.

If the writer is to secure the permission, the editor should explain the kind of letter to be written. The letter must inform the publisher of the exact words to be quoted, the publication in which the quotation will appear, and the name and address of the publisher. I like to add that the publication is distributed among the churches for a nominal price. The writer should keep a carbon of his request to use the copyrighted material. The letter granting permission to use the material should be sent to the editor when the manuscript is sent in.

Much copyrighted material requires a fee for its use. Who is to pay the fee? Writer and editor should have an understanding at this point. Some publishers secure permission and charge all fees to the writer. In some cases the publishers pay the fees.

6. *Style*. The matter of style should be a subject for early consideration. Will the style be formal, conversational, or colloquial? Will it be permissible to follow the present trend toward the use of contractions, such as "didn't" and "can't"? Will the information to be given be conveyed through simple exposition or through an imaginary conversation between Mr. Smith and Mr. Jones? Will the material be written in the first person or in the third person?

7. *Taboos*. If a writer has a notion that he can escape the clutches of taboos, the editor will soon disabuse his mind. Taboos, much as we hate them, are with us constantly. Like a bad heart, one has to learn to live with them.

EDITORS AND WRITERS, A TWO-WAY STREET

Park Hays Miller

Dr. Park Hays Miller, until his recent retirement, was Editor-in-Chief of the Board of Christian Education of the Presbyterian Church in the U.S.A. He has given many years to the writing and editing of church school literature. For some years he was the honored chairman of the Committee on Uniform Lessons of what was then known as the International Council of Religious Education. Among his several books are The Holy Spirit in Christian Experience *and* Christian Doctrine for Sunday School Teachers.

EDITORS AND WRITERS should be partners. They have many interests in common. Writers can sell their manuscripts only if editors can sell their publications. Writers attract the attention of editors only if their manuscripts are good; likewise, editors attract good writers only if their publications are of high standard.

Editors do much to improve the manuscripts which they publish, and the writers should be grateful for the editorial changes made in the manuscripts they send in. (However, there is a limit to the editor's rights in this respect. For example, he may not misrepresent the writer's point of view or convictions.) Some writers profit by the editor's corrections. These writers grow. Other writers disregard these corrections and in their writing continue in the old rut.

Suggestions and ideas should be exchanged between writers and editors. The writers should try to carry out the editor's ideas, if they appeal to him. A writer should never write about something that does not appeal to him. The writer, on his part, may ask the editor if he would be interested in an article or story of a certain type. Suppose the writer is encouraged to proceed and submits his manuscript. He should bear in mind that his manuscript, even then, will have to be fully satisfactory or it will not be accepted. The Presbyterian Board, like most Boards, has a rule covering the relationship of editor and writer while work is in progress. It is as follows:

The editor reserves the right to reject, at any stage of its preparation, a manuscript which does not meet the requirements of the Board
of Christian Education, and no payment will be made for a manuscript
until it has been finally approved for publication.

Obviously, a writer should not deliver a manuscript in person
and expect immediate judgment. The manuscript must speak for
itself.

Editors are eager to discover new and promising writers; and
young authors should realize that the religious publications offer
them a fine opportunity to become established.

Needless to say, the writer needs a knowledge of his subject.
Because he is writing on a religious topic, his task is not less difficult
but more difficult. He should be willing to do some genuine research.

The writer should have also a knowledge of the public for whom
he is writing. He should know its point of view. His expression
should be clear and vigorous. His organization should lead progres-
sively up steps and never let go of the subject. Writers should be
very careful to meet schedules set up by editors. In all events, writers
and editors should be partners, not contestants in a tug of war.

THE EDITOR KEEPS THE SPARK

HAROLD L. PHILLIPS

*Rev. Harold L. Phillips is the capable and energetic Editor-in-Chief
of the Publication Board of the Church of God (Gospel Trumpet
Company), Anderson, Ind. His address, "The Editor Keeps the Spark,"
is filled with rare wit as well as with editorial wisdom. In it he shows
that he himself possesses both the spark and the spunk of which he
speaks so entertainingly and helpfully.*

To BEGIN WITH, the editor, if he is to "keep the spark," needs a first-
class pair of specs (colloquial for "spectacles") to aid his vision. An
editor too blind to recognize a good manuscript when he sees it, is
mired down in a hopeless situation. Even though he may be sur-

rounded by manuscript readers of unusual skill, if he cannot exercise some judgment beyond their opinions, has he not in reality vacated his perch? Or is not the spark already cold?

The editor also needs specs for spotting potential writers. No self-respecting editor can just sit and wait for whatever the fame-seeking and money-hungry writing public chooses to dump onto him. He must pursue an active policy of writer-hunting, writer-cultivation, and writer-training. Through the editor's specs the actual number of highly proficient writers in his field always seems drastically limited.

The editor's specs, by all means, should be bifocals, especially when he uses them on his writers. While busily engaged in the scrutiny of a finished manuscript, he needs to shift from the close-range vision of its particularities to the distant writer as a person. Writers have feelings, as every editor knows; and some of the best of them wear those feelings on their sleeves, readily available for the next editor-injury. Shall I confess for the editors that we wound writers unnecessarily when we fail to focus our specs on their peculiar viewpoint?

Perhaps the editor needs an extra pair of specs for judicious loaning. As the occasion and the need arise, he should interpret the policies, problems, and goals of his publications for the benefit of his writers. At opportune times he might even explain the background of those irritating taboos that forever hang over his head like the sword of Damocles. Through the writer's specs they seem silly; through the editor's specs they are more understandable. After all, complete freedom of speech obtains only in never-never land. Not all the sacred cows reside in the Orient. Every editorial department has a few of them hitched to the principal desks. In the comparative safety of his study at home, the writer finds it easy to forget them or ignore them. But the editor—never! He has had painful experience. And he remembers!

If the editor keeps the spark, he needs not only specs but also spirit. The desk job of an editor has its dangers. Day after day we grind away at a never-ending mess of minutiae. We cannot keep the spark without finding ways of renewing our souls. From time to time we must find ways to renew our sense of high calling. With this effort will come a humbling sense of reliance upon divine resources that lie beyond our human abilities.

Much more could be said about "spirit," but we must now move on to "spunk." Here we are to consider the editor's need for courage. Somebody is always ready to dump cold water on the spark; the editor's task includes sentry duty. The onslaughts come from many areas, but we will note three: (1) management, (2) writers, (3) subscribers or consumers.

Differences of approach and opinion do arise between editorial and management personnel. We simply do not sit in the same seats. Our specs are ground on a different formula. An editor naturally tends to maintain the viewpoint of an educator. "Expense be hanged," he says; "we've got to put persons and principles first." This attitude fails to impress the watchdog of the publisher's treasury. And amid the give-and-take, the editor must know both how to yield gracefully at some points and how to fight like a cat being dragged out by the tail at others. Blessed be the editor with enough spunk to raise his hackles when the best interests of his work seem threatened by undue management pressure. Likewise, blessed be the editor who refuses to carry a chip on his shoulder or to condone a perpetual running fight between his department and others.

Also in his relationships with writers, an editor occasionally needs spunk. Writers can be, and sometimes are, persons of tenacious disposition. If I were to write a book entitled *Authors I Have Known,* an interesting chapter might be given to the type of writer who lets out a blood-curdling scream if an editor dares to cross a "t" or dot an "i" on the beloved manuscript. What is an editor to do when he knows that certain changes in a manuscript are simply mandatory, but the writer maintains a bulldog grip for the original text—unrevised, unexpurgated, unedited, and eventually . . . unpublished?

Fortunately, what is described here rarely occurs. But if and when it does happen, the editor needs spunk. As for me, I would rather go to the mat with an irate author than to stomach the fellow who constantly seeks to lick the editorial hands with a saccharin tongue. The dual problem for the editor here is that of holding to his principles and policies and, if at all possible, holding the good will of those who write for him. But woe to the editor who skulks in the editorial cave whenever some Philistine Goliath troubles the peace of Israel! Verily, the spark has died. Incidentally, though, we need to remember that the need for spunk makes no excuse for the ulcerous disposition that constantly threatens the editor. Spunk is commendable; pettiness is despicable.

Have you ever attended a rodeo? And did you ever see a rider rowel a range pony for the purpose of furnishing you entertainment? Believe it or not, the distance from the riding lot to the editorial sanctum is not very great. Editors are entertained by an almost perpetual rodeo. They furnish the broncos; the subscribers do the riding and the roweling. A good time is had by all, provided the editor learns how to yield gracefully to saddle and bridle. As the editor seeks adjustment to this situation, he might even be willing to admit that this subscriber-spur actually helps rather than hinders his work.

If the editor is to keep the spark, he must avoid two extremes when he detects the jingling spurs headed his way. He must not just stand there and tremble and heave, or fall to the ground. Neither should he fly at his tormentor with flailing hoofs. The better technique is to canter away gracefully or else to manage a brief but pleasant word-ride.

But the very best approach to this "spur" business is a good laugh. To assist us in this, I offer a brief system of classification for the editor's fan mail. This applies only to the "Dear Sir! You Cur!" type of letters with which all editors are familiar. Here are a few pigeonholes:

1. The *Barker*. You will readily recognize this fellow. He threatens to cancel his subscription unless . . .

2. The *Baiter*. The fellow who issues a ringing challenge for debate on some point of doctrine or biblical interpretation. He usually oozes with self-confidence and describes with modesty (!) how much more he knows about the subject than the editor. One such wrote: "I am willing to give your doctrine a fair hearing before I rip it to shreds"!

3. The *Biter*. Matters are not going too well over in the local parish, so this fellow gets worked up. Some family or community frustration is eating away at his equanimity. So what does he do? He sits down to his typewriter and bites the editor—a convenient victim at a safe distance. He makes the paper sizzle and curl with the epithets he would use at home, if he dared.

4. The *Bitter*. Here the rancid perfume known as "sour grapes"

has soured the milk of human kindness. Everyone is out of step but him. The whole universe is out of joint; cursed spite that he was born to set it right! So he pours out his bitterness upon an editor.

5. The *Bellower*. A letter from this type has more sound than sense. Rising to histrionic heights, with adjective piled on adjective, it climaxes with some brash threat.

Other less exciting but needed spurs should be mentioned in passing. Did you hear about the editor who spent three weeks in the hospital after getting caught at the intersection of two deadlines? Deadlines keep us spurred to deliver all there is of us and in us. We must read much, and write at least a little. We must form the collecting habit, storing away observations, experiences, ideas against that day when the spark of inspiration becomes feeble and a spur to the mind is needed.

WRITER-EDITOR RELATIONSHIPS

Benjamin P. Browne

For a brief biographical note concerning Dr. Benjamin P. Browne, turn to his address entitled "Training Writers with a Christian Purpose," beginning on page 13.

Because the editor and writer should be good friends, it is important that they keep their fences of friendship in repair. Each must respect the other's work. To that end, I offer some suggestions which may help to cement cordial understanding and firm friendship between editors and writers.

Let us begin with mutual admiration. The editor would starve without the writer, for he lives by the contributions which come to him or by the assignments which he makes to the craftsmen of the writing profession. By the same token, it would be hard for writers to dispose of their manuscripts if there were no eager editors to receive

o

them and, incidentally, to pay for them. Therefore, a most essential need exists for complete understanding between these two groups, both of which are working at all times on a very high plane of literary interests.

William Adams Brown reported in *The Education of American Ministers*, a three-volume survey made in 1934, that in a testing of 12,000 students for all vocational pursuits, the highest intelligence group went into literary professions such as writing, journalism, editing, publicity (I.Q. 173). The next groups in order down the line were: science (163); art, drama, and engineering (158); law and diplomacy (157); business executives (150); medicine (146); agricultural experts and officials (145); accountants and business management (142); smaller forms of business (132); teaching (122); farming (109). Thus it becomes evident that editors and writers belong to an extremely intelligent group. Yet, despite this high rating of writers and editors, you will soon come to know that the editor is a man of human foibles and prejudices. Sometimes by the very nature of his work the editor is inclined to be irritable over what many people regard as trifles, but which from his viewpoint are very far from being trifles. He lives on the razor edge of disaster. One misspelled word, going into print and circulated by the tens of thousands through the mail beyond recall, may do him irreparable damage.

On one occasion, one of our editors caught a misspelled word just before the type was locked into the press. The article was an evening program for young people in which the writer had thought up the clever idea of a candlelight service with singing as the climax. Can you imagine the horror of reading the following words intended to be circulated among young people in the churches: "And now, as the climax of the service, turn out all the lights and let the young people sin softly by candlelight." Just the careless omission of the letter *g*, making the word read *sin* instead of *sing*, would have stirred up a hornet's nest had we not fortunately caught the error in the nick of time.

This is why the editor sometimes seems to you unreasonably upset over misspellings, loose phrases, and poor construction, and why he seems always to be insisting like a martinet upon precision, accuracy, and exactitude. What gets frozen into type may be loaded with dynamite. The little words and the single letters, therefore, are of the utmost importance.

May I suggest that if you want to write for the editor's magazine, you do him the courtesy and yourself the favor of reading his magazine? Familiarize yourself with its content and its concerns. Do this over a period of weeks or months. Editors receive scores of articles which indicate as plainly as a pikestaff that the writer is completely ignorant of the type of magazine to which he has addressed his manuscript. You would not, for instance, send an article on how to teach solid geometry to a magazine for kindergarten children, nor would you send an article on the latest Paris women's fashions to a magazine intended for the plumbing trade. In order, therefore, to write upon the subjects which interest the editor and which are slanted to the needs of his periodical, you must live with his magazine for some time. Do not be afraid to buy it, read it, and if need be, put it under your pillow and sleep on it.

Now, having read the magazine, do not address your article to "The Editor"—that anonymous person whose name apparently you do not regard worth the trouble of looking up. You could, of course, find his name in the masthead of the magazine. Certainly Dale Carnegie would tell you that people like to see their names in print, as well as to hear them frequently spoken. When you address your article to "The Editor," by making him a nameless person, you are missing an opportunity to build up the editor's ego by showing him that you regard it as very important for you to write his name. In other words, get on a friendly basis and not on a stilted, anonymous one.

Before you write the article which you have an urge to send to his magazine, first sit down and write him a friendly letter. Tell him the story you have in mind to write, or the feature article you wish to present. Ask him frankly if this interests him, and how he would like it handled. Ask if you may send him an outlined suggestion of what you can do in this article. Such a letter will save you time and will give him an opportunity to make some important suggestions to you before you have gone to all the work of producing your manuscript. Furthermore, the editor will appreciate the fact that you have let him in on your intention and that you have sought his advice and guidance at the outset. This type of approach makes for more harmonious, satisfactory, and creative results than the usual method of simply sending a cold manuscript addressed to an anonymous person.

It may be that this is the moment to say something about the appearance of the manuscript when you finally do send it to the editor. Needless to say, it should be typed on a good quality of paper. You cannot afford to use cheap paper if you want to impress the editor; and by all means be sure that you do not make a poor impression by careless and sloppy typing. It would be better to have your manuscript typed by a professional typist than to take the chance of presenting a raggedly typed manuscript.

The typing, of course, should be double-spaced with generous margins. The paper should be kept clean, free of smudges and unsightly erasures. Let the manuscript glisten with neatness. Be sure the type has been cleaned and that the typewriter ribbon is not worn out. Please remember that misspelled words are simply unforgivable. The dictionary is a simple device for avoiding the misspelling of words. If a writer is too lazy to check a word with the dictionary, then the chances are that the editor gains a poor impression of the quality of work which that writer is able to do.

Recently I received a manuscript from the hands of a college professor. The professor had sent the manuscript to his father, who also was a professor. The father sent it to me for publication. Thus the manuscript had passed through the hands of two thoroughly educated men. Yet, there was in the very first sentence of that manuscript a shocking misspelling. This seemed inexcusable, and as a result I had to drag myself mentally by the scruff of the neck to read the rest of the manuscript.

May I suggest not only double checking your manuscript before you send it to the editor, but triple checking it just to make very sure. The better the impression you make, the greater the chances of the acceptance of your manuscript. It pays to remove the stumbling blocks and the barriers to the smooth and enjoyable reading of your manuscript when it comes to the editor's desk. An editor friend of mine, who must receive regularly certain manuscripts on particular subjects, has decided to give no consideration to the manuscripts of a very able author who appears to think that because he has a reputation he can ignore spelling, grammar, punctuation, and neatness of copy, allowing the editor to do all this work for him. This editor finally chose to use a less well-known writer, and indeed a less able writer, because *his* manuscripts are always the acme of accuracy, neatness, and correctness. In other words, the editor got tired of doing the other man's work, and was willing to select the writer who left but little work for the editor to do.

Make sure, therefore, that you do all of the chore work related to your manuscript; do not leave it to the editor. For example, carefully check all your quotations. Never, never guess at them, and never trust your memory. You may be dead sure that you know a Scripture verse perfectly, but when you check it with the Bible itself you may find that your memory has played a trick on you and that one word is misplaced. If the editor gets to know that all of your quotations can be depended upon for accuracy, again he will gain a very fine impression of you as a writer, and he will grow to like your work.

If you quote copyrighted material, it is your job as a writer to secure permission for its use. Do not use copyrighted material without permission. There are many reasons why you should secure the permission rather than expect the editor to do it. In the first place, the editor is too busy to be writing around to all of the publishing houses for permissions for the quotes that occur in the mountain of manuscripts that come to him. In the second place, if the editor writes to the publishing house for permission, there is likely to be a charge that he must pay since publishing houses are often competitors. If, on the other hand, the author writes for permission, publishing houses generally assume that he is a poor person; therefore their hard hearts, somewhat touched with sympathy, are more willing to give permission. This they would not be inclined to do for a publishing house.

Recently I received several manuscripts from a writer who had packed his articles with liberal quotations. If I had purchased these manuscripts, it would have been necessary for me to write twelve letters to twelve different persons and publishers. You can see why, therefore, with a desk already piled too high with mail, I returned these manuscripts to the author with a statement that if he cared to take the trouble to secure the permissions I would be glad to consider his articles. After a couple of months he returned his manuscripts. As you may well have imagined, he had reduced the quotations to only one, for which he had secured permission. He had not relished writing a dozen letters to secure permissions. Why then had he expected that the editor would be enthusiastic about doing it?

It goes without saying that your manuscript should carry your name and address, and that with it you should enclose a self-addressed, stamped envelope. The editor is not expected to pay the postage for returning your manuscript. You are asking a service of him.

Writers may be interested to know that every publishing house receives a flood of manuscripts and employs clerks and readers to give careful attention to these manuscripts. For example, when a manuscript is received it is carefully recorded in a card index file which includes the date it is received, the name and address of the author, and the editor or reader to whom it is given. In the same way, a careful record is made of its disposition—whether returned or accepted. Busy editors give hours of service to reading scores, even hundreds, of manuscripts. Yet experience in our office indicates that we can actually accept for publication only 5 per cent of the manuscripts received. In other words, we render, without benefit to ourselves, the service of readership and criticism of 95 per cent of the manuscripts that come to us. Doubleday & Company has reported that in a recent year its staff read 5,000 unsolicited book manuscripts which were not accepted.

This leads me to say also that no one should be disturbed by a rejection slip. In the first place it may not mean that your manuscript is a poor piece of work. It may mean only that the editor has a full backlog awaiting publication; or that no specific need for your particular manuscript exists at the time; or that it was a good manuscript, but written over the heads of his readers. One of the chief difficulties of the self-conscious writer is the tendency to write in an academic vein, through fear that he may not be regarded as superior if he writes in very simple, readable English. To illustrate, we may recall the story that Alex F. Osborn relates in his book, *Your Creative Power* (quoted in *Grass Roots,* a service supplied by the School of Journalism of the University of Missouri).

"A plumber wrote the National Bureau of Standards that he had found hydrochloric acid would work wonders in clogged drains, but wanted to know whether its use would do any harm. A technical member of the staff replied: 'The efficiency of hydrochloric acid is indisputable, but the corrosive residue is incompatible with metallic permanence.' The plumber wrote back and thanked the Bureau for telling him that his method was okay. This upset the federal scientist. So he consulted his superior, who then wrote the plumber: 'We cannot assume responsibility for the production of toxic and noxious residue with hydrochloric acid and suggest you use an alternative procedure.' But even that did not close the file.

"The plumber replied how glad he was that the Bureau was crazy about hydrochloric acid for use in drains. In despair the two scientists appealed to the head of the Bureau. He closed the file by dictating this: '*Don't use hydrochloric acid. It eats the devil out of the pipes.*' "[1]

Readers as well as editors resent forced, involved, tortured language which goes around the periphery of a subject instead of making a beeline to the center. Rudolph Flesch, in his book, *The Art of Plain Talk,* cites a horrible example by way of an excerpt which he took from a popular book of science. After quoting the involved sentence, Flesch exploded: "I've read that sentence ten times, and I haven't the slightest idea of what—if anything—it says." The greatest words are really the simple words like hope, love, and faith.

Rejections of manuscripts should not be disturbing since it is good discipline to write, rewrite, and write again. Lincoln wrote the Gettysburg Address at least three times, and there are some who say he wrote it four times. Indeed, those who get rejection slips are in a glorious company. Ben Ames Williams reported to a Philadelphia audience that he had accumulated three hundred rejection slips before he sold his first story. It is reported that *The Magnificent Obsession* by Lloyd Douglas was rejected by six publishers, including Harper & Brothers. *Lorna Doone* by Blackmore was rejected by twelve publishers, and that best seller, *Peace of Mind* by Rabbi Joshua Liebman, was rejected by twenty-two publishers before it was finally accepted by Simon and Schuster. Thus it is easy to see that many of the great writers have faced the discouragement of repeated rejections.

Just as there is body surgery and tree surgery, so there is manuscript surgery. Skillful surgery not only can beautify a manuscript; it can give it a glowing personality. Cut your manuscript to the right length and to tightness. Frank Yerby, author of several best-selling novels, says that he writes not with the pen but with the knife. He cuts his manuscript, and cuts it again and again. The writer must develop the intestinal ruggedness to cut out even brilliant passages if they do not fit into his article or advance his story. The working over of your manuscript may become even more important than the original writing, and frequently takes more time.

You will want to check your metaphors and similes to make sure that they do not get mixed. You know the author who wrote: "If they don't stop shearing the sheep that lays the golden egg, they are going to pump it dry." You may also recall the writer who waxed eloquent with the words—"We need to stand face to face, shoulder to shoulder, backing each other up."

If you would have the good will of the editor, please remember that he lives under the constant threat of deadlines. Deadlines never wait and cannot be postponed. They are ordered by the printing presses, by the U. S. mails, by the daily calendars, and by the clock, and certainly by the readers' demands. These five forces join hands to shout in the editor's ears the ghostly warning—deadlines, deadlines, deadlines!

It will not help your friendly relations with the editor if your manuscript which was due on August 2 fails to arrive at all, but in its place there comes on August 5 a letter explaining that you have had company in your house and that your mother-in-law was sick and that consequently you hope to get the manuscript to him by August 15 or 20. His love for you will wane decidedly. You see, you have no regard for his precious deadlines. You treat these dear deadlines with careless irreverence—an attitude which he cannot tolerate. You have deserted him in the hour when he needed you and depended upon you. Now he is embarrassed and caught in an emergency. Naturally he will not be eager to have you produce further embarrassment and more emergencies for him. Increasingly he will turn to those persons who rigidly respect the sanctity of deadlines.

It is true that when you write your original manuscript, you will not have time to worry about all these details; for you must write in the pure glow and ardor of your urge and interest. You must be "bursting and blazing," as Carlyle says, with your subject. You must write with a kind of resistless fury. Later, you can correct with caution and concern. Let the pen strike while the fire burns, and then revise when the mind has recovered enough poise to take the objective viewpoint of the reader. When you revise your manuscript, keep the reader in mind.

You are not writing for yourself, but for those persons who are to read what you write. The trouble with most curriculum writers is that they write for other curriculum writers and not for the homespun folks. They write, as do so many of our modern poets, with an obscurity which can be understood only by other poets and not by the people.

For those of us who are engaged in Christian writing, it is important to keep in mind the group for which we write. We tend to overestimate the intelligence of our audience. No writing for adults should be over the eleventh grade. It might be even better to keep it down to the tenth grade. Similar care should be taken in writing for other age levels.

If you are writing for the busy housewife who is a Sunday school teacher, your teacher-helps must be simple, direct, practical, pointed, and inspiring. She will lose her way on Saturday night in that three-quarters of an hour's preparation if you use big words, involved sentences, hard-to-understand terms, and if you are wordy and dull. Keep your reader in your mind's eye all of the time. When you write for Sunday school boys and girls, please remember how uninteresting the Sunday school quarterly often seems to them. Make your writing sparkle, and write it with the lift of spiritual vitality. While you write, remember John Bunyan's famous words, "I wrote what I did feel and what I did feel smartingly."

We must write what we feel, what we believe, and what we practice. Our Christian writing must grow out of our experience and out of the reality of our own Christian faith and life. We must write out of a full knowledge of the gospel, a mastery of the New Testament, and out of a deep conviction of the necessity of the gospel. We must believe that God will give piercing power to his word as we interpret it. We do not write alone, for God is with us to illumine our minds. We must write out of deep and great convictions.

It may be recalled how *Ben Hur* came to be written. General Lew Wallace was riding on the train one day when he fell into conversation with the infidel, Robert Ingersoll. Ingersoll denounced the deity of Christ as myth and rubbish, and went on to say, "The preachers have no influence over me." Wallace, at that time, was himself an unbeliever, but he was so shocked and horrified by the ghastly unbelief revealed in Ingersoll's words that he determined to investigate for himself and to discover whether or not Christ was divine. Gathering a library of books, he studied for years until he became a convinced believer in the Christian gospel. Afterwards he went to the Holy Land and accurately traced the journeys of Christ. His great novel, *Ben Hur,* which has sold millions of copies, grew out of his own deep convictions.

All writing that is to endure and have power must grow out of the depth of our own faith and out of our own struggles. As Christian writers we must proclaim always the gospel; we must miss no opportunity to give forth its redemptive message. That this can be done by Christians even in the secular press is evident from the case of Vaughn Shoemaker who has been alert to seize the opportunity. He is a Pulitzer Prize-winning cartoonist of the *Chicago Daily News,* who says, "I do not draw my cartoons alone, God helps me draw them."

A few years ago, Shoemaker was searching for an idea for a Christmas cartoon for the front page of the Chicago paper. He drew a Bethlehem picture with the star gleaming down on the manger; across the body of the cartoon he wrote the words of John 3:16.

The day of the editorial conference came when the decision was to be made on his Christmas cartoon. He feared that a great daily Chicago newspaper would never print such a religious drawing. While the editors had no complaint concerning the drawing, they said that their non-religious readers would be offended by the John 3:16 quotation. Shoemaker was stubborn and would not yield to omitting the Bible verse. When the editors said that it could not be used, one of the editors, in the impasse, said, "We'll have to take this to the publisher himself and let him decide."

The publisher listened patiently, then finally said, "Shoemaker's right. We'll run the cartoon."

It made the greatest hit of anything he had ever done. Now for eight successive years it has been run on the front page of the *Chicago Daily News* on Christmas morning. It has carried a message to millions in a great commercial city. Now, the editors keep asking Shoemaker, "When are you going to draw for us another gospel cartoon?"

Shoemaker says, "It is never easy going, but the Christian can go forward in confidence. With God as his partner, he cannot fail.

When God guides pen or brush, sword or hammer, plow or hoe, the Christian has no need to fear or falter."

One of the most delicate problems which editors and writers face is that of the editor's revisions of the writer's manuscript. One asks, "Does not the writer have the right to insist that the manuscript be printed as he wants it, rather than as the editor wants it? Is it ethical for the editor to change words and phrases and to cut out sentences and paragraphs?" The editor's knife on the manuscript is very painful to the writer. Even the changing of a word by the editor can be most annoying to the writer. It must be remembered that the editor, not the writer, takes the final responsibility for publication. The letters of criticism descend upon the head of the editor; they do not descend upon the head of the writer. The cancellations of subscriptions come to the editor, not to the writer. The writer, therefore, must have sufficient appreciation of the editor's final responsibility to grant him a sympathetic understanding. The writer also needs to remember that the publication is the editor's "baby." He has nurtured it in the cradle and protected it through the hazards of stormy weather and periods of illness and depression, and, therefore, he does have a paternal and protective regard for his publication.

My own plan is usually to accept manuscripts on the clearly written understanding that the writer grants the customary editorial license to make such changes as seem necessary to fit the manuscript to the needs and desires of our readers. If, as rarely happens, some writer says that he cannot give consent to changes, then I find it necessary to return his manuscript and refuse publication. The writer and editor must establish mutual trust. As an editor I may be forced to abbreviate a manuscript because of space limitations, and I may change a word or phrase in order to make the article more acceptable to our readers. The editor usually knows the prejudices of his audience much better than does the writer.

If there are any really radical changes in the manuscript, then it should be resubmitted to the writer. If the changes are too much for the writer to take, he can certainly make his protest and may even withdraw the manuscript if he so desires. These things can work out with happy results. While now and again a writer will be disappointed because some pet phrase or some beautiful sentence has been omitted, in the long run the writer will come to feel that the editor is his friend who seeks only to improve his manuscript and to give it the widest possible acceptability.

Let the writer and editor then be friends, good friends who work together for great ends, and who find unending joy in the service of God.

THE BOOK OF MY DREAMS

Miles W. Smith

For a brief biographical note concerning Dr. Miles W. Smith, turn to his address entitled "Taboos for Religious Writers," beginning on page 168.

Those of you who have been regular attendants at these Christian Writers and Editors' Conferences doubtless have concluded by now that I am afflicted with a perverse fondness for giving unpalatable advice. I say "unpalatable advice" because—human nature being what it is—a person welcomes only such advice as flatters his vanity or encourages him to pursue a course he has already chosen. Last year, when I attempted to point out that the writing of a worthy and publishable book was not so easy as falling off the proverbial log, some felt that my words were very discouraging and might better have been left unsaid. I am inclined to believe, however, that my words did no more than sound a warning to would-be writers who lack the determination and stamina to pursue the stern disciplines which every first-rate writer must undergo.

Certainly, one should gain some proficiency in the shorter literary forms—the story, the essay, and the article—before undertaking a full-length book. Incidentally, books usually are not so profitable to their authors as are short stories and articles, when one takes into account the much greater length of time required to write them. Indeed, if one hopes to find in writing an easy way to earn money, one is due for a disappointment. To all such, I would recommend baby sitting as a much more lucrative form of employment. As for those who already are under contract to produce a manuscript or who labor under a strong inner compulsion to put their thoughts on paper, I am sure that nothing I have said, or may say, will stop them, or should stop them. My words will be only so much counsel with respect to various procedures.

The Book of My Dreams! Someday there may come into my office a book manuscript which measures up to all of my specifications, for I do not believe that my specifications are unreasonable or impossible of attainment. It will be in the shape that every manuscript should be put before it is submitted to an editor. But frankly, I've been waiting for that manuscript now for quite some time. I'm becoming a bit discouraged. Perhaps it will never come to hand. But I can dream, can't I? If that expression is too colloquial for the purists who are present, let me change it to "One may dream, mayn't one?"

1. This Book of My Dreams will be a finished literary work. I do not say this unkindly, but I have sometimes suspected that many writers are so eager to receive their payment checks that they do not take time really to finish their manuscripts. They suppose that it will be sufficient if they merely set down a few ideas and observations. The editor, of course, will organize their material, correct the mistakes, make a presentable article or book out of their suggestions and jottings. Is not that what editors are paid to do? Well, not entirely. Interestingly enough, an editor frequently will give such help. He will care for all the things which the author has left undone. But it is not wise to presume too much upon an editor's friendship and patience. It is just possible that he may discover that morning a manuscript which needs less editorial attention, and choose to publish it instead of yours.

So do not be in too much haste to submit your manuscript. One of my teachers was fond of giving this advice: "Write with fury; correct with phlegm." By which he meant: "Get down on paper all that you possibly can while your heart is still aglow with enthusiasm for your subject; then, having laid aside your enthusiasm, proceed with phlegm (calmness, equanimity) and all the critical judgment which you can muster to look at what you have written; and correct, revise, and improve." This "working over" frequently is more important than the original writing and may take five times as long.

I advise letting a manuscript cool off before submitting it to an editor. That is to say, when the manuscript has been finished, lay it aside for a week or a month; then come back to it. You then can read it more impersonally. It will be almost as though you were reading something written by another person. You will see what your manuscript lacks and be able to revise it accordingly. Only then will the manuscript be representative of your best work.

It may seem that I am counseling a wholly unreasonable amount of labor, but there is no other way by which a really good book can be written. I understand that Flaubert, when writing *Madame Bovary,* spent three days on eight lines. Even then, he was not satisfied with them. I read recently *A History of the Cure of Souls,* by Dr. John T. McNeill, professor of church history at Union Theological Seminary. Tucked away in the preface, I found this modest statement: "This volume has been half a lifetime in preparation, but it is only about twelve years since I resolved to complete it in the form of a general history." Half a lifetime spent in gathering material, twelve years spent in writing, and only 371 pages! Will the book repay the author for the amount of time spent on it? Not in dollars and cents, but in the satisfaction of having made an important contribution to human knowledge.

2. This Book of My Dreams will be written in the author's best literary style. There is a recognizable difference between the spoken word, intended to be heard, and the written word, intended to be read; so much difference in fact, that addresses or sermons stenographically reported or preserved on a wire recorder, as a rule, need much revision before they can be printed.

There is no law against good writing. If you are of a mind to write a book—and who isn't?—it is not enough that you shall have something to say; you should seek also to say it well. Unless you are compiling a telephone book or a city directory, put into your sentences all of the movement, all of the color, and all of the music that you possibly can. Try to say everything so well that no one else will ever need to say it again. Remember that your sentences, if carefully worded, can conjure up precious memories, stir men's blood, or set men's feet on paths of high adventure.

Style is so much an expression of one's own personality that no editor can impart it to an author's manuscript. The editor, if he is charitable and patient, can correct the author's errors of fact, the faulty grammar, the incorrect spelling, and the haphazard punctuation, but he cannot make the manuscript a true expression of the author's personality. The most that he can do is to rewrite the manuscript in his own style, for him an onerous task and for the author, in all likelihood, an unacceptable result. Consequently, you must put your own personality into your manuscript, otherwise it will never get there. Saying that a writer should have his own individual style is, of course, something quite different from saying that a writer is privileged to be eccentric.

Good writing demands clarity of meaning. If the writing can possess force and elegance also, well and good. But, above all, it must be clear, understandable. Please, no speaking in tongues, whether those tongues be ancient languages or modern jargons! And no gobbledygook! Hear the admonition of the apostle Paul: "Except ye utter by the tongue words easy to be understood, how shall it be known what is spoken? for ye shall speak into the air" (1 Cor. 14:9).

3. The Book of My Dreams, when at last it comes to hand, will be a unified literary work. It will be devoted wholly to the exposition of a single topic. It will not be a potpourri of literary exercises, however brilliant they may be. It will not be marred by long excursuses (what an awful plural!), however much those excursuses may contribute in the way of background information. The Book of My Dreams will announce its subject or contention—no guessing contest, please, as to what the manuscript is about—and then will proceed in logical fashion to explain that subject or to defend that contention. Six or eight sermons on various texts, for example, do not constitute a unified book. They may be samples of a man's better preaching, but the assembling of them is accidental and artificial. On the other hand, six or eight sermons based on texts chosen from Paul's letter to the Philippians may serve as an inspiring exposition of that epistle. It is true, of course, that occasionally books are published bearing such titles as *Collected Essays of Mr. So-and-So*. Those books do not establish the reputation of Mr. So-and-So; they are published because Mr. So-and-So already has an established reputation, and because many have come to desire a complete, definitive edition of his writing.

This principle of unity holds good with respect to books which, to the eye, present three or four major divisions. An excellently written treatise, *Our Religious Traditions,* by Sterling P. Lamprecht, has three major parts: The Heritage of Judaism, The Genius of Catholicism, and The Adventure of Protestantism. But a brief introduction informs the reader that the author will undertake to show what each of these three major faiths can contribute to today's world. The conclusion sums up the author's findings and challenges the reader to consider whether or not it is possible to achieve some synthesis of the three which will benefit all mankind. I am not defending the author's contention; I am merely pointing out that behind his threefold division of material he has a single constructive purpose.

Similarly, I read recently a manuscript which might fittingly be entitled *Three Freedoms.* It discusses spiritual freedom, ecclesiastical freedom, and political freedom. The author finds spiritual freedom exemplified in the life and writings of the apostle Paul. He finds ecclesiastical freedom exemplified in the life and writings of Balthasar Hübmaier. In the life and writings of Thomas Paine, he finds a shining example and convincing exposition of political freedom. Now, observe that so long as the idea of freedom, whether spiritual, ecclesiastical, or political, is kept to the fore, the book possesses unity. Paul, Hübmaier, and Paine merely illustrate the various phases of freedom. But should the author in his enthusiasm for these heroes undertake to write a complete biography of each, should he permit the idea of freedom to drop into the background, immediately the book would lose its unity. We then would have merely three biographical sketches brought mechanically within the covers of one book.

Perhaps you have had six or eight articles published in various periodicals. Each article is excellent in its own way; each has received warm commendation. Do you not see, in the light of what has been said, that these articles will not necessarily constitute a truly unified book?

4. The author of the Book of My Dreams will watch his figures of speech. He will use sufficient metaphors and similes to give his writing a pictorial quality; he will refrain from using so many of them as to make his manuscript involved, fanciful, and affected. He

will, of course, avoid the trite; he will shun the clichés, and equally the incongruous and far-fetched. He will seek aptness rather than alliteration; he will choose the durable homespun in preference to the diaphanous raiment affected by the socialites of Greek mythology. Do not change from one figure of speech to another when you are still in the midst of your sentence. For example, the amendments to our national Constitution may be likened to massive cords binding together our body politic. Well and good, but do not then permit those massive cords suddenly to extend hands of welcome to the refugees who seek our shores. Cords do not possess hands.

Beware, therefore, of mixing your figures of speech. One writer confused the writings of Jonathan Swift with the Holy Scriptures. Remembering *Gulliver's Travels,* he said that one man had Lilliputian courage and that another had Goliathan courage. But the opposite of Lilliputian is not Goliathan, but Brobdingnagian. The opposite of Goliathan, I suppose, would be Davidic. You cannot have one term out of one pair and the other term out of the other pair.

5. The author of the Book of My Dreams will exercise care also in the handling of quotations. It is easy to go astray in this matter, especially if one quotes from memory. One of our writers had in his manuscript a sentence concerning America. He thought to conclude it with a familiar quotation. The sentence read: "I can just see this country of ours. . . . There are the tropical land of Florida, the winter snows in New England, the milder climate of the West, and on both sides of our country 'ocean waves beat shores.' " The last four words, "ocean waves beat shores," were in quotes. I suppose he was trying to quote from Faber's hymn, reading, "Hark, hark, my soul! angelic songs are swelling o'er earth's green fields and ocean's wave-beat shore." But "ocean" should have been "ocean's"; "waves" should have been "wave"; "beat" instead of standing alone as a verb, should have been joined by a hyphen to "wave," making the compound adjective "wave-beat"; and "shores" should have been "shore." Out of four words, not even one was right! Furthermore, the words, if correctly quoted, would not have fitted into the author's sentence. The author had no right to change them to suit his convenience.

Much the same thing frequently happens when an author attempts to weave into his manuscript quotations from the Scriptures.

P

The Scriptures, when quoted, must be quoted correctly, and preferably always from the same version. In weaving in the Scripture words, one must be on one's guard lest the quotation introduces an abrupt and ungrammatical shift of subject from singular to plural, or from plural to singular, or a change of tense from present to past or from past to present. One may not alter the Scriptures to suit one's convenience.

6. Furthermore, the author of the Book of My Dreams will remember that he is writing a book to be read, not a Ph.D. thesis to be entombed in a university library. He will not feel called upon to document every statement; and he will bear in mind that footnotes do not add beauty to the printed page.

Many writers make entirely too many quotations from current books. Is it because they have nothing of their own to say? If the writer must quote, let him quote with meticulous accuracy. And let him indicate in full the source of his quotation. By "in full," I mean, not the name of the book and author only, but the publisher, and—most important—the number of the page from which the quotation was made. This information is needed when writing to the publisher for permission to include the quotation in the published work. Permissions often are difficult to secure; sometimes a charge is made for them. It is well, therefore, to avoid quotations which are not essential to the book. Anyway, you will want your book to stand on its own merits, not to be dependent upon the merit of quotations you have made from other writers.

If I were writing a book, I would secure all the needed permissions before submitting the manuscript to a publisher. The author has more time in which to secure these permissions than the editor has. Furthermore, the author has at hand the reference books from which he has drawn his material, whereas the editor may need to secure them from a library. Finally, the owner of the copyright is more likely to be generous to an author than to another publishing firm, which presumably is able to pay well for the material requested.

7. Finally, in the Book of My Dreams, all such mundane matters as consistency in spelling will have been taken care of by the author. I recall that Mark Twain once said that he did not have much regard for a writer who knew of only one way to spell each word. I do not hold with that point of view. As an editor, I want each word

BOOKS AS A PUBLISHER SEES THEM

FRED C. BECKER

Mr. Fred C. Becker has been active in the book trade for many years, and by his wide experience is well qualified to discuss the merchandising of books from both the production and the distribution points of view. For eight years he was connected with the Methodist Publishing House, Boston. Since 1935 he has been with Harper & Brothers. He now has a supervisory responsibility in connection with Harper & Brothers' Religious Book and Bible Departments, but comments: "I am still a book peddler at heart; I love books and I love to sell them."

T HE FUNCTION of a book publisher is to serve as the medium by which an author with a worth-while story or idea, set down on manuscript paper, reaches an audience of readers in the form of a printed book. The publisher's operations in carrying out this function fall into three divisions: (1) editorial, (2) manufacturing, (3) distribution or sales. It is his responsibility and stewardship to perform these publishing operations usefully and to return to the company a reasonable profit to reward those who provide the capital.

At Harper & Brothers, three main criteria motivate the choice of a manuscript, and none of them is concerned primarily with the author's religion or theological position: (1) Does the manuscript state a valid position and does it contain ideas which are worth promulgating or which add to our verifiable knowledge? (2) Is the material well organized, lucid, and attractively presented? (3) Is there a clearly defined group of readers that can be reached effectively?

The books on each Harper seasonal list, so far as origin is concerned, fall in the following categories: manuscripts received from authors of previous books on the Harper list, usually on subjects of their own special interests; manuscripts resulting from the editor's request for books needed in fields in which the authors are eminently qualified; manuscripts from authors, new or old, who have been recommended to our firm by friends, agents, British publishers, or other Harper authors; and, finally, books selected from the very large number of unsolicited manuscripts received from persons unknown to us in any of the above ways.

In 1950 over six hundred unsolicited religious book manuscripts were received by our department. Perhaps three to five of them were accepted by us for publication, and I would hazard a guess that possibly ten of the others were taken later by other publishers. This avalanche of manuscripts is read by us without cost to the authors because of the firmly fixed tradition that any manuscript sent to an editorial office, regardless of origin, should have every consideration.

Now it is obvious that Mr. Eugene Exman, our editor, cannot himself read all these hundreds of manuscripts each year. However, trained readers go over the manuscripts. It is admitted that in some cases only part of a manuscript is read, but as George Horace Lorimer once said, "You do not have to eat all of a rotten egg to know that it is rotten."

If the first reader sees any possibility in a manuscript, it will then be given to a second reader. In special fields, outside professional authorities are consulted. If a manuscript continues to be recommended, it finally reaches the desk of Mr. Exman for ultimate decision. Thus he becomes a reader of opinions about manuscripts. It is highly unlikely, however, that a first reader will summarily decline and send back with a rejection slip a first-class manuscript. If he did this twice, he would be looking for a new job! In fact, it is as unlikely that such a manuscript will be rejected on one reading as it is that Mr. Exman will contract for a poor manuscript. The good manuscript, if offered, may not be taken, but it will not be ignored or treated lightly. Finally, a good editor tries to keep ahead of the crowd, but not too far ahead. He tries to know what people are thinking and wanting before they themselves fully realize it, and to recognize the author or manuscript that will build future trends of thought.

At this point a brief discussion of the manufacturing phase of publishing is appropriate. The rising costs of labor and materials are altering the whole aspect of this side of our business. Books have never had to contend with price ceilings, even in wartime; yet with all their freedom of price movement, books have risen less in price than any other commodity or article that you and I can name. Whereas publishers' costs have risen about 100 per cent in the past ten years, and whereas the price of almost every article, whether it be an auto, a pair of shoes, or the good old American hot dog, has risen 100 per cent, and food in general nearly 120 per cent, books have increased in price no more than 30 per cent, and religious books even less than that.

How has the publisher performed these gymnastics and stayed in business? Frankly, his profit margin has been cut to the bone, and in many cases his first printings show a loss, even when all copies are sold. He is more and more dependent on book club adoptions and subsidiary rights to show a black figure on his ledger. He cuts corners in manufacturing to keep the retail price down. During the war, the "slim" book found its way into the field. By using lighter weight paper, by reducing margins, and by reducing type sizes, we produced a book which was half the former size, yet contained the same content. Actually, the small book has numerous advantages to the consumer—in appearance, in ease of handling, and in stacking on library shelves. At the same time, since thin paper is lighter in weight than thick paper, the publisher was able to produce twice as many books from the paper poundage quota allowed him by the governmental agencies.

Since the war, we have begun to make use of plastic plates, which are cheaper than metal plates. In many cases, when we are not sure that the book will be reprinted, we print from type, thereby eliminating the expense of plates. And there has been developed a new and less expensive three-piece binding which is composed of a cloth spine and paper-over-board covers. When reprinting, we put ten to twenty-five books of similar size through at the same time, thus effecting savings in the make-ready of the presses. This may hold up needed books for several weeks until the entire group is ready, but it helps to keep prices down. These are a few of the ways by which a publisher battles constantly the increases in costs and prices.

Another cost area is that of royalty. With the first-printing picture so gloomy, a publisher may ask the author to help initially on the first 1,000 or 2,500 copies by accepting a 5 per cent, instead of a 10 per cent royalty, perhaps with a compensating increase on later printings. Thus, what may seem to an author at first like a real sacrifice may prove to be the final factor in pricing the book correctly and thereby securing the maximum sale and income for author, publisher, and bookseller alike.

I think that now all the economies that can be reasonably effected have been made. Prices must reflect costs in the book business as they do in milk and autos. The public must soon be asked to pay fairly for books, and I believe it will; if not, we had best find out. In our field, the public will buy at a reasonable price any good and needed book. The marginal book may suffer; but perhaps everyone will be better off as the result.

Now to state a few specific phases of the manufacturing process. The manuscript has been accepted and the contract signed. It is then put in the hands of a stylist; this is one of the most important steps in publishing. This person, sometimes called a "professional comma chaser," checks the manuscript for style, spelling, and punctuation before the printer gets it for setting into type, thus cutting down very expensive proof-correcting charges.

After being styled, the manuscript goes to the designer, who will ask some specific questions. How many pages are wanted? (This will be determined by the length of the manuscript and the retail price desired.) What do the editors have in mind as to size and kind of type? Should extracts be set in body type and indented, or should they be set in smaller type and full measure? How are footnotes to be handled? Will there be an index and illustrations? If so, should the illustrations be half tones, line cuts, or a folio of offset illustrations bound in the front, back, or middle of the book? Is the book to be printed from type or from electroplates? What kind of paper shall be used? (The longer the prospective life and usefulness of the book, the better must be the quality of the paper.) What should be the bulk of the book? (A pocket reader, for example, should be as thin as practicable.) Should the title and author's name be stamped on shelf-back only? Shall we use gold ink or try an attractive two-color ink stamping? Would a pasted label be appropriate? Decisions need to be made also regarding the color and style of binding cloth, and whether the jacket shall be an ordinary typeset wrapper or one designed by an artist. Publishers spend a lot of time and money on the jacket, so that it will attract the attention of the ultimate consumer and reflect the contents of the book itself.

Contrary to general belief, most publishers do not do their own type composition, printing, and binding. They let this work out on bids to firms especially equipped to do book work economically and attractively. The publisher, however, must have a manufacturing department to carry on the detailed and intricate job of shepherding a book from manuscript form to composing room, to foundry, to pressroom, and finally to the bindery—and to watch the pennies.

In the period since 1935, the minimum quantity of books that can be printed on first editions (and the publisher *just break even*) has steadily increased, due to rising costs and the penalty which the printer is now imposing on small runs. Prior to the war we often printed 1,250 to 1,500 copies of a book by a new author or of a specialized character, being content to break even in the hope that a sufficient number of our books would go beyond the first edition and show a profit. During the war this minimum quantity rose to 2,500, and within the past twelve months this figure has risen to 3,500 or higher. This is only the break-even point on a given religious title, priced as realistically as we can forecast. This situation is going to create some casualties along the way, but it probably will result in the publication of better books, and in the long run it will make for better authors and better eventual sales.

To give an idea of the time schedule set up for a book, let us suppose that a manuscript was accepted for publication and the contract signed January 1. It is likely that the book will not be scheduled for publication before October. This allows four months (January to April) for the necessary editorial work. Between May and August the firm's salesmen are calling on the trade and taking advance orders. These orders give some indication of the number of copies which may wisely be printed. Five months may be thought of as the very *minimum* of time for the average book to go from the manuscript stage to the finished book. Manuscripts that require technical supervision by the manufacturing department may take much longer. When a "quickie" is put through in a shorter period of time, some other book suffers a delay. There are today no soft spots in the book manufacturer's schedule. Books start to the West Coast three to four weeks prior to publication. Books for nearer points are sent a little later. Theoretically, all stores have a stock ready for sale on publication day.

The publisher will use all available means to advertise the book and to promote its sale. The amount of money to be spent on paid advertising in books and magazines, of course, is limited. The advertising budget is determined by the character of the book, the size of the edition, the wholesale price, etc.

Furthermore, the publisher usually sends from seventy-five to one hundred complimentary review copies to magazines and newspapers, and to people he believes can help the book by word-of-mouth. Selecting the most advantageous hundred review media and individuals is a task worthy of Solomon's wisdom! There are not only book editors of newspapers, magazines, and the religious press to consider, but also columnists, radio reviewers, public personages, authors, teachers, and denominational officials. Each book demands close attention, lest we waste copies or give away our business. Review copies are mailed two to four weeks in advance of publication, in an attempt to synchronize the review-break with the publication date of the book.

It is not wise for an author to put on a disguise or go into a bookstore incognito and ask for his book. There are ten thousand books published annually, and every title cannot possibly be in the most prominent spot. Booksellers are enterprising people; they want to sell books. If there is a market for your book in their stores, they will seek you out and ask for autographed copies; and they will increase the space and promotion as the demand accelerates. In fact, in a good many cases your local bookstore will create the demand. Instead of being a house detective, therefore, let your publisher know in what cities you are known. Keep him informed of your speaking engagements and addresses four to six weeks in advance. He will see that copies of your book are available either through your denominational house, local bookstore, or through the local person in charge of the meetings. We find this to be one of the best ways to sell books, and by letting the publisher handle the arrangements it relieves the author of any embarrassment he might feel in connection with the promotion and sale of his own book.

Religious book publishing has become big business during the last fifteen years. We have seen our books appear on the best-seller lists. We have seen their acceptance and promotion in general bookstores; sales by department stores have increased perhaps tenfold. The next great growth in the field of religious books is going to come in the churches. The preacher who has his congregation for an hour on Sunday can increase his ministry a hundredfold by recommending good religious books to his parishioners for their inspiration the other six days of the week.

RELIGIOUS PUBLISHING HOUSES AND EDITORS-IN-CHIEF

COMPILED BY BENJAMIN P. BROWNE

ADVENT CHRISTIAN CHURCH

Board of Religious Education of the Advent Christian General Conference
Secretary, Rev. (Mrs.) Susie W. Davis, 615 Randolph Street, Charleston 2, W. Va.

Editor of Denominational Paper and Young People's Paper, Dr. J. A. Nichols, 160 Warren Street, Boston, Mass.

Editor of Sunday School Lesson Quarterlies, Dr. L. J. Carter, 16 Van Zandt Street, East Norwalk, Conn.

Advent Christian Publication Society, 160 Warren Street, Boston 19, Mass.

AFRICAN METHODIST EPISCOPAL CHURCH

Board of Christian Education, 414—8th Ave., S., Nashville 4, Tenn.

Editor-in-Chief of Religious Literature, Dr. Charles W. Abington, 1277 W. 25th Street, Los Angeles, Calif.

African Methodist Episcopal Sunday School Union Press, 414—8th Ave., S., Nashville 4, Tenn.

AFRICAN METHODIST EPISCOPAL ZION CHURCH

Christian Education Department, 128 E. 58th Street, Chicago 37, Ill.

Editor of Church School Literature, Dr. J. S. Nathaniel Tross, Box 1828, Charlotte, N. C.

African Methodist Episcopal Zion Publishing House, Box 1047, Charlotte, N. C.

AMERICAN BAPTIST CONVENTION

The American Baptist Publication Society, The Board of Education and Publication, 1701-1703 Chestnut Street, Philadelphia 3, Pa.

Executive Director of Division of Christian Publications, Dr. Benjamin P. Browne

Editor of Youth Publications, Rev. Lawrence P. Fitzgerald

The Judson Press, 1701-1703 Chestnut Street, Philadelphia 3, Pa.

Director, Book Publishing Department, Dr. Miles W. Smith

AMERICAN LUTHERAN CHURCH

Board of Parish Education, 57 E. Main Street, Columbus 15, Ohio

Editor of Sunday School Literature, Dr. C. E. Linder

Wartburg Press, 55-59 E. Main Street, Columbus 15, Ohio

AUGUSTANA EVANGELICAL LUTHERAN CHURCH

Board of Parish Education, 2445 Park Avenue, Minneapolis 4, Minn.

Editor of Uniform Lessons, Dr. Daniel Nystrom, 639—38th Street, Rock Island, Ill.

Augustana Book Concern, 639—38th Street, Rock Island, Ill.

BAPTIST FEDERATION OF CANADA

Chairman, Dr. Waldo C. Machum, 8 Market Square, Saint John, New Brunswick

Baptist Publications Committee of Canada, 299 Queen Street, W., Toronto 2 B, Ontario

Editor of Canadian Baptist, Rev. Thomas Bruce McDormand, 223 Church Street, Toronto 2, Ontario

CHRISTIAN SCIENCE

The Christian Science Publishing Society, Norway Street, Boston, Mass.

Editor, Miss Viola S. May

CHURCH OF THE BRETHREN

Christian Education Commission—General Brotherhood Board, 22 S. State Street, Elgin, Ill.

Editor, Dr. E. G. Hoff

Brethren Publishing House (The Elgin Press), 22 S. State Street, Elgin, Ill.

CHURCH OF CHRIST (HOLINESS), UNITED STATES OF AMERICA

National Publishing Board (National Publishing House), 44th and St. Lawrence, Chicago, Ill.

Editor of Truth Messenger, Mr. L. F. Dunn

CHURCH OF ENGLAND IN CANADA

General Board of Religious Education, Church House, 604 Jarvis Street, Toronto 5, Ontario

Editorial Secretary, Dr. D. B. Rogers

CHURCH OF GOD

Board of Christian Education, 1303 E. 5th Street, Anderson, Ind.

Editor-in-Chief and Chairman of Publications Committee, Rev. Harold L. Phillips

Editor of Church School Literature, Miss Lottie M. Franklin

Associate Editor of Youth-Adult Publications, Rev. Kenneth Hall

Gospel Trumpet Company (Warner Press) (Triumphant Art Publishers), Anderson, Ind.

CHURCH OF JESUS CHRIST OF LATTER-DAY SAINTS

Salt Lake City, Utah

Editor, George A. Smith

CHURCH OF THE NAZARENE

Department of Church Schools, 2923 Troost Avenue, Kansas City 10, Mo.

Editor-in-Chief, Dr. Albert F. Harper

Nazarene Publishing House (Beacon Hill Press), 2923 Troost Avenue, Kansas City 10, Mo.

CUMBERLAND PRESBYTERIAN CHURCH

Board of Publication and Christian Education, McKenzie, Tenn.

Editor of the Cumberland Presbyterian, Rev. Ray Dobbins, 117—8th Ave., S., Nashville 3, Tenn.

THE DANISH EVANGELICAL LUTHERAN CHURCH IN AMERICA
Council of Elementary Religious Education
Editor of Denominational Paper, Rev. H. Strandskov, 25 Chippewa Street, Dwight, Ill.
Editor of Sunday School Paper, Mrs. Viggo Nielsen, Tyler, Minn.

DISCIPLES OF CHRIST
United Christian Missionary Society, Division of Christian Education, Missions Bldg., Indianapolis 7, Ind.
Christian Board of Publication (Bethany Press), 2700 Pine Blvd., St. Louis 3, Mo.
Editor-in-Chief of Church School Publications, Dr. Glenn McRae
Editor of Young People's Publications, Rev. Ray L. Henthorne

EVANGELICAL AND REFORMED CHURCH
Board of Christian Education and Publication, 1505 Race Street, Philadelphia 2, Pa.
Director of Publications and Curriculum, Dr. Fred D. Wentzel
Christian Education Press, Philadelphia 2, Pa., and St. Louis 3, Mo.
Heidelberg Press, 1505 Race Street, Philadelphia 2, Pa.
Eden Publishing House, 1724 Chouteau Ave., St. Louis 3, Mo.
Central Publishing House, 2969 W. 25th Street, Cleveland 13, Ohio

THE EVANGELICAL UNITED BRETHREN CHURCH
The Board of Christian Education, 1900 U. B. Bldg., Dayton 2, Ohio
The Evangelical Press, 3rd and Reily Streets, Harrisburg, Pa.
Publisher, Dr. Roy H. Stetler
The Otterbein Press, 240 W. 5th Street, Dayton 2, Ohio
Editor of Sunday School Literature, Dr. O. O. Arnold

FREE METHODIST CHURCH OF NORTH AMERICA
Winona Lake, Ind.
Editor-in-Chief of Sunday School Literature, Dr. B. L. Olmstead
Editor of Youth Papers, Dr. LeRoy M. Lowell, 1626 W. Troy, Ferndale 20, Mich.

THE MENNONITE CHURCH
The Mennonite Publishing Company, 616 Walnut Ave., Scottdale, Pa.
Editor-in-Chief, Dr. Paul Lederach

THE METHODIST CHURCH
The Board of Education—Division of the Local Church, Box 871, Nashville 2, Tenn.
Editorial Division, 810 Broadway, Nashville 2, Tenn.
Executive Editor, Dr. C. A. Bowen
Editor of the Church School, Rev. Walter N. Vernon, Jr.
Editor of Youth Publications, Dr. J. Emerson Ford
Methodist Publishing House (Abingdon-Cokesbury Press)
Publishing Agents
   Mr. Lovick Pierce, 810 Broadway, Nashville 2, Tenn.
   Dr. Roy L. Smith, 740 Rush Street, Chicago 11, Ill.
Abingdon-Cokesbury Press
   810 Broadway, Nashville 2, Tenn.
   150—5th Ave., New York 11, N. Y.

MISSOURI LUTHERAN SYNOD
Concordia Publishing House, 3558 S. Jefferson Ave., St. Louis 18, Mo.
Editor, Henry Rische

NATIONAL BAPTIST CONVENTION OF AMERICA
National Baptist Publishing Board
Department of Education—Sunday School Congress, 523—2nd Ave., N.,
Nashville 3, Tenn.
Editorial Secretary, Dr. E. H. Borden, 1205 Gladys St., Beaumont, Texas

NATIONAL BAPTIST CONVENTION, UNITED STATES OF AMERICA (Inc.)
Department of Christian Education, 4th Ave. and Cedar Street, Nashville
3, Tenn.
Editor-in-Chief, Dr. George W. Harvey

NORTH AMERICAN BAPTIST GENERAL CONFERENCE
Editor, Dr. J. C. Gunst, 7308 Madison Street, Forest Park, Ill.

PRESBYTERIAN CHURCH IN CANADA
Board of Sabbath Schools and Young People's Societies, 63 Saint George
Street, Toronto 5, Ontario
Editor of Publications, Rev. N. G. Smith, 165 Elizabeth Street, Toronto
2, Ontario

PRESBYTERIAN CHURCH IN THE UNITED STATES
Board of Education, Presbyterian Bldg., 8 N. 6th Street, Richmond 9, Va.
Division of Religious Education
Editor-in-Chief, Dr. Holmes Rolston
Editor of Youth Materials, Miss Ruth D. See

PRESBYTERIAN CHURCH IN THE UNITED STATES OF AMERICA
Board of Christian Education, Witherspoon Bldg., Philadelphia 7, Pa.
Division of Education in Home, Church, and Community
Editor-in-Chief, Rev. Norman F. Langford
Editor of Uniform Lesson Materials, Dr. Earl F. Zeigler
Editor for Young People's Publications, Miss Margaret G. Hummel
The Westminster Press, Witherspoon Bldg., Philadelphia 7, Pa.

PROTESTANT EPISCOPAL CHURCH
Department of Christian Education, National Council, 281—4th Ave., New
York 10, N. Y.
Editor-in-Chief, Canon V. O. Ward

REFORMED CHURCH IN AMERICA
Board of Education, 156—5th Ave., New York 10, N. Y.
Director of Department of Publication (Half Moon Press), Dr. Bernard
J. Mulder

SEVENTH-DAY ADVENTISTS
Review and Herald Publishing Association
Editor, H. H. Votaw, Takoma Park, Washington 12, D. C.

Q

SEVENTH-DAY BAPTISTS

Board of Christian Education, Alfred, N. Y.
Editor of Adult Bible School Helps, Rev. Erlo Sutton, 601 Marine Street, Boulder, Colo.

SOUTHERN BAPTIST SUNDAY SCHOOL BOARD

The Broadman Press, Nashville, Tenn.
Editor-in-Chief, Dr. Clifton J. Allen
Youth Publications, J. E. Lambdin, Dr. C. Aubrey Hearn

UNITARIAN

The Beacon Press, 25 Beacon Street, Boston, Mass.
Editor, Melvin Arnold

UNITED BRETHREN IN CHRIST

Department of Christian Education, 402 United Brethren Bldg., Huntington, Ind.
Editor of Sunday School Literature, Rev. J. L. Towne
United Brethren Publishing Establishment, United Brethren Bldg., Huntington, Ind.

UNITED CHURCH OF CANADA

Board of Christian Education, 299 Queen Street, W., Toronto 2B, Ontario
The United Church Publishing House, 299 Queen Street, W., Toronto 2B, Ontario
Book Steward, Dr. C. H. Dickinson
Editor, Dr. George A. Little
Associate Editor, Dr. Archer Wallace

UNITED LUTHERAN CHURCH IN AMERICA

The Parish and Church School Board, 1228 Spruce Street, Philadelphia 7, Pa.
Editorial Staff
Dr. Theodore K. Finck, Dr. Arthur H. Getz, Dr. Gustav K. Wiencke

THE UNITED MISSIONARY CHURCH

Editor of Bethel Series of Sunday School Literature, Dr. J. A. Huffman
The Bethel Publishing Company, 1819 S. Main Street, Elkhart, Ind.

UNITED PRESBYTERIAN CHURCH OF NORTH AMERICA

Board of Christian Education, 209—9th Street, Pittsburgh 22, Pa.
Associate Secretary and Editor-in-Chief, Dr. Richard W. Graves

WESLEYAN METHODIST CHURCH OF AMERICA

General Sunday School Board, 330 E. Onondaga Street, Syracuse, N. Y.
Editor of Sunday School Literature, Rev. Rufus D. Reisdorph, Houghton College, Houghton, N. J.

INTERDENOMINATIONAL

The Friendship Press, 156 Fifth Ave., New York, N. Y.
The American Bible Society, 450 Park Ave., New York 22, N. Y.
  Editor, Rev. Francis Stifler
American Tract Society, 21 W. 46th Street, New York 19, N. Y.
  Editor, Henry S. Perry
The American Sunday School Union, 1816 Chestnut Street, Philadelphia 3, Pa.
  Editor, Dr. William J. Jones
Association Press, 291 Broadway, New York 7, N. Y.
  Editor, James Rietmulder

NON-DENOMINATIONAL

David C. Cook Publishing Co., Elgin, Ill.
Zondervan Publishing House, Grand Rapids, Mich.
  Editor, T. W. Engstrom
Moody Press, 820 N. LaSalle Street, Chicago 10, Ill.
World Publishing Co., 2231 W. 110th Street, Cleveland 2, Ohio
  Manager, Religious Dept., Rev. C. L. Bathrick
The Standard Publishing Co., Cincinnati 10, Ohio
The Highley Press, Butler, Ind.
The Scripture Press, 434 S. Wabash Ave., Chicago 5, Ill.
The Warner Press, Anderson, Ind.
The Union Gospel Press, P. O. Box 6059, Cleveland 1, Ohio
The Gospel Light Press, Oakland, Calif.
Van Kampen Press, Wheaton, Ill.
Light and Life Press, Winona Lake, Ind.
Wm. B. Eerdmans Publishing Co., Grand Rapids, Mich.

MARKET CHART FOR LEADING RELIGIOUS PERIODICALS

As there is no official compilation of religious publishing markets, this partial listing was compiled mainly through correspondence with the editors. Rates and policy may have since varied slightly.

FOR ADULT PERIODICALS

THE LUTHERAN (Lutheran)

1228 Spruce Street, Philadelphia 7, Pa. Articles and fiction: 100-2,000 words. Payment: 1c-2c a word. Preference: (1) personal religious experience; (2) human interest stories pertinent to the church press; (3) instructive articles on Christian ideology; and (4) various aspects of the church at work in the world. Note from editor: "Popular style of writing and concrete details. No editorializing."

THE CHRISTIAN CENTURY (Non-denominational)

407 S. Dearborn Street, Chicago 5, Ill. Articles: 1,500-6,000 words. Payment: $15-$100 per article. Preference: subject matter where religion affects politics,

economics and social welfare. Interested in theological discussions provided they have relation to some current topic.

THE CHRISTIAN HERALD (Non-denominational)

27 E. 39th Street, New York 16, N. Y. Fiction: (1) Short stories, 2,500-3,500 words. Payment: $50-$150. (2) Short-shorts: 1,000-1,500 words. Payment: $40-$100. (3) Serials: 15,000-20,000 words. In 5 or 6 parts. Payment: from $300 to $750. Preference: all themes common to modern living. Themes need not be primarily religious in the narrowest sense of the term—and definitely not be "preaching." Acceptable are stories bearing on any social, domestic, religious, philosophical or historical subject. No juveniles. Articles: Human interest features, 800-1,500 words, with candid-type photographs. Payment: $35-$50. Crusade-type article: 1,500-2,500 words. Payment: $50-$100. Preference: Feature-type articles dealing with comparative unknowns—humble persons who do something or achieve something which should be inspiring to others. Crusade-type articles telling the story of some person or group that does something about an injustice or neglect in the civic or social field. Word from editor: "Material to be presented in a crisp, lively manner, shorn of all clichés. All material to be pointed up with anecdotes apropos of the theme being handled."

CHRISTIAN LIFE (Non-denominational)

434 S. Wabash Ave., Chicago 5, Ill. Fiction: (1) Short stories, 2,000-3,000 words. Payment: 1½c a word. (2) Storiettes: 900-1,300 words. Payment: $25. (3) Serials: Payment: 1½c a word. Articles: Short features, 400-600 words on pet hobbies or interests of Christians. Most include a picture. Payment: $20. Quizzes or puzzles on contemporary or historical rather than biblical material. Devotional fillers: 600-800 words. Payment: $10 and up. Christian service articles: 500-800 words. Payment: varies. Word from editor: "Most of the manuscripts rejected fall into two classes—either wrong from an evangelical point of view (and those do not appeal to the conservative membership) or else they have the evangelical Christian approach but violate the principles of good writing."

CHURCH MANAGEMENT, INC. (Non-denominational)

1900 Euclid Ave., Cleveland 15, Ohio. Articles: 1,500-2,000 words. Payment: varies, with an average of 1c a word. Preference: Church management, finance, church law, architecture, real estate, special-day programs, sermons, publicity, and public relations. Word from editor: "Most free-lance writers fail to make our market because they interpret the church in the light of one local church which may or may not be representative. All material is directed to the local church and the minister of the local church."

THE CHRISTIAN ADVOCATE (Methodist)

740 Rush Street, Chicago 11, Ill. Articles: 1,200-1,500 words. Payment: $25-$30 or more. Prefer pictures to illustrate. Types in demand: (1) Articles dealing with religious viewpoint on world problems; (2) heart-warming articles or sermons based on personal religious experience; (3) human-interest short stories and articles; (4) personality sketches; and (5) church methods articles. Note from editor: "Each issue has a representative of one of the above classifications."

HEARTHSTONE (Disciples of Christ and American Baptist Convention)
2700 Pine Blvd., St. Louis 3, Mo. Articles: 1,500 words. Payment: ½c-1c a word. Preference: Articles on Christian home life. Methods of bringing the church into the home.

BAPTIST LEADER (Baptist)
American Baptist Convention, 1703 Chestnut Street, Philadelphia 3, Pa. Articles: up to 1,500 words, preferably accompanied by one or two photographs. Payment: up to $7.50 per 1,000 words. Preference: (1) Articles for church school workers with children up to 12 years of age. Subject matter: child psychology and teaching technique methods, and trends in Christian education. (2) Junior High Leader: methods, experiences of teachers and leaders, and how to make equipment for the church school at a low cost. (3) Young People's Leader: articles offering guidance for adult counselors of young people. (4) Adult Leader: subjects of interest to leaders of adults and young adult groups.

ADULT CLASS (Baptist)
American Baptist Convention, 1703 Chestnut Street, Philadelphia 3, Pa. Articles: 400-1,500 words, preferably accompanied by photographs. Payment: usually ½c a word. Photographs: $2-$5. Articles dealing with activities of successful church school classes and departments. Poetry.

HOME (Baptist)
American Baptist Convention, 1703 Chestnut Street, Philadelphia 3, Pa. Articles: 400-1,500 words. Payment: usually ½c a word. Poetry. Features dealing with homes and family life.

WAR CRY (Salvation Army)
The Salvation Army, 719 N. State Street, Chicago 10, Ill. Fiction: 1,800-2,000 words. Articles: 1,200-1,800 words. Poetry. Payment: rates vary. Preference: stories may have either biblical or modern background. Prefers general type article rather than seasonal. Word from editor: "Where a story is given a Salvation Army slant, the portrayal must be convincing. Prefer inspirational or religious slant but no moralizing. Fast-moving action stories preferred."

THIS DAY (Lutheran)
Missouri Lutheran Synod, Concordia Publishing House, 3558 S. Jefferson Ave., St. Louis 18, Mo. Fiction: 1,000 words and up. Articles: 1,000 words and up. Payment: varying rates. Human-interest features and articles which bring Christianity into the home. Photographs of outstanding merit.

CHRISTIAN HOME LIFE (Disciples of Christ)
Standard Publishing Co., 20 East Central Parkway, Cincinnati 10, Ohio. Fiction: 1,500 words and up. Articles and features: 1,000 words and up. Payment: varying rates. Well written features which show Christianity operating within the home. Short articles demonstrating child and youth psychology.

LIBERTY (Seventh-day Adventists)
Takoma Park, Washington 12, D. C. Articles: 1,000 words and up. Payment: varying rates. Features dealing with the preservation of individual liberty and social problems.

LINK (Non-denominational)
General Commission on Chaplains. 122 Maryland Ave., Washington, D. C.
Articles: 1,000 words and up. Payment: rate varies. Articles dealing with
soldiers' problems and the Christian resolution of these problems.

CHRISTIAN SCIENCE MONITOR (Church of Christ, Scientist)
1 Norway St., Boston, Mass. Essays: 1,000 words. Payment: 2c a word.
Feature articles: Payment: $7 a column. Interviews, human interest, current
events.

PRESBYTERIAN LIFE (Presbyterian)
3217 S. 4th Street, Philadelphia 6, Pa. Articles: 1,500 words. Photographs and
fillers. Payment: 2c a word. News-type feature articles.

FOR YOUNG PEOPLE'S PERIODICALS

CLASSMATE (Methodist)
810 Broadway, Nashville 2, Tenn. Payment: 1c a word.

FORWARD (Presbyterian)
Presbyterian Board, 930 Witherspoon Bldg., Philadelphia 7, Pa. Fiction.
Articles: 1,000 words. Payment: 1c a word and up.

FRONT RANK (Disciples of Christ)
Disciples of Christ, 2700 Pine Blvd., St. Louis 3, Mo. Fiction: 1,000-2,500
words. Articles: 1,000-2,500 words. Illustrations. Poetry. Payment: 1c a word.

GIRLHOOD (Non-denominational)
20 E. Central Parkway, Cincinnati 10, Ohio. Fiction: 1,800-2,000 words.
Articles: 100-1,500 words. Payment: ⅓c per word and up.

HIGH CALL (Baptist)
American Baptist Convention, 1703 Chestnut Street, Philadelphia 3, Pa.
Articles: max., 1,200 words. Payment: articles, $7.50-$10; short items, $2-$3;
verse, $1-$3; photographs, commercial rates.

HIGH ROAD (Methodist)
1444 Astor Street, Chicago 10, Ill. Articles: 750-3,300 words. Payment: ¾c
a word.

LOOKOUT (Non-denominational)
20 E. Central Parkway, Cincinnati 10, Ohio. Fiction: 1,000-1,500 words.
Articles: 1,000-1,500 words. Photographs. Payment: 1c a word and up.

OUR YOUNG PEOPLE (Evangelical Lutheran)
425 S. 4th Street, Minneapolis 15, Minn. Fiction. Articles. Fillers. Illustrations. Payment: $4 per 1,000 words.

SUNDAY DIGEST (Non-denominational)
David C. Cook, Elgin, Ill. Fiction: 1,500—— words. Articles: 100-1,500
words. Fillers. Payment: 1c a word and up.

VISION (Disciples of Christ)
2700 Pine Blvd., St. Louis 3, Mo. Fiction: 2,000 words. Articles: 100-1,000
words. Fillers. Illustrations. Poetry. Payment: ½c a word and up.

YOUNG PEOPLE (Baptist)

American Baptist Convention, 1703 Chestnut Street, Philadelphia 3, Pa. Fiction: 2,000-3,000 words. Serials, installment: about 2,500 words. Articles: 1,000-2,500 words. Payment: short stories, $20; serials, $20 a chapter; features and articles, $5-$10; photographs, $3-$6; poetry, $2-$4.

YOUNG PEOPLE'S PAPER (Non-denominational)

1816 Chestnut Street, Philadelphia 3, Pa. Fiction: 1,800-2,000 words. Articles: 1,500 words and up. Fillers. Illustrations. Poetry. Payment: ½c a word.

YOUNG PEOPLE'S STANDARD (Nazarene)

2923 Troost Ave., Kansas City 10, Mo. Fiction: 2,000-2,500 words. Articles: 500-1,000 words. Fillers. Illustrations. Poetry. Payment: $3.75 per 1,000 words.

YOUTH (Church of God)

5th and Chestnut Streets, Anderson, Ind. Fiction: 1,000-2,500 words. Payment: $3 per 1,000 words.

YOUTH FOR CHRIST (Non-denominational)

130 North Wells Street, Chicago 6, Ill. Fiction: 1,000 words. Articles. Payment: up to 1c a word.

YOUTH TODAY (Swedish Baptist)

912 Belmont, Chicago 14, Ill. Fiction: 1,500-2,000 words. Articles: 500-2,000 words. Payment: ⅔c and up a word.

YOUTH'S COMRADE (Nazarene)

2923 Troost Ave., Kansas City 10, Mo. Fiction: 2,000-2,500 words. Articles: 500-1,000 words. Illustrations. Poetry. Payment $3.75 per 1,000 words.

FOR JUNIOR HIGH PERIODICALS

CANADIAN BOY (United Church of Canada)

299 Queen Street, W., Toronto 2-B, Ontario, Canada. Payment: ½c a word and up.

CANADIAN GIRL (United Church of Canada)

299 Queen Street, W., Toronto 2-B, Ontario, Canada. Payment: ½c a word and up.

CHILDREN'S FRIEND (Church of Jesus Christ of Latter-Day Saints)

36-40 Bishops Bldg., Salt Lake City, Utah. Fiction: 800-2,500 words. Payment: 1c a word.

THE CHILDREN'S HOUR (Non-denominational)

Ages 9-14 years. Christian Education Company, 1222 Mulberry Street, Highland, Ill. Fiction: 1,000 words——. Payment: $2.50 per 1,000 words.

CHRISTIAN TRAILS (Non-denominational)

Ages 9-16 years. Christian Missionary Alliance, 3rd and Reily Streets, Harrisburg, Pa. Fiction: 1,500 words. Payment: varies.

FRIENDS (Evangelical United Brethren)

Ages 12-14 years. Otterbein Press, Dayton 2, Ohio. No fiction. Articles: 100-1,200 words. Payment: ¼c a word.

OUR YOUNG PEOPLE (Lutheran)

Ages 12-18 years. 425 S. 4th Street, Minneapolis 15, Minn. Fiction: 2,500—words. Payment: $4 per 1,000 words.

SENTINEL (Baptist)

Ages 9-14 years. Southern Baptist Convention, 161—8th Ave., N., Nashville 3, Tenn. Fiction: 1,500-1,800 words. Articles: 500-1,000 words. Poetry. Payment: ½c a word.

'TEENS (Baptist)

Ages 12-15 years. American Baptist Convention, 1703 Chestnut Street, Philadelphia 3, Pa. Fiction: 2,000 words. Articles: 800 words. Payment: short stories, $15-$20; serials, $20 a chapter; articles, $8-$12; photographs, $3-$6; verse, $2-$4.

UPWARD (Baptist)

Ages 13-16. Southern Baptist Convention, 161—8th Ave., N., Nashville 3, Tenn. Fiction: 2,500-3,000 words. Articles: 500-1,500 words. Illustrations. Poetry. Payment: 1c a word.

VENTURE (Presbyterian)

Ages 12-15 years. Presbyterian Board, 930 Witherspoon Bldg., Philadelphia 7, Pa. Fiction: 1,500-2,500 words. Articles: 500-1,000 words. Payment: 1c a word and up.

VISION (Disciples of Christ)

2700 Pine Blvd., St. Louis 3, Mo. Fiction: 2,000 words. Articles: 100-1,000 words. Poetry. Payment: $5 per 1,000 words.

YOUTH'S COMRADE (Nazarene)

2923 Troost Ave., Kansas City 10, Mo. Fiction: 200-2,500 words. Articles: 500-1,000 words. Poetry. Payment: $3.75 per 1,000 words.

YOUTH'S STORY PAPER (Non-denominational)

American Sunday School Union, 1816 Chestnut Street, Philadelphia 3, Pa. Fiction: 1,200-1,500 words. Some poetry. Payment: ½c a word.

FOR JUNIOR PERIODICALS

CHILDREN'S ACTIVITIES (Non-denominational)

Ages 3-12 years. 1018 S. Wabash Ave., Chicago 5, Ill. Fiction: 1,200 words. Fillers. Illustrations. Poetry. Payment: 2c a word and up.

CHILDREN'S FRIEND (Evangelical Lutheran)
Ages 9-12 years. 425 S. 4th Street, Minneapolis 15, Minn. Fiction: 1,500 words. Articles: 1,500 words. Illustrations. Payment: $4 per 1,000 words.

COMRADE (Church of God)
Ages 9-11 years. S. E. Cor. 5th and Chestnut Street, Anderson, Ind. Fiction: 800-1,500 words. Some poetry. Payment: $3 per 1,000 words.

THE EXPLORER (United Church of Canada)
299 Queen St., W., Toronto 2-B, Ontario, Canada. Payment: 1c a word and up.

JUNIORS (Baptist)
Ages 9-11 years. American Baptist Convention, 1703 Chestnut Street, Philadelphia 3, Pa. Fiction and articles: 1,200-2,200 words. Payment: up to $7.50 per 1,000 words. Verse: $1-$4. Photographs: $3-$6.

JUNIOR WORLD (Disciples of Christ)
Ages 9-12 years. 2700 Pine Blvd., St. Louis 3, Mo. Fiction: 1,500—— words. Articles: 100-1,000 words. Poetry. Payment: $4-$5 per 1,000 words.

For Kindergarten and Primary Age Group Periodicals

DEW DROPS (Non-denominational)
Ages 6-8 years. David C. Cook Publishing Company, Elgin, Ill. Fiction: 700-900 words. Articles: 150-300 words. Payment: 1c a word and up.

HIGHLIGHTS FOR CHILDREN
Ages 2-12 years. 968 Main Street, Honesdale, Pa. Fiction: 950—— words. Payment: Liberal rates.

LITTLE FOLKS STORY TIME (Non-denominational)
Ages 4-8 years. Christian Education Company, Box 31, Highland, Ill. Payment: $2.50 per 1,000 words.

STORIES (Presbyterian)
Ages 4-8 years. Presbyterian Board, 930 Witherspoon Bldg., Philadelphia 7, Pa. Fiction: 400-800 words. Articles: 500 words. Poetry. Payment, ½c a word and up.

STORIES FOR CHILDREN (Church of God)
Ages 5-9 years. 5th and Chestnut Streets, Anderson, Ind. Fiction: 300-500 words. Payment: $3 per 1,000 words.

STORY LAND (Disciples of Christ)
Ages 4-9 years. 2700 Pine Blvd., St. Louis 3, Mo. Fiction: 300-1,000 words. Articles: 300-500 words. Payment: $4-$5 per 1,000 words.

STORY TIME (Baptist)
Ages 4-8 years. Southern Baptist Convention, 161—8th Ave., N., Nashville 3, Tenn. Fiction: 400-700 words. Articles: 100-300 words. Poetry. Payment: ½c a word.

STORY WORLD (Baptist)

Ages 6-8 years. American Baptist Convention, 1703 Chestnut Street, Philadelphia 3, Pa. Fiction: 500-700 words. Articles: 400-500 words. Some fillers. Payment: up to $7.50 per 1,000 words. Verse: $1-$4. Photographs: $3-$6. Puzzles and Miscellaneous, $1-$6.

WEE WISDOM (Unity)

Ages 4-13 years. Unity School of Christianity, 917 Tracy Ave., Kansas City 6, Mo. Fiction: 1,000 words. Some poetry. Payment: 1c a word and up.

NOTE: The grading is not uniform. It differs with the denomination, but in general it tends to follow the public school grading.

SELECTED BIBLIOGRAPHY ON RELIGIOUS JOURNALISM

PREPARED BY LAWRENCE P. FITZGERALD

GENERAL

A. S. Burack, ed. *The Writer's Handbook,* The Writer, 1946. $4.50.

W. S. Campbell, *Professional Writing,* Macmillan, 1939, $4.15.

John E. Drewry, *Book Reviewing,* The Writer, 1946, $2.50.

Fred Eastman, *Writing the Religious One-Act Play,* Friendship Press, 1947, paper, 50 cents.

Julie Eidesheim, *Editor at Work,* Farrar & Rinehart, 1939, $2.00.

Rudolf Flesch, *The Art of Readable Writing,* Harper, 1949, $3.00.

Robert van Gelder, *Writers and Writing,* Scribners, 1946, $3.50.

Scott Meredith, *Writing to Sell,* Harper, 1947, $2.75.

Jack Woodford, *How to Write for Money,* Garden City, 1944, 95 cents.

RELIGIOUS FICTION

Harold Blodgett, *The Story Survey,* Lippincott, 1950, $3.50.

W. S. Campbell, *Writing Magazine Fiction,* Doubleday, 1940, $2.50.

August Derlith, *Writing Fiction,* The Writer, 1946, $2.50.

Maren Elwood, *Characters Make Your Story,* The Writer, 1942, $3.50.

Maren Elwood, *Write the Short Short,* The Writer, $3.50.

Foster-Harris, *The Basic Formulas of Fiction,* University of Oklahoma Press, $2.50.

Pearl Hogrefe, *The Process of Creative Writing,* Harper, 1947, $3.00.

J. Edward Lantz, *Stories of Christian Living,* Association Press, 1950, $2.50.

Dorothy McCleary, *Creative Fiction Writing,* The Writer, 1947, $2.50.

FEATURE WRITING

Robeson Bailey, *Techniques in Article Writing,* Appleton-Century-Crofts, 1947, student ed. $2.50.

Ernest Brennecke, Jr. and Donald Lemen Clark, *Magazine Article Writing,* Macmillan, 1947, $4.50.

W. S. Campbell, *Writing Non-Fiction,* The Writer, 1944, $3.00.

Dewett Reddick, *Modern Feature Writing,* Harper, $4.00.

CURRICULUM WRITING

Philip Henry Lotz, *Orientation in Religious Education,* Abingdon-Cokesbury, 1940, $6.50.

Frances Cole McLester, *Teaching in the Church School,* Abingdon-Cokesbury, 1940, paper, 75 cents.

A. J. William Myers, *Teaching Religion Creatively,* 1932, Revell, $2.00.

Paul Vieth, ed., *The Church and Christian Education,* CPA, Bethany Press, 1947, $2.50.

CHURCH PUBLICITY

W. Austin Brodie, *Keeping Your Church in the News,* Fleming H. Revell, 1942, $1.50.

Stewart Harral, *Public Relations for Churches,* Abingdon-Cokesbury, 1945, $1.25.

Stanley Stuber, *Public Relations Manual for Churches,* Doubleday, 1951, $3.00.

INDEX

Date Due

Date Due